King and Country: monarchy and the future King Charles III

King & Country

Monarchy and the future
King Charles III

Robert Blackburn

POLITICO'S

First published in Great Britain 2006 by
Politico's Publishing Ltd, an imprint of
Methuen Publishing Ltd
11–12 Buckingham Gate
London
SW1E 6LB

10 9 8 7 6 5 4 3 2 1

A CIP catalogue record for this book is available from the British Library.

ISBN-10 1-84275-141-7
ISBN-13: 978-1-84275-141-1

Typeset by SX Composing DTP, Rayleigh, Essex
Printed and bound in Great Britain by Cromwell Press

For
Paula, Sophie, Amy & Eden

Contents

Preface and acknowledgements

Monarchy today, as a friend once commented, is 'a cultural reality'. It defies rational analysis in so many respects, yet still manages to fit into the rhythm of our constitutional and social way of life.

That it may continue to do so, however, depends very largely upon the person who is on the throne. Queen Elizabeth II has by near universal acclaim been 'one of the most respected people of our times . . . a truly remarkable source of constancy and strength', as the Prime Minister told the House of Commons in April this year, paying tribute on her eightieth birthday. But after Elizabeth, what will the situation be? This book offers a commentary on a range of royal topics affecting the Prince of Wales as heir apparent, together with the issues and opportunities he – and we as a country – will face when he ascends the throne as King Charles III.

Chapter 3 of this book contains material, in revised form, that was earlier published as articles by me in the journal *Public Law*, entitled 'Monarchy and the Personal Prerogatives' and 'The Royal Assent to Legislation and a Monarch's Fundamental Human Rights'.

My warm thanks go to my publishers at Politico's, Alan Gordon Walker and Jonathan Wadman, for their exceptional efficiency and support. I am grateful to my friends Raymond Plant, George Jones and Geoffrey Bindman for reading and commenting on drafts of the work. As always, my final words of gratitude go to my family, not only for welcome distractions and tolerating my absences when writing, but for helping to put everything into its proper perspective.

Robert Blackburn
June 2006

1

Two monarchs: Queen Elizabeth II and King Charles III

2005–6 as a watershed in royal history

Considered in retrospect, the period of 2005–6 will be seen as a watershed in the contemporary history of the British monarchy. Three events of particular significance stood out, all of them serving to highlight the personal and constitutional position that the present Prince of Wales, Charles Philip Arthur George, will hold when in due course he becomes King.

One of these was simply the eightieth birthday celebrations being organised for Elizabeth II in 2006.* This outstanding monarch had now served as head of state for over half a century, fifty-four years, since her accession on 6 February 1952. The prospect of her being unable to continue forever, and the certainty that the performance of her royal functions would progressively need to be passed on to the person next in line to the throne, positioned the Prince of Wales more centrally within the world of politics than ever before.

The second significant event was public realisation of the extent to which the future Charles III privately expressed strong views on political affairs and

---

* On 26 October 2005, a statement from Buckingham Palace set out the formal events taking place to celebrate the Queen's eightieth birthday in 2006, mostly in the period between her actual birthday on 21 April and her official birthday on 17 June, marked by the Trooping of the Colour. On 19 April, a House of Commons address expressed its 'appreciation of Her Majesty's unfailing devotion to the duties of state, the Nation and Commonwealth'. On 21 April, the Prince of Wales gave a television broadcast in tribute to his mother, and hosted a birthday dinner with the royal family at Kew Palace. A National Service of Thanksgiving at St Paul's Cathedral took place on 15 June.

participated in political dialogue with government ministers. Ever since a young man, the Prince had been well known for the serious and thoughtful side of his personality, reflected in many speeches and articles on matters relating to the natural world, the human environment, architecture and spirituality. But of real constitutional significance was the fact that in 2005–6 it was acknowledged at the highest levels that the future King did take a stand on certain political matters and actively lobbied the government to try to achieve his aims.

This public realisation arose out of a legal action the Prince brought in February 2006 against the publishers of a national newspaper, the *Mail on Sunday*, claiming breach of copyright and confidentiality in publishing extracts from one of his personal journals.[1] This had been typed up and circulated to various members of his family, close friends and advisers. The content of the published material was remarkable in revealing the depth of the Prince's feelings on various politically related matters. More generally, the case was significant for the evidence produced by the newspaper in support of its public-interest defence. This included a sworn statement by a former deputy private secretary of the Prince, giving a description of the future King's dealings with ministers and the media with regard to political affairs on which he held strong views. This episode was smoothed over by the Prime Minister, Tony Blair, when questioned about its constitutional implications at his monthly Downing Street press conference on 23 February 2006.

Mr Blair prefaced his comments by referring to the successful charity work conducted by the Prince's Trust, which the future King founded thirty years ago and of which he is president, saying, 'I think that Prince Charles does an amazing job for the country.' He then went on to support the future King's utterances on public affairs:

> I think he is perfectly entitled to express his views and personally I find no problem with it at all . . . I find that what Prince Charles certainly has talked to me about and written about is exactly what you would expect. I think it is completely unreasonable not to expect that he has views or that he transmits them to government ministers . . . I personally do not think it has ever caused difficulties for ministers.

An opinion poll commissioned by the *Daily Telegraph* showed that Mr Blair was in tune with popular feelings on Prince Charles's right to speak out.[2] Some 75 per cent of respondents felt that Charles as heir to the throne had 'the right to communicate his views on controversial political matters, in private, to government ministers and other important people'. Others, however, took a different stance, both on the significance of this event and on the right of the next monarch to be expressing political opinions. For whatever rights Prince Charles may legitimately possess as a human being are not necessarily the same thing as the rights or entitlement of a constitutional monarch and head of state. As the author and journalist Peter Riddell observed, 'at last the secret is out. Senior ministers, from Tony Blair downwards, have been protecting the Prince of Wales from himself. Far from acting as closet republicans, New Labour has safeguarded the monarchy by keeping publicly silent about the often highly controversial interventions by Prince Charles.'[3]

The reactions from across the political parties were mixed. Most Conservatives broadly supported the approach of the Prime Minister, with most Liberal Democrats voicing concern that the Prince was exploiting his position and destabilising the political neutrality of the monarchy, and many Labour backbenchers resenting his 'interference' in politics.* The event as a whole therefore evoked controversy and a serious question on the constitutional legitimacy of the future King Charles's interventions in politics and government, something that had never come close to being an issue in the case of the Queen.

The third major landmark in royal history was the marriage of the Prince of Wales to Mrs Camilla Parker Bowles, now Her Royal Highness the Duchess of Cornwall. For the many millions of people in the United Kingdom, the Commonwealth, and around the world where the British monarchy is a subject of immense curiosity and fascination, this was the climax to a long-running, much-publicised, controversial, and deeply troubled story.

---

* On 22 February 2006 the following comments were made to the press, published the next day in the *Times*. The Conservative MP Oliver Heald, shadow Secretary of State for Constitutional Affairs, said, 'Our party is very supportive of the Prince. Certainly every time I talk to former ministers who were approached by him they all welcomed his comments.' Paul Holmes MP, chairman of the Liberal Democrat parliamentary party, said, 'Either the monarch is the neutral head of state that the armed forces can swear to, or they are politically active. If they are politically active, they can't be the monarchy. If he's trying to exploit his position as future monarch then that's unacceptable.' According to Paul Flynn MP, a Labour backbencher, 'his actions are suicidal. The only reason why the monarchy and the Queen are successful is that she has kept out of all political decisions, and the only way it can continue to survive as an institution is if the monarchy is seen to be above politics. If he is going to find it irresistible to interfere in politics – sometimes on the side of sense, sometimes on the side of nonsense – then the monarchy would be in grave peril with him as head of state. It would collapse.'

On one level, it was perceived as a private story in the public eye. This was a very human drama of broken marriages, marital infidelity and dysfunctional families, but one involving two major world celebrities – the heir to the British throne and his former wife, the hugely popular and iconic Diana, Princess of Wales. Inter-twined in the story, purportedly justifying the intrusive nature of the mass media's sensationalist coverage of the Prince's private life, was the extraordinary range of constitutional, religious and legal complications arising from Charles and Camilla's relationship. This was a relationship that had been the subject of a huge amount of ongoing commentary and analysis since the Prince's official separation from Diana was announced by the then Prime Minister, John Major, to the House of Commons on 9 December 1992.

Throughout that thirteen-year period since the Prince and Princess's formal separation, the questions that were asked and commented on time and again in the media and public discussion revolved around whether Charles's liaison with Camilla would precipitate a constitutional crisis. Would it subvert or be contradictory to Charles ever becoming King and head of the Church of England? Would the public stand for Camilla becoming Queen and, if not, could this lead to another abdication crisis similar to that of 1936 or even cause the downfall of the monarchy itself?

The proper answer to all these questions remained the same, and indeed was given by the author to media interviewers on numerous occasions. However, the non-sensationalist nature of this answer attracted considerably less attention than the voices of prophets of doom and disaster if a marriage between Prince Charles and Mrs Parker Bowles ever took place. There were no insuperable legal obstacles, and there would be no constitutional crisis. Whilst some problems clearly existed, especially ones of a religious nature, there were no impediments that precluded this royal marriage.

The determining factor in constitutional terms would be the opinion of the Prime Minister, and it was unimaginable that Tony Blair would do other than support the union and future happiness of Prince Charles and Mrs Parker Bowles. In reaching his opinion, the Prime Minister would consult various other interested bodies, notably the Archbishop of Canterbury and the heads of government of Canada, Australia and other Commonwealth countries where our monarch serves as head of state. But it was to be expected that Mr Blair would be persuasive in guiding others towards his own judgement, as head of government of the core state, the United Kingdom, where the monarchy operated. Finally, if the Prince and Mrs Parker Bowles wished to marry, then it was far better to do so now while Charles was heir apparent, rather than subsequently as Charles III, for it was clearly preferable in diplomatic terms for the King to be married rather than to be co-habiting with his partner.

Questions arising from Charles's marital affairs

More subtle and fundamental questions relating to the monarchy itself would arise out of the royal marriage, however. A consequence of the royal marriage, during all the preparations, ceremonies and celebrations surrounding it, was that it provided a powerful focal point for contemplating the future of the British monarchy itself. Life events in the royal family, be they births, deaths or marriages, regularly trigger a flurry of commentary and speculation in the mass media about the monarchy and how the new event might change things. But this particular royal episode raised questions and thoughts – and some doubts – about the whole institution of the monarchy and its processes, in a way that none other had done for many decades – probably not so powerfully since the abdication of Edward VIII in 1936. It projected Charles into the public imagination as our King, together with his new wife Camilla as his legitimised consort, in a far more vivid manner than had ever previously been the case.

This was certainly a marriage conducted in the full glare of publicity and controversy, despite all the attempts by Clarence House – the Prince's official household – to keep it as low key and private an affair as possible. It was the wedding of the 56-year-old heir apparent, whose reigning parent, Elizabeth II, was approaching her eightieth birthday the following year, 2006. It was a marital union with a divorcee, by a royal divorcee and one who would eventually be head of the Church of England. It was the marriage of a Prince of Wales who already has two sons, the elder of whom, Prince William, appears to be considerably more popular and at ease with the public and the new media age than his father.

Throughout the eight-week period between their engagement on 10 February 2005 and the marriage on 9 April the broadcasters' airwaves and the printing presses of the daily papers and celebrity magazines dwelt on the personalities involved and the human interest side of the occasion, which best sells news stories. In general terms, many feature articles and television reports offered views on what the impact of the wedding might be upon the future of the monarchy. What was more surprising was a number of unexpected complications, some legal and constitutional, that arose during the unfolding drama of the preparations, ceremonies and celebrations.

The first complication was the question whether the royal marriage could actually take place inside Windsor Castle, as originally planned. This proved impossible when it was realised that the grant of a marriage licence for the castle would entail opening its doors to anyone who wanted to get married there, so the wedding was re-located to the town's guildhall. Then a media furore erupted around the question of whether the Prince of Wales could lawfully wed in a civil marriage service at all. Was an English civil register office more or less suitable than a Christian wedding in Scotland, in the earlier example of the divorced Princess Royal? When the Pope died a week before the scheduled wedding date, should the ceremony be postponed (which it was)? On what doctrinal basis did the Archbishop of Canterbury give the Church's blessing to the marriage of two divorcees whose involvement had been a factor in the dissolution of the Prince's prior marriage to Princess Diana? Had Camilla Parker Bowles ever taken communion in the Roman Catholic Church during her marriage to her Catholic first husband and, if so, did this affect Charles's claims to the throne under the Act of Settlement? Why were the television cameras and therefore the public excluded from the royal wedding ceremony itself yet permitted to attend its blessing by Dr Williams in the castle? Was this, or any, royal wedding a private or public event? All these questions emerged against the background of the social and constitutional truism that the monarchy is in fact a far more complex institution than is commonly supposed.

What was most notable about the royal wedding of the future Charles III and Mrs Parker Bowles, from a constitutional perspective, was how the political and religious establishment united in its support of the couple's union, sweeping aside all objections laid before it. This was strikingly different from the occasion of Edward VIII's expressed desire to marry the American divorcee Mrs Wallis Simpson in 1936, when the establishment united in its utter condemnation of the union, insisting that such personal conduct would be in breach of the King's public duties.

But in what senses was the royal marriage a constitutional issue at all? This goes to the heart of what always has been, and remains, the central conundrum for hereditary monarchy in the modern era. For everyone, marriage is a private business; except for the monarch. The public duties and expectations imposed upon the private individual who would be King are still considerable, whether they are regarded as anachronisms or not. Most obviously, a royal head of state is ex officio Supreme Governor of the Church of England, and as such is expected by many to provide a religious and moral example to Anglicans everywhere. He is head of the royal family, a public institution in its own right since Queen Victoria projected it into the public domain to support the monarch and to be emulated by her subjects as a model for family values and responsibilities. Secular aberrations such as civil marriage and divorce were not traditionally applicable to the royal family in the same way as for normal citizens.

The marriage of an heir apparent most directly affects the politics of the country, or may potentially do so, because of the possibility of children, who may succeed their parent to the throne and become our constitutional head of state. This consideration may not be applicable in the instant case of Mrs Parker Bowles, though clinically today it is not impossible. But this is why there are ancient statutory provisions governing succession to the throne, laying down conditions and disqualifications. Most famously, the Bill of Rights and Act of Settlement preclude anyone who marries a Roman Catholic from being or becoming the royal head of state,[4] since in the seventeenth and early eighteenth centuries the religious leadership and official faith of the state was a deeply serious political issue.

Of course, there may very well be good reasons for reforming – 'modernising' – the legal and constitutional furniture within which the monarchy sits. Certainly, one interesting component in the mix of issues thrown up by the royal marriage was the question of constitutional reform generally. What was put in prospect were not just matters of substance or regulation affecting the institution of kingship itself, but the subtle way in which the revolutionary mass of constitutional reforms since 1997 had made further reform across the whole political and legal terrain easier to contemplate and achieve. So too arose questions relating to the manner in which the government now seeks to change or re-mould our constitutional law, even on matters of great longevity and antiquity. For example, the historic legal exception of members of the royal family from the Marriage Act – meaning they must contract their marriages through a religious service – was circumvented in an entirely non-judicial and non-legislative manner. To facilitate the wedding of the Prince of Wales and Mrs Parker Bowles, a government minister, Lord Falconer, simply issued a ministerial statement to Parliament declaring that he believed royal civil marriages now to be lawful, and this was treated as final and authoritative by the Windsor superintendent registrar.[5]

To shrug off the future King Charles's marriage, and the monarchy in general, as being politically unimportant or irrelevant is too simplistic by far. So too is the glib assertion that one might be 'against the monarchy'. Combined with those positions is a programme of tangential constitutional and public considerations. To start with, the monarchy and the House of Lords – the second chamber of our legislature – are inextricably linked in their aristocratic associations. So too is the system of honours – Sir Mick Jagger, Jonathan Ross OBE (Officer of the Order of the British Empire) and so on. It is the Crown that appoints members of the second legislative chamber and recipients of the various orders of heraldry and chivalry. As well as the monarch's ex officio role as head of the Church of England – a worldwide Christian denomination – there are the powers vested in the Crown for selecting and appointing religious leaders, from the Archbishops of Canterbury and York downwards. What detailed schemes of replacement does the abolitionist have in mind for these institutions of great public importance?

Opposition to the monarchy means being in favour of a presidency, but what kind of president? Would she or he be directly elected by the people, or appointed by politicians, as is the Speaker of the Commons? To whom would she or he be accountable, and what extra powers would she or he possess? In contemplating alternatives to monarchy, we must bear in mind that the Crown is the legal basis and ultimate source of legitimacy in the British political state. We have Her Majesty's Government, Her Majesty's Loyal Opposition, the Royal Courts of Justice and so on. Even 'Parliament' is shorthand for its proper title of 'Queen-in-Parliament', and all parliamentary legislation requires the assent of the monarch. And all the basic functions of government – extending to national security, inter-state treaty making, and ministerial appointments – are carried out in the name of and under the authority of the Crown and the royal prerogative, which is part of the common law of the land. Those who are against the monarchy are ipso facto in favour of drafting a new written constitution, raising all the difficulties and questions involved in finding alternative models for virtually all our major political and governmental institutions. These are not insuperable obstacles, of course, and written republican constitutions are the norm around the world. But abolitionists must be clear on the implications of what it is they may be too glibly lending their support to.

So was Prince Charles's second marriage a defining moment in the history of the monarchy? There are good grounds for maintaining that it was. Above all, a touch of realism has now entered the public persona of the institution. Traditional notions and expectations of a monarch have been tested and found to be neither realistic nor necessary in the modern world. The establishment accepted that it was no longer a vital purpose to provide a fairy tale story of endless happy families for others to find vicarious enjoyment in. Today, it is to be regarded more in the fashion of a pragmatic piece of constitutional machinery, one we have inherited from our ancient past, that continues to fit in with our political arrangements. It should be appreciated and evaluated on that basis.

What the future King's public position will be

The public role of the monarch is, first and foremost, to serve as the constitutional head of state. Under the British system of government, this means performing a limited number of formalities and ceremonies that are essential to the structure and existence of our government, and which can only be legitimately exercised by the person who is King or Queen. These acts of state relates to some of the most important and basic facets of our democratic life, the most important of which are the appointment of a Prime Minister, the dissolution of Parliament (prior to a general election), and Royal Assent to legislation. They are formidable powers in appearance but ones whose exercise is circumscribed by constitutional convention, leaving no room for the personal views of the monarch.[6] There are a number of other governmental functions routinely performed by the monarch. These include formalising the business carried out by the Privy Council (such as legislative orders and proclamations), and confirming in law a wide number of appointments (such as new peerages in the House of Lords, and Anglican bishops).

The monarch performs a ceremonial role at state occasions. A leading instance is the Queen's/King's Speech at the state opening of Parliament, an annual event at the start of each annual session. This is a royal act devoid of personal involvement or independence, with the monarch reading out a speech every word of which has been written in advance by 10 Downing Street. As the Duke of Windsor, formerly Edward VIII, once dryly commented, 'nothing could be more calculated to remind the monarch that he is only a figurehead'.[7]

As a symbol of the nation, or the authority of the state, the monarch takes a lead at national ceremonies or commemorations, such as on Remembrance

Day at the Cenotaph in Whitehall each November. The monarch is officially commander in chief of the armed forces and every year attends numerous military events (such as inspecting guards of honour, launching ships, presenting colours and honours) as well as presiding at anniversaries such as the Trooping of the Colour, which celebrates the Queen's official birthday. This military dimension of monarchy is essentially a symbolic role, though several leading members of the royal family have personally served in the forces and seen conflict. It is said to be upon the Crown as an institution, and upon the individual monarch as a person, that the armed forces psychologically and emotionally focus their loyalties, rather than upon the party politicians of the day (who may be disliked) or government policy (which may be disagreed with).

In many respects similar to royal ceremonial functions is the international public relations and goodwill diplomatic role performed by the Queen. A principal function of a British monarch is to preside over meetings and banquets with visiting heads of state or other top government dignitaries from abroad. Again, this is a public role to be carried out at the request of our elected government, even where the individual personalities or policies of the foreign power represented may be at odds with the private views of the Queen or our future King. At home, these occasions are usually held at Buckingham Palace, the official residence of the British monarchy,* where the Grenadier Guards and horsemen of the Royal Household are able to perform a quasi-theatrical ceremony of impressive grandeur. In the further performance of this diplomatic role, the royal head of state travels extensively abroad, sometimes assisted or represented by other leading members of the royal family.

There are two special positions that Elizabeth II holds as British monarch with respect to foreign affairs. The first is that she is monarch and head of state not only in the UK but in a wide number of other countries around the world, as a result of the former Empire. Those countries which have not created their own separate head of state are Antigua and Barbuda, Australia, the Bahamas, Barbados, Belize, Canada, Grenada, Jamaica, Mauritius, New Zealand, Papua New Guinea, St Christopher & Nevis, St Lucia, St Vincent & the Grenadines, the Solomon Islands and Tuvalu. In those countries, the legal and constitutional powers and functions of the monarch as head of state are represented and exercised by a governor general. The constitutional

---

* Queen Elizabeth's main domestic residence is at Windsor Castle; Prince Charles's is at Highgrove, near Tetbury in Gloucestershire, though he also regularly resides in London at Clarence House, where his business offices are.

principle is that a monarch acts on the advice of his or her United Kingdom ministers on all occasions and wherever he or she is travelling, except when within one of those states where he or she is retained as monarch, in which case he or she acts on the advice of that country's Prime Minister.

Elizabeth II has also served as Head of the Commonwealth, a title created in 1949 as a result of India's desire on independence to become a self-governing republic but to remain within the Commonwealth. The title is symbolic and there is no constitutional role attached to it. The Commonwealth itself has no formal constitution and is a unique voluntary association of independent self-governing states, almost all being former colonies of the British Empire, fostering international goodwill and reaching agreed declarations on matters such as inter-racial relations. As part of the ceremonial bonding of these relationships, the Queen opens the biennial meetings of the Commonwealth and gives a televised message to the Commonwealth on Christmas day each year and a Commonwealth Day message in March. When delivering these speeches or statements as Head of the Commonwealth, she acts free from ministerial advice, though as a matter of courtesy they are usually shown to the Prime Minister in advance. The speeches represent over 50 per cent of her own personal work, including choice of topic and the writing of the first and final drafts.[8]

When Charles III ascends the throne, there is no guarantee the title of Head of the Commonwealth will be bestowed upon him. The title is not vested in the Crown, but in the combined authority of the parliaments of all the member states of the Commonwealth. It will be a Commonwealth heads of government meeting, held after the demise of Elizabeth II, that will determine the next recipient of this title, and whether or not it is to descend upon any other person at all.

The present expectation is that the future Charles III will become ex officio the 'supreme head on earth, under God, of the Church of England'. In the Sovereign's Declaration, which prefaces the Church's *Thirty-Nine Articles of Religion*, the monarch describes himself as 'being by God's Ordinance, according to Our just Title, Defender of the Faith and . . . Supreme Governor of the Church of England'. The national Anglican Church, established in the sixteenth century by Henry VIII, has been of immense significance to the life of the country, spiritually, socially and politically. The monarch makes all the formal appointments of archbishops and bishops. He or she summons and dissolves the General Synod of the Church. His or her assent is required before new ecclesiastical canons take effect. Worldwide across the globe, from Africa to North America to Australia, there are forty-four Christian churches with seventy-seven million adherents in communion with the Church of England. All bishops and priests of the Church of England are required to take a personal oath of loyalty and obedience to the person who becomes monarch including, in due course, the future King Charles.

Finally, there is the social dimension of monarchy, involving the popular affairs of the country. The monarch, and members of the royal family, act as patrons of charities and worthy causes, to raise the profile of those bodies.* As Prince of Wales, Charles has been innovative and highly successful in establishing his 'Prince's Charities', raising around £100 million for charitable activities of a wide variety. The best known of these is the Prince's Trust, offering support to disadvantaged young people, such as through training, mentoring, or grants for set-up business costs. Members of the royal family lend support to a host of public bodies by regular visits to attend anniversary or achievement events. In law, the monarch is 'the fountain of honours'. There are regular investitures by Queen Elizabeth, or the heir apparent on her behalf, at Buckingham Palace to confer honours, titles and medals upon those marked out for distinction by the government, which controls their distribution. A small number of exclusive honours are reserved for award at the monarch's own personal pleasure.

In constitutional terms, it is difficult to give any tangible meaning to this social or philanthropic function of the monarchy, if indeed it can be said to exist as a formal role at all. Yet undoubtedly, the degree of personal charm with which the monarch performs these socially interactive, non-constitutional tasks is perhaps the greatest factor in influencing the popularity of a monarch at any particular time. The huge popularity of Diana, Princess of Wales, for example, was due to her immense personal charm and ability to enthuse popular feelings towards her personally, though she performed no role at all in the functioning of the monarchy as a piece of constitutional machinery.

Monarchy, constitution and prerogative

Any legal or constitutional study of the monarchy needs to explain what 'the

* Queen Elizabeth II is patron or president of more than 700 organisations.

Crown', in theory and in reality, means and involves with regards to our system of public law and government as a whole. Other European monarchies have been subsumed into a written constitution that lays down a description of the government. This sets out the parameters of the head of state, which is then subordinate to the written constitution document itself. In cases of dispute, the courts or a special tribunal will apply the basic law to the Crown. Ancient theories of ultimate royal authority have thereby been superseded by the legal reality of a modern republican state.

This is not so in the United Kingdom. With us, the legal source of government authority in the state is the Crown. Indeed, some jest that the Queen *is* the constitution, and this is an accurate portrayal in so far as all government activities operate in the name of the Crown. So too do the Crown and those who govern in its name possess a vast number of inherent powers, privileges and immunities – known as the royal prerogative – with which to govern and rule the country. These executive powers and rights are derived not from any constitutional or parliamentary written source, but simply from the ancient common law – in other words, by virtue of de facto judicial recognition as having existed from time immemorial. The executive authority of the royal prerogative controls the entire administrative machinery of government: what departments of state there are, who its ministers are,* and when parliaments are summoned and dissolved. It alone, without the legal necessity for any parliamentary involvement, determines the requirements of national security including decisions on defence, treaty making, declarations of war and entry into military conflict.[9]

Questions arising from Charles's involvement in political affairs

The restraint of Elizabeth II
In terms of royal personality, the heir apparent stands in striking contrast to his mother in one important respect. Queen Elizabeth II has been highly

* Even the office of Prime Minister – the head of government in the United Kingdom – is not the creation of any constitutional law. Occasionally politicians forget the distinction between head of state and head of government, subconsciously linking the greater executive power of a Prime Minister with the more elevated status of a head of state. Thus in an interview with the *Guardian* newspaper Jack Straw, then Foreign Secretary, responded to a question about Tony Blair's air shuttle diplomacy in the immediate aftermath of 9/11 by saying, 'The more critical an issue, the more a head of state is going to be involved with September 11 and the use of our military action – of course the head of state is going to be involved.' (*Guardian*, 28 January 2002).

restrained in expressing her views on public affairs, however far removed they be from the centre of party political debate. As a general rule her public utterances have been made only on the direction of the government or after careful consultation with 10 Downing Street, such as prior to her meetings with visiting heads of state at Buckingham Palace, on her overseas visits or at Commonwealth occasions. There are hardly any known instances of her writing to government ministers, asking them to take her views into account in the formulation of ministerial policy. Only at her weekly meetings with the Prime Minister, which are private and where no minutes are taken, might she presume to offer some opinions and then only in the knowledge that the Prime Minister of the day values or wishes to hear them.[10] For us, the Queen's views on public affairs can only be guessed at.

Charles's ventures into political affairs

How different the situation is in the case of the heir apparent, Prince Charles. The future Charles III feels compelled to take a stand on a wide range of public issues, some well within the field of political controversy.

It is now well known that he makes his personal opinions felt both in the public eye and regularly within the corridors of power, on subjects which are mostly, but not all, at the margins of party politics. A widely held view of Prince Charles, as expressed by Anthony Sampson in his best-selling book *Who Runs This Place?*, is that 'as he grew older he became more eccentric and opinionated, displaying strong views about almost everything'.[11] There is a long list of his forays into government policy in recent years. He gives regular public speeches and, increasingly, writes articles for the press on topics close to his heart, such as education policy, rural communities, the architecture of public places, the public use of genetic science and alternative medicine.[12] Significantly, his most challenging opinions are expressed personally to government ministers in the numerous personal meetings he asks for with them and through the large number of letters he has written, and continues to write, to them.*[13]

As mentioned earlier, the Prime Minister, Tony Blair, has himself publicly

---

* According to Jonathan Dimbleby's authoritative biography, *The Prince of Wales*, during a twelve-month period Prince Charles had private meetings with ten government ministers and three with leading members of the then opposition, and he wrote over 1,000 personal letters including 'missives to Cabinet ministers'. Elsewhere, it has been reckoned the Prince wrote over 100 letters to government ministers during the period between Labour taking office in 1997 and 2002, a frequency of one every three weeks.

stated that he does not mind the letters he receives from Prince Charles. 'He is perfectly entitled to do it. I find the letters helpful. I don't have any problem [with them] at all.'[14]

Political subjects close to Charles's heart

An earlier known instance of the Prince's intervention in 2002 concerned one of the Labour government's most important constitutional reforms, the Human Rights Act. This had just recently come into force in 2000. Writing to the Lord Chancellor, then Lord Irvine, berating the corrosive effects of the Human Rights Act, the future Charles III appended his comments on the Act by adding:

> As the Prime Minister has warned me, I am sure you will not agree with much of this, but I should welcome the chance to talk through these issues with you privately in more detail when we next have the chance to meet! – perhaps when I come to see the pictures in your London apartment![15]

In separate letters to the Lord Chancellor dated 26 June 2001 and 13 February 2002, he protested that 'over the last few years, we in this country have been sliding inexorably down the slope of ever-increasing, petty-minded litigiousness'. He spoke of increasing quantities of 'bureaucratic red tape', 'ever more proscriptive laws' and 'the blame culture', adding that 'our lives are becoming ruled by a truly absurd degree of politically correct interference'. On the undesirability of Labour's human rights legislation, he said, 'The longer term effect of the Human Rights Act will be to provide opportunities which – whatever the sanity and reasonableness of our own judges – will only encourage people to take up causes which will make the pursuit of a sane, civilised and ordered existence ever more difficult.'

It is not just United Kingdom central government but the newly devolved administrations that appear to be subject to lobbying by Prince Charles. It seems that the heir apparent regularly makes personal contact by telephone or letter with the Scottish First Minister on a range of devolution issues. In recent years, these are said to have included salmon farming, fox hunting and the Scottish Parliament building. In 2002 it was reported that the Prince had telephoned Henry McLeish, First Minister from 2000 to 2001, in order to lobby him over changes to the Land Reform (Scotland) Bill, giving rights to roam and purchase properties on large Scottish estates.[16]

On the range of subjects raised by the future King Charles, he has made frequent attacks on the methods of the teaching establishment and the alleged failures of the educational policies of successive governments. In a lecture in 1991 he said:

> It is high time that the bluff of the so-called 'experts' was called . . . There are terrible dangers, it seems to me, in so following fashionable trends in education . . . that we end up with an entire generation of culturally disinherited people . . . Here in Britain, we seem to get it wrong almost before we have begun.[17]

Earlier, in 1985, he had forcefully described 'the desperate plight of inner city areas . . . the hopelessness left in such communities is compounded by decay all around', calling for a more coherent government strategy to alleviate the situation. The controversy this generated in the press is said to have angered the then Prime Minister, Margaret Thatcher, who was in New York and telephoned Buckingham Palace to express her disapproval of the heir apparent's intervention.[18] Some commentators, including the leader writer for the *Times*, compared the episode with Edward VIII's famous statement that 'something must be done' in response to the unemployment and poverty he found when visiting the towns of south Wales in 1936.

Stimulating and guiding public debate appears to be a deliberate strategy and purpose of the Prince. In 1999, he launched his Prince of Wales website, inviting people to 'join the Prince's online forum', alongside a photograph of himself, captioned 'The Prince of Wales wants to hear your views'. The public policy issues varied from time to time; on 8 November 1999, for example, it was 'The Prince of Wales asks: Should we revive the fortunes of old buildings and unused land in our towns and cities – rather than build on green fields?' The phraseology of this question makes it obvious in which direction the future King wants government policy to proceed.

At the height of the hugely sensitive public controversy over a ban on fox hunting in 2002, whilst the largest mass demonstration seen in post-war Britain was being planned by the Countryside Alliance, it was revealed that Prince Charles had written a passionate letter to the Prime Minister, complaining about government policy towards the countryside. The Prince himself, and the Duchess of Cornwall, have been enthusiastic fox hunters and were widely believed to be opposed to the ban. In his letter to the Prime Minister, the future King said he agreed with what a Cumbrian farmer's had said to him, that if, 'we as a group were black, other ethnic minorities or other minority groups, we would not be victimised or picked upon'.[19]

Foreign policy and China

Perhaps more serious have been the future King's powerful opinions and personal stance in the field of foreign policy, where in the future he will be expected to play a key diplomatic role as head of state, offering goodwill and hospitality to visiting heads from other countries.

A well-known flash point revolves around UK relations with China, a country which has emerged as a major power on the global political stage after its long period of insularity. It has entered a period of tremendous growth and will shortly overtake the UK as the fourth largest economy in the world, almost certainly becoming the largest economy in place of the USA inside the next half-century. Good relations with its government are therefore of very great importance to the UK, especially with new opportunities opening up for British businesses to trade in a country with a massive population of more than 1.3 billion people.

The future Charles III meanwhile appears to be bitterly opposed to China's occupation of Tibet and its suppression of religious freedoms. He is believed to be an admirer of the exiled Tibetan spiritual leader, the Dalai Lama, whom he first met in 1991. In 1999, during the state visit to the UK by China's President Jiang Zemin, Prince Charles was widely reported as having effectively boycotted the Chinese state banquet given in honour of the Queen, and failed to accompany President Jiang on any of his engagements during his visit. More recently, in November 2005 the heir apparent was once again a noticeable absentee during a Chinese state visit, this time failing to attend the state banquet given at Buckingham Palace in honour of China's new leader, President Hu Jintao. On both occasions, the Prince's office offered public reasons for the absences: in 1999, because of an earlier arranged private dinner; in 2005, on the basis that he was jet-lagged, having just flown back from a tour of the United States.

This distancing from and widely viewed conflict with Foreign Office diplomacy was prominently reported across the British press, along with the embarrassment it caused the government. On his absence from the 1999 banquet, for example, the headlines in the newspapers read 'Prince Charles boycotts Chinese banquet' and 'Charles Chinese snub infuriates ministers'.[20] The Prince's deputy private secretary at that time, Mark Bolland, has stated:

> The Prince chose not to attend the return state banquet at the Chinese embassy but to attend instead a private dinner at his home with Camilla Parker Bowles and close friends. He did this as a deliberate snub to the Chinese because he did not approve of

the Chinese regime, and he is a great supporter of the Dalai Lama, whom he views as being oppressed by the Chinese.[21]

The leader writer for the *Daily Telegraph*, the monarchy's most loyal newspaper, pointed out the public implications of this personal gesture: 'In the longer term, his boycott of the banquet would seem to rule out any state visits involving a future King Charles unless there has been a substantial change in Chinese politics.'[22] The *Sunday Times* compared Prince Charles's action with that in 1920 of the Prince of Wales at that time, Edward (later Edward VIII), during a tour of the Empire. In that year, Prince Edward referred to the governors of Hong Kong and Singapore as 'fossilised clerks', causing a famous rebuke from the then Prime Minister, David Lloyd George: 'If you are one day to be a constitutional King, you must first be a constitutional Prince of Wales.' The *Sunday Times* also published a number of politicians' opinions indicating a similar irritation today, including one who said, 'He doesn't seem to understand that a state visit is at the invitation of the elected government and it is the responsibility of the constitutional monarch and her family to welcome the country's guests.'[23]

Extraordinarily, it has been claimed that the Prince not only deliberately snubbed the Chinese state visit but that he took active steps to make it known publicly that he was doing so. According to Mr Bolland, who was in charge of the heir apparent's press relations at that time, 'I was given a direct and personal instruction by the prince to draw to the media's attention his boycotting the banquet. This I did, as he knew, by briefing the press, as did a number of his friends.' If true, this would seriously compromise the constitutional limits of tolerance surrounding the expressions of political opinion by members of the royal family, especially the future King. Naturally, all individuals are entitled to their own private and personal points of view – it is impossible for anyone as an individual not to hold opinions on matters on which they are both interested and knowledgeable, and futile to suggest otherwise. But what strays beyond the boundaries of constitutional legitimacy is when private royal opinions on sensitive political issues are deliberately aired in the public domain.

If any diplomatic offence was caused by the future King's non-participation in the state banquet in honour of the Chinese President in 2005, it is likely to have been made much worse by publication of some rude and disparaging private comments he made about Chinese government officials. These surfaced in the press within days of the President's departure from his state visit to the UK, but this time not by any alleged design of the heir apparent. It transpired that Prince Charles writes journals of his foreign visits, and subsequently has these photocopied and circulated to selected staff, family and friends. A journal he wrote in 1997 described the ceremonies he attended in Hong Kong to mark its reversion to Chinese government. This had the title *The Handover of Hong Kong or The Great Chinese Takeaway* and included some descriptions of Chinese personnel and affairs, now made infamous through their repetition in the press, such as his view of the Chinese diplomats surrounding their President as 'appalling old waxworks'.*[24] One might consider it indiscreet, and arguably careless, to propagate such private views by photocopying the journal to dozens of other people, creating the risk of a 'leak', as did in fact occur. But it was not the Prince's intention that these personal opinions should be published in his lifetime.

How the future King sees his public role

On one level it is entirely laudable that the Prince wants to make a difference, sets about creating new public initiatives and tries to have a voice in the formulation or re-formulation of government policy. But on another, it is questionable whether the privilege of active citizenship is appropriate to the office of a politically neutral monarch.

Furthermore, the scope of the constitutional principles guiding the Prince's involvement in public policy matters remains unclear, especially where the tools and channels of the political influence he seeks to exert are secret letters and confidential meetings. Jonathan Dimbleby's revealing biography of Charles shows that the heir apparent has adopted a highly

---

* As mentioned earlier, the Prince commenced a legal action against Associated Newspapers, publisher of the *Mail on Sunday*, for breach of copyright and confidentiality, seeking an injunction to prohibit further publication of this journal (the 'Hong Kong journal') and future publication of the other seven journals the newspaper had in its possession. In justification, a spokesman for the newspaper said, 'This was not a private journal. It was widely distributed and viewed, as Clarence House confirmed to us, as a historic document intended for eventual publication. The story raised important questions about Britain's relations with China and the Prince's influence on British political thinking.' (*Times*, 19 November 2005). The judgment handed down on 17 March 2006, *HRH The Prince of Wales v. Associated Newspapers* [2006] EWHC 522 (Ch), was a partial victory for the Prince. An injunction and damages were granted against the newspaper in respect of the Hong Kong journal, though, as the judge pointed out, 'the contents of the journal are now fully in the public domain' (para. 6). Regarding the injunction applied for to prevent publication of the Prince's other seven journals, Mr Justice Blackburne forwarded the matter to trial later in the year.

proactive interpretation of the Victorian constitutional writer Walter Bagehot's famous dictum, that a monarch has 'the right to be consulted, the right to encourage, the right to warn'.[25] Indeed, the dictum appears to have been extended with the addition of a 'right to protest', both in his role as Prince of Wales and as future King, coupled with an appetite for holding 'dissident' views.* It seems the Prince feels possessed of not only a right but a duty to involve himself when he 'has a view'.[26]

In Mr Dimbleby's biography, the future Charles III is quoted as saying in one of their numerous conversations, 'I think you could invest the position [of King] with something of your own personality and interest but obviously within the bounds of constitutional propriety'.[27] But the real issue, in terms of constitutional implications, may well be precisely the future King's personal impulses and interests. For, as he himself says, 'the trouble is I always feel that unless I rush about doing things and trying to help furiously I will not (and the monarchy will not) be seen to be relevant and I will be considered a mere playboy'.[28] This is the irony and contradiction of the situation. In truth, a more inactive, less anxious, non-initiating, and 'holding back' personal style is the one in tune with the needs of a contemporary monarchy.

The phlegmatic and tolerant reaction of the present Prime Minister to Prince Charles's royal intrusions into government policy should not blind us to the exasperation regularly felt by other parliamentarians and government ministers. There was a much-publicised 'spat' between Charles Clarke, then Secretary of State for Education, and Prince Charles in November 2004 – the 'war of the Charleses', as it was caricatured at Westminster – which is explicable precisely because of such ministerial resentment. The episode arose out another of the future King's memoranda, made public during the course of an employment tribunal case brought by a former employee, in which the Prince had poured scorn on the 'learning culture at schools . . . which admits of no failure'.† When questioned about the Prince's comments during an interview on BBC radio's *Today* programme on 18 November

---

* According to the Prince's diary, the former Conservative Prime Minister Sir Harold Macmillan said to him after they had had dinner together on 11 November 1970, 'My boy, the sovereign has the right to be informed, to protest and to warn': quoted in Dimbleby, *Prince of Wales*, p. 153. The Prince's self-description of 'dissident' was attributed to him by Mr Bolland in his written statement in *HRH The Prince of Wales v. Associated Newspapers*: 'He often referred to himself as a "dissident" working against the prevailing political consensus.'

† The memorandum went on to say, 'and tells people that they can all be pop stars or High Court judges, or brilliant TV presenters – heads of state! – without ever putting in the necessary work or effort, or having the natural abilities': quoted in the daily press, 19 November 2004.

2004, Mr Clarke displayed irritation at the Prince's intervention and comments, saying, 'To be frank, I think he is very old fashioned and out of time and he doesn't understand what is going on in the British education system at the moment. And I think he should think carefully before intervening in that debate.'

Being a modern monarch as Charles III, as with being the heir apparent as the Prince of Wales, could be interpreted as a thankless task. Today few of our public professions appear to be regarded very highly by society, especially politicians and those working in positions in government. In this vein, significantly, Prince Charles appears to feel that he too is under-appreciated by the British people. In a personal interview for the US television network CBS's *60 Minutes* programme, broadcast on 30 October 2005 on the eve of his American tour, Prince Charles was asked by the interviewer, Steve Kroft, if he felt he was making a difference. His reply was, 'I don't know. I try. I only hope that when I'm dead and gone, they might appreciate it a little bit more. Do you know what I mean? Sometimes that happens.' Some other exchanges related to his public role, as follows:

Kroft: Most of us in our lives have to fill out applications listing our profession and occupation. You don't have to do that.

Charles: No. Not always, but sometimes.

Kroft: If you did, what would you put down?

3 | 2066598.

Charles: I would list it as worrying about this country and its inhabitants. That's my particular duty. And I find myself born into this particular position. I'm determined to make the most of it. And to do whatever I can to help. And I hope I leave things behind a little bit better than I found them. It's hard to say, but I think it is a profession, actually, doing what I'm doing. Because if you tried it for a bit, you might find out how difficult it is.

Kroft: [On the Prince's Trust, which over thirty years has helped to provide job training for more than a half a million young people] Do you think if you weren't doing this stuff, that it would get done?

Charles: If I wasn't doing it? No.

Kroft: What is the most difficult part of your job? I mean except for talking with people like me.

Charles: I think that the most important thing is to be relevant. I mean, it isn't easy, as you can imagine. Because if you say anything, people will say, 'It's all right for you to say that.' It's very easy to just dismiss anything I say. I mean, it's difficult. But what I've tried to do is to put my money where my mouth is as much as I can, by actually

creating, like here, models on the ground. I mean, if people don't like it, I'll go away and do it.

Kroft: How do you deal with [avoiding politically contentious issues]?

Charles: Well, years of practice, perhaps.

Kroft: Does it get you in a spot of trouble from time to time from certain people?

Charles: Oh, inevitably. But it seems to be part and parcel of the thing. I mean, if I wasn't, I think, doing these things, I would be accused by people like you, of doing nothing with my life.

The modern role for a constitutional King

But the precedent and conduct of Elizabeth II clearly contradict this approach. The way the Queen has conducted her public role and work has been universally admired. Popular approval ratings of the Queen have remained consistently high, including in comparison to projections of how Charles will fare as monarch. Asked whether the Queen should step down and let Prince Charles become King, 80 per cent of respondents disagreed, compared with 20 per cent who agreed. On being asked who was their favourite living member of the royal family, 47 per cent stated the Queen and only 11 per cent Prince Charles.[29] Instead of seeking political involvement, Elizabeth II has quietly performed her royal duties with a dignity and self-assurance for which she has earnt the deep affection and loyalty of the political establishment and the broad mass of the British people. The isolated occasions when there has been the remotest public indication of a parting of minds has been on a matter of process, such as the Queen's reported dismay in 1986 at Margaret Thatcher's divisive style of diplomacy at Commonwealth meetings.[30]

It would be a grave mistake to confuse intervention and energetic involvement in government with being 'modern'. To the contrary, as is discussed in Chapter 3 on the powers and duties of a monarch, Elizabeth II has been the epitome of a 'modern monarch' in loyally supporting her democratically elected government's decisions and reconciling her private feelings to her public duties. As to a monarch's ministerial meetings and correspondence, there is a major distinction to be drawn between the receiving and the giving of information. For a constitutional monarch, the primary purpose of the weekly meetings with the Prime Minister is to be briefed on significant domestic and international developments, not to have the opportunity to enter into intellectual discourse on the philosophical direction of the government.

Identity swap: Charles III or 'George VII'?

It has been assumed that the heir apparent, Prince Charles, will succeed to the Crown as Charles III. His first name is Charles, and that is the name he is called by in the family. When communicating directly with people, he usually presents himself in the rather detached manner of 'The Prince of Wales', but he is known and referred to by everyone as Prince Charles. It would seem to follow naturally and automatically that he will ascend the throne as Charles III.

However, he could choose to give himself a different regal name, and the most likely alternative is George VII. It is believed he has contemplated this option, and this was the subject of comments given by two 'trusted friends' of the Prince direct to the media during the Christmas season of 2005. Indeed, one such person went so far as to comment that 'there have been many conversations with the Prince about this. It is an assumption among us all that it will happen.'[31]

As with so many factual developments affecting the monarchy, it is difficult to establish for certain whether this report is tittle-tattle from a bogus 'friend' or an instance of covert Clarence House media briefing to either prepare or test public opinion. One former member of Charles's private office has recently testified as to the covert use of media briefings by the Prince or his staff. Mark Bolland, deputy private secretary from 1997 to 2002, has said that during his period of royal employment,

> the Prince viewed the media as a useful vehicle for getting across to the wider public his views on issues that were important to him. He used the media in two ways: he would directly deal with the media, mainly by writing articles, but also, for example (though this was before my time with the Prince, but is a matter of public record), by co-operating with Jonathan Dimbleby in his authorised biography of the Prince, by participating in the 1994 documentary (again before my time) in which he admitted adultery during the term of his marriage; or by 'briefing' the media by authorising friends and employees such as myself to make the Prince's views known.[32]

It is believed that this form of authorising 'friends' to speak directly to the media as a means of expressing royal news or points of view to the public is indeed a prevalent practice. There is good reason, therefore, to suppose that what was essentially a briefing to the media in December 2005 does represent serious consideration behind adopting the royal name of King George.

A key advantage of being George VII lies in the public relations and presentational effect in distancing the man from all the personal baggage that has gone before as 'Prince Charles'. In other words, this royal personage would re-brand himself. 'New Charles' would become 'King George', the start of a new era for King and country. Christened Charles Philip Arthur George, his other given names are unlikely to appeal to him: Philip is associated with his father, Prince Philip, and surely no one would take 'King Arthur' seriously, having too strong an ancient flavour to it.

Though the first four King Georges all had some negative features to them, the two most recent, who served during the twentieth century, were regarded positively as excellent and much-loved monarchs. George V is generally viewed as a highly dignified, outstanding constitutional monarch. George VI – the Queen's father – gained the huge public respect and affection of the British people for reluctantly taking over as King from his brother Edward after the abdication crisis, and for his conduct working alongside Winston Churchill during the dark days of World War II. The name George, therefore, has a feelgood factor to it.

By contrast, the name Charles has negative connotations in our con-stitutional history, especially ones relating to the survival or well-being of the monarchy. Charles I precipitated a bloody civil war and was eventually beheaded in 1649, following which a republic was established by Oliver Cromwell that lasted for eleven years. In 1660, Charles II was restored to the throne; he is best known for his racy private life – the 'merry monarch' – and for having a string of mistresses, the best known of whom was Nell Gwyn. The other famous royal Charles was the Jacobite 'young pretender' to the throne in the eighteenth century, Bonnie Prince Charlie – called 'King Charles III' by his supporters – who was finally defeated at the Battle of Culloden in 1746.

A final decision on the future King's name will be made at the time of his accession. Legally and constitutionally, the name and title of every new monarch is proclaimed by a body called the Accession Council, which meets to declare the legitimate right of the new monarch to take the throne. The Accession Council is convened within a matter of days following the demise of the incumbent monarch, so clearly some consideration and discussion of the options on a name is indeed desirable now by Clarence House. There are certainly precedents for choosing a name as King that differs from that held as prince. Most recently, for example, the Christian names of the Queen's father were Albert Frederick Arthur George. He was known to his family as

Bertie and in the country as Prince Albert. Yet he chose the name of his father and was proclaimed monarch in the name of George VI.

The significance of the hereditary principle

A perfectly defensible democratic case can be made for a constitutional monarchy, but a principled case can be made for republicanism in Britain.[33] The basic assumption of republicans such as Tony Benn, the veteran former Labour Cabinet minister, is that political power should rest upon consent and that the elective principle is basic to securing such consent to the exercise of power. The case for a constitutional monarchy, on the other hand, relies upon the monarch's withdrawal from, and political neutrality in, the political process. Indeed, its one crucial advantage in comparison to a presidency lies precisely in its lack of being tainted by prior political involvement and partisanship in the life of the nation. This is what makes it preferable to most people over the thought of a President Margaret Thatcher, David Owen or (when available) Tony Blair.

It is important to be clear about the nature of heredity when considering the monarchy's place in the constitution and political process. The essential point about a hereditary monarchy is that the constitutional furniture into which the monarch arrives must be shaped to cope with whatever the accident of birth produces. There is absolutely no guarantee the hereditary principle will produce a monarch who is capable of symbolising the nation and its values. If one wants a head of state who can symbolise the whole nation, or at least a majority in it, then this is probably a stronger argument in favour of an elected head of state than a hereditary one. Because the hereditary principle enshrines the accidental and the unpredictable, the corollary of accepting the hereditary principle is that the institution of monarch should accept a narrowly drawn political place in the system of government. That said, popular attitudes towards the monarchy regularly confuse two separate issues – claims about the legitimacy of the hereditary principle and claims about the character and virtues of the monarch and heir apparent.

The propositions on which future developments depend

There are a number of truisms about the monarchy's place in our present and future political life which bear emphasis before turning to the particular subjects and issues discussed in the later chapters. Put simply, they are these:

- The personality of the King or Queen directly affects the working of the institution of monarchy, how it carries out its functions, how it is perceived and evaluated and its level of popular support. People find it hard to distinguish between their support for the institution and for the person who happens to be King or Queen.
- After a very long period with Queen Elizabeth on the throne, by projecting into the future with a different person as royal head of state, King Charles III, this allows us more clearly to evaluate the institution of monarchy itself, the constitutional furniture within which it sits today, and where the prospects for reform and future development lie.
- Contemporary constitutional commentators – republicans apart – be they parliamentarians, ministers, or university professors, are unanimous in their view that Elizabeth II has been a model of democratic constitutional sovereignty in her fifty-four years upon the throne. Her place as an exemplary monarch of this country is guaranteed, resting on her deep-rooted sense of constitutional duty inherited from her father and her subordination of the considerable potential influence she possesses in public affairs to the policies and primacy of her elected ministers.
- Monarchy under Charles III could prove very different to that which most British people have known all their lives. He will be, as his relative the former King Constantine of Greece calls him, the 'philosopher King'. His most famous biographer describes him as a personality of soul-searching disposition, prone to the 'assertion of conviction which those around him would increasingly have to reckon with'.[34] One day, he could choose to make use of the elevated authority and access to powerful individuals he will enjoy as head of state to promote his views on any issue of the day and to further the causes and beliefs he now already espouses.
- Some might find this royal involvement welcome, particularly those who might share the future King's views on the particular matter in question, be it genetically modified crops, complementary medicine, the education curriculum, architecture or foreign policy on Tibet. But for others, it could breed resentment. There would be grave dangers to the

institution of monarchy if the King's dealings with ministers, or his communications of opinion with people outside government influential in shaping public opinion, ever came to be regarded as unwarranted interference, tantamount to unconstitutional conduct.

But if the working of the institution will almost certainly evolve according to a new personality on the throne, so too will the circumstances in which King Charles starts his new reign be of a markedly different nature to those which were inherited by Elizabeth II in 1952. Liberalisation, a classless society, secularisation, globalisation and the European Union – these alone present a very different context for the succession of Charles to the Crown to that inherited by his mother.

2

The marriage of the future King and Mrs Camilla Parker Bowles

The announcement and timing of the royal wedding

'At last' – resolution of a troubled royal romance
The overarching theme of the day's press the morning after the public announcement of the engagement of Prince Charles and Camilla Parker Bowles was 'At last'. For the two human beings concerned, the royal engagement and eventual marriage ceremony that took place on 9 April 2005 at Windsor Guildhall were very happy occasions. They were the culmination of a private romance that, despite numerous obstacles in its path, had survived its course and the vicissitudes of fortune over the space of thirty-four years.

Foremost among the causes of these difficulties was the fact of their earlier respective marriages along the way since their first meeting in 1970 and subsequent young romance. Both those respective earlier legal unions, that of Miss Camilla Rosemary Shand in 1973 to Brigadier Andrew Parker Bowles, and that of Prince Charles in 1981 to the hugely popular and glamorous Lady Diana Spencer, had produced families. The children were, of course, in Charles and Diana's case the Princes William and Harry, the first of whom will one day be King and head of state, and in Brigadier and Mrs Parker Bowles's case Tom and Laura. These two first marriages were legally dissolved, with the divorce of the Prince and Princess of Wales taking effect on 28 August 1996. Earlier, the Prince had admitted his adultery, though only after his marriage had irretrievably broken down, in a national television interview broadcast on 29 June 1994;[1] and the Princess referred to Mrs

Parker Bowles as a factor in her marital breakdown in a national television interview on 20 November 1995.* On 31 August 1997 Princess Diana tragically died in a motor accident in Paris. Andrew and Camilla Parker Bowles's divorce had been completed in March 1995, and the following year Brigadier Parker Bowles had married his present wife, Rosemary.

The official announcement of the royal engagement came from Clarence House in the early morning of Thursday 10 February 2005. The press announcement read:

Announcement of the Marriage of HRH The Prince of Wales and Mrs Camilla Parker Bowles

It is with great pleasure that the marriage of HRH The Prince of Wales and Mrs Camilla Parker Bowles is announced. It will take place on Friday 8th April 2005 at Windsor Castle.

The Prince of Wales has said: 'Mrs Parker Bowles and I are absolutely delighted. It will be a very special day for us and our families.'

Princes William and Harry released a joint statement: 'We are both very happy for our father and Camilla, and we wish them all the luck in the future.'

Mrs Parker Bowles will use the title HRH The Duchess of Cornwall after marriage. It is intended that Mrs Parker Bowles should use the title HRH The Princess Consort when The Prince of Wales accedes to The Throne.

The wedding will be a largely private occasion for family and friends. It will comprise a civil ceremony in Windsor Castle. There will subsequently be a service of prayer and dedication in St George's Chapel at which the Archbishop of Canterbury will preside.

The timing of this announcement was brought forward because of a leak of the pending news to the London *Evening Standard.* The plan had been to break the news to the public during the week commencing Monday 14 February, Valentine's Day. However, in its early morning edition on 10 February, the newspaper exclusively published details of the engagement and wedding date of 8 April. Its royal correspondent, Robert Jobson,[2] had been closely investigating developments at Clarence House ever since the previous December, when he reported in the *Evening Standard* that Prince Charles believed he would soon be free to marry, under the front page headline

---

* BBC *Panorama* interview by Martin Bashir, 20 November 1995, during which Princess Diana famously commented, 'There were three of us in this marriage, so it was a bit crowded.'

'Exclusive: Charles prepares the way to wed Camilla'. As soon as Clarence House learnt of the *Standard*'s pending publication, it immediately issued the official announcement of the royal engagement through a press release and on its website, supplemented by statements from various spokesmen. The Prince and Mrs Parker Bowles were reported to be understandably irritated by the leak. It upset their intentions for a sensitive and more finely tuned release of the news to their family and close friends, of whom only a handful such as Princes William and Harry, and Tom and Laura Parker Bowles, had received advance notice.

Concern over the timing of a 2005 wedding, however, paled into insignificance in comparison to the much wider, long-running issue of whether a marriage of the future King Charles and Camilla Parker Bowles could ever take place at all. The heir apparent and his advisers had been working for many years at planning, or rather managing, a process on this issue which involved resolving three key points.

- The first of these was to answer the question of whether he and Mrs Parker Bowles wished to get married, or were content simply to remain in an extra-marital relationship.* Termination of their romantic liaison altogether – the solution adopted by Princess Margaret in 1955[3] – was out of the question, it seemed, so far as the Prince was concerned. Their relationship was 'non-negotiable', as he let it be known and understood. This was a sentiment similar to that of his great-uncle the Duke of Windsor regarding his affair with the divorcee Mrs Wallis Simpson, which led to his enforced abdication as Edward VIII.
- If the answer to this was that they wished to marry, then a public relations exercise was required gradually to promote and establish Mrs Parker Bowles with a positive image in popular opinion as a suitable consort to the future King. This required strategic long term planning and great patience, which most regard has having begun six years earlier

---

* On 21 December 1995 Prince Charles had issued a statement through his spokesman at St James's Palace that he had no intention of re-marrying after his pending divorce from Princess Diana. Lord St John of Fawsley, a former Cabinet minister and constitutional specialist, commented in the *Times* for its edition on 22 December 1995, 'While he has a perfect right to marry or change his mind, that statement is to be very warmly welcomed. It removes a source of gossip and speculation.' In July 2000 the Prince, through his then private secretary, Stephen Lamport, complained to the Press Complaints Commission about a misleading press article 'Charles explores Scottish wedding with Camilla', asserting, 'There is no intention of remarrying.'

on 29 January 1999, with a carefully staged photo-opportunity of the couple making a public appearance together to attend a fiftieth birthday party celebration at the Ritz.

• Closely linked to the task of gaining popular acceptance for Mrs Parker Bowles as consort to the future King was the question of the constitutionality of such a marriage. A favourable resolution of the complex mix of political and religious factors involved required a careful strategy of gaining support from influential people within the corridors of those places – in political, royal and ecclesiastical circles – where a determination of this question would be made.

After so long – why now?

When Sir Michael Peat, the Prince's private secretary, came personally to deliver the news of the royal engagement to the staff at Clarence House, the human response was one of great emotion and enormous relief. According to those present, several people burst into tears and there was hardly a dry eye in the house.[4] The Charles–Camilla question was one that had hung over the Prince's household like a dark cloud for so long, it seemed to many unbelievable that at last some blue was appearing in the sky.

'The issue of marriage has been considered by them for a long time and they, like any couple, felt now was the right time to get married,' one of Charles's aides commented to the press.[5] Another added, 'They are very much a couple and have shown their commitment to each other for many years. It is a natural conclusion for their loving relationship.' The presentational pitch of the Clarence House public relations team, therefore, was one that focused on the private and personal human dimension of their predicament. The positive emotional support of the children featured prominently in the elucidation of and comments on the engagement as presented to the media by Clarence House and Buckingham Palace staff. Of William and Harry, a close aide of Prince Charles said they had been kept informed of developments throughout and were extremely happy about the news: 'They are delighted. They want their father and Mrs Parker Bowles to be happy. These things have been discussed within the family.'

The reality is that privately Charles and Camilla are likely to have wished to be married far earlier, certainly from 1999 onwards. It was public factors, rather than private considerations, that determined the most appropriate time for them getting married. The factors in the public decision were as follows. First, despite ongoing public and media controversy about the relationship and its potential for precipitating a constitutional crisis, the balanced view of most experts and advisers – or at least the most sensible ones – was that the marriage could go ahead and that there were no insuperable legal or constitutional problems.[6]

Furthermore, while these balanced constitutional opinions nonetheless recognised that the Charles–Camilla relationship was not good for the institution of monarchy and would have some destabilising effect, this disadvantage was considerably outweighed by the more serious negative public problems in them not being married when Charles became King.* Considering the huge importance of protocol and diplomatic etiquette bound up in the public work of the monarch as head of state, for example meetings and dinners with foreign heads of state or government, the non-status of the King's partner would have been extremely difficult to manage. And once Charles was King, the announcement of his engagement and the event of his marriage would attract far more sensational publicity and occasion for mischief than was the case in 2005. As Prince of Wales, his marriage could just about pass public acceptance as a private event of sorts. As King and head of state, his marriage to Camilla would far more obviously have been a de facto state event, whatever presentational gloss and arrangements were made. From a constitutional perspective, the royal marriage of Charles and Camilla taking place sooner rather than later had become the lesser of two problematic scenarios.

There were other elements in the equation that served to galvanise or amplify these difficulties at the time of the engagement. One was simply the Queen's age, and the fact that she was not eternal. In 2005, Elizabeth would turn seventy-nine years of age. Prince Philip, upon whom she relies so much, would be even older – eighty-four. Although there is some longevity in the family, the prospect of Charles III on the throne was getting ever nearer. For the present, out of necessity the Queen would be starting to devolve more and more state work upon Charles as heir apparent, especially in the area of foreign travel, which the Queen's and Prince Philip's age was making increasingly arduous.

---

* Indeed, if the whole controversy had been raised when he was King, it would have powerfully evoked references, memories and comparisons with King Edward VIII and the royal abdication crisis in 1936. The presence of personal traumas associated with past royal strife over questions of divorce, notably in 1936 and in 1955, was lessened when the Queen Mother and Princess Margaret died in 2002.

The need for the 'non-negotiable' partner to acquire official status
The need for Camilla to acquire some formal status was materialising in other ways too, including ones symptomatic of the mixed public-private lifestyle of the royal family. To take examples drawn from the three months prior to the royal engagement, in November 2004 at a society wedding attended by the Queen as godmother to the groom, Camilla was allocated seating away from Charles. This was widely seen as a snub and was allegedly the reason causing him to withdraw his acceptance and not attend at all. Next month, Camilla was prevented from joining Charles for Christmas, which the royal family by tradition hold at Sandringham House in Norfolk, because royal etiquette dictates that only members of the royal family may attend. Then on 5 January 2005, there was another seating issue at the funeral of Sir Angus Ogilvy, husband of the Queen's cousin Princess Alexandra. Charles and Camilla arrived together by car, but were then split up for the service, Camilla with the ordinary mourners and Charles sitting with his mother and father. As construed by the press, Camilla was 'frozen out' and 'forced to sit away from Charles at funeral'.*

The question had also arisen as to the legitimacy with which Camilla could, or should, be supported financially out of the Prince of Wales's accounts. As a mere friend and unmarried partner to the heir apparent, the idea that her daily activity expenses should be met out of public funds was open to possible criticism and objection. This issue had recently attained much greater prominence as a result of some details about the Prince's public income and expenditure being published for the first time in an annual report in June 2004. In this report, Mrs Parker Bowles was mentioned twice under expenditure items. Referring to the Prince of Wales's household, it said there were eighty-four members of staff paid to support the Prince's official and charitable work, and twenty-seven others as 'personal staff for himself, Prince William and Harry, and Mrs Parker Bowles'. Elsewhere in the report it was said that 'income from the Duchy of Cornwall is used to meet personal expenditure for The Prince of Wales, Princes William and Harry, and some personal costs of Mrs Parker Bowles'.

This raised eyebrows when reported in the press, and at the London

---

* *Daily Express*, 6 January 2005. Two months later, at the service of remembrance held for Sir Angus at Westminster Abbey on 2 March, things were different. Camilla – now bearing the status of fiancée to the heir apparent – represented the Prince, who was abroad on a tour of Australia, and was seated close to the Ogilvies and members of the royal family, though not the Queen, who did not attend.

briefing for journalists on the report, the Prince's private secretary, Sir Michael Peat, was said to have 'appeared flustered only under questioning about Mrs Parker Bowles's presence in the Prince's accounts'.[7] Any anxieties of the Prince's senior advisers were made worse when the House of Commons Public Accounts Committee then indicated that it wished to inquire into the Duchy of Cornwall's finances, using the annual report as the basis for an oral examination of the leading figures in the work of the duchy. Given the ease with which even the most trivial royal matter can be sensationalised out of all proportion in the mass media, the urge of the Prince's household to try to maintain confidentiality about all the Prince's affairs is understandable. Initially, Paul Clarke, the chief executive and clerk of the Prince's Council, was resistant to the Public Accounts Committee's proposal that it scrutinise the Duchy of Cornwall's finances by way of an oral hearing.[8] However, the claims of the Public Accounts Committee were well founded and could hardly be resisted. In the event, the question of the expenses of Mrs Parker Bowles did not arise during the evidence-taking session, and it is likely an agreement was reached as a pre-condition for the hearing taking place that matters of personal expenditure would not be raised. Nonetheless, this whole episode had increased the level of sensitivity about how defensible it was that the Prince be supporting his unmarried mistress out of duchy funds, whereas if married, there could be no dispute that the expenses of the heir apparent's spouse were entirely legitimate.

In terms of public opinion and popular acceptance of the future King Charles being married to Mrs Parker Bowles, attitudes towards a possible marriage seemed to have reached a favourable plateau. By the time of the announcement of the royal engagement, levels of downright hostility had declined and the great majority of people were now expressing lukewarm support or were apathetic about the matter. A Populus opinion poll conducted on 10 and 11 February 2005, commissioned immediately upon the engagement by the *Times*, indicated that only 22 per cent disapproved, 43 per cent approved and 30 per cent did not care. This was favourable progress on nine months previously, when in June 2004 the respective figures found by Populus had been that 29 per cent disapproved, 32 per cent approved and 22 per cent did not care. Within the establishment, a judgemental point of critical mass had now been reached. Of the three options available, abdication, King with an unmarried partner, or royal marriage to a divorcee, a consensus now converged around the last of these as the route forward.

The media leak the news: the couple's announcement brought forward
Who had leaked the news? Some suspected that electoral advantage was being gleaned from the royal occasion by Labour's strategists in 10 Downing Street, with the May general election in prospect. Thus one Conservative shadow Cabinet member told the press, 'It was clearly part of the spin to try to give Blair a feelgood factor.'[9]

At the daily No. 10 press briefings, when the Prime Minister's official spokesman was asked several times whether Tony Blair's famous former 'spin doctor' and communications chief, Alastair Campbell, had had knowledge of the engagement in advance, the response was that the news had not been passed on to Mr Campbell. The Prime Minister's spokesman strongly rejected the suggestion that someone at 10 Downing Street had leaked the news, saying this was 'categorically wrong'. In his view, it was simply a straightforward *Evening Standard* scoop. According to Trevor Kavanagh, the veteran political editor of the *Sun*,

> the conspiracy theory is that Downing Street blew the gaffe on Charles and Camilla to boost the PM in the run-up to a May 5 General Election. But it doesn't stack up. Many people are against the marriage. Charles is widely seen as a dithering wimp who should never be King and most people blame Camilla for ending his marriage to Di. The news has wiped politics off the front pages and it will eclipse Labour's spring conference. We all love a wedding, but there is precious little goodwill for this one.[10]

This reception in parts of the media, from the leaking of the news before the couple had even told their friends, to unkind or downright rude press commentary on them as human beings, was no doubt the key factor in determining that the period of the royal engagement would be extremely short. Any married couple, particularly if they have organised any kind of ceremony for their nuptials, knows full well the large amount of planning and organisation there is to do. The period the couple allowed, just two months, would for most people would be near impossible for sorting out all the paperwork, bookings, printing, notifications, catering arrangements and so on. The royal couple and their advisers, aware of the mischief and distress the media and others might cause, resolved for a wedding to take place at the earliest humanly possible date.

The response of the Queen and the Royal Household

The Queen's support for her family

The response from Buckingham Palace, immediately following the official announcement of the royal engagement on 10 February 2005, was for its press office to issue the following statement on behalf of the Queen:

> The Duke of Edinburgh and I are very happy that The Prince of Wales and Mrs Parker Bowles are to marry. We have given them our warmest good wishes for their future together.

Over the years the marital difficulties of three of her four children (first Anne, then Andrew and finally Charles) had clearly been a source of great personal unhappiness for the Queen. The traditions of her own family background and her constitutional and religious duties powerfully endorsed the institutions of marriage and the family. However, she remained stoically supportive as a parent throughout.

Princess Anne (the Queen's second child), then aged twenty-three, married Captain Mark Phillips in a glittering ceremony at Westminster Abbey on 14 November 1973. They had two children, Peter and Zara, born in 1977 and 1981 respectively, but agreed to separate in 1989 and divorced in 1992. On 12 December 1992, she married Captain Timothy Laurence in a Church of Scotland service at Crathie kirk, Balmoral. The matrimonial breakdown of Prince Andrew, Duke of York (the Queen's third child) and his wife, Sarah, was more painful, aggravated by embarrassing media and photographic coverage of the duchess's private affairs. They had been married in Westminster Abbey in 1986, and had two daughters, Beatrice and Eugenie, born in 1988 and 1990 respectively. They separated in 1992, with the marriage being formally dissolved in April 1996.

The earlier divorce of the Prince and Princess of Wales

Neither of these two sets of matrimonial episodes could match the highs and lows of Charles and Diana's marriage, however. They were married in a 'fairy tale' wedding ceremony at St Paul's Cathedral on 29 July 1981. In the Archbishop of Canterbury's address at the marriage, he said, 'This is the stuff of which fairy tales are made; the Prince and Princess on their wedding day . . . Those who are married live happily ever after the wedding day if they persevere in the real adventure which is the royal task of creating each other and creating a more loving world.'[11] There were national celebrations before and after and a grand procession across London, the streets were lined with a million people who had specially come to watch, and every moment was broadcast on television across the world to an estimated audience of three quarters of a billion viewers. Two children followed, the Princes William and Harry on 21 June 1982 and 15 September 1984 respectively.

According to the Prince's most authoritative biography, by Jonathan Dimbleby, 'by 1986, their marriage had begun slowly to disintegrate in what were, for both of them, the most excruciating circumstances'. Among the confidential private papers made available to Mr Dimbleby by the Prince of Wales during the course of his research, Charles wrote in a letter dated 18 November 1986, 'How awful incompatibility is, and how dreadfully destructive it can be for the players in this extraordinary drama.'[12] The Prince and Princess of Wales began to live separate lives, which posed no major public problem until 1992, when a book by Andrew Morton, *Diana: Her True Story*, serialised in advance by the *Sunday Times*, exposed the full extent and nature of their marital problems.

On 9 December 1992, Buckingham Palace issued a written statement to the press announcing the official separation of the Prince and Princess of Wales, in the following terms:

> It is announced from Buckingham Palace, that, with regret, the Prince and Princess of Wales have decided to separate . . . The Queen and the Duke of Edinburgh, though saddened, understand and sympathise with the difficulties that have led to this decision. Her Majesty and His Royal Highness particularly hope that the intrusions into the privacy of the Prince and Princess may now cease. They believe that a degree of privacy and understanding is essential if Their Royal Highnesses are to provide a happy and secure upbringing for their children, while continuing to give a whole-hearted commitment to their public duties.

The Prime Minister, then John Major, simultaneously read out the Queen's message to the House of Commons, adding that 'the decision to separate has no constitutional implications' and that ' the succession to the throne is unaffected by it'.[13] The Queen's overriding concern for the feelings and stability of the future heir to the throne, Prince William, as well as his brother, Prince Harry, has been evident throughout, not only during the collapse of Charles's first marriage, but in the proceedings leading up to his re-marriage in 2005.

From 1992 to 1996, the most private and personal actions, foibles and conversations of Charles or Diana, together with any suggestions of conflict or indiscretion, were grotesquely pored over and amplified by the media on purported grounds of public interest and constitutional importance. To some extent it is true, as the Calcutt report on press behaviour in respect of personal privacy in January 1993 suggested, that the media could not be entirely blamed for intruding into their personal affairs because of Charles and Diana's own deliberate utilisation of it.[14] And indeed, the final climax of media sensationalism on the couple's relationship was triggered by Diana herself when she gave a secretly filmed interview with Martin Bashir for the BBC's *Panorama*. This programme, broadcast on 20 November 1995, was watched by an audience of 22.8 million people, and made mass headline coverage on virtually every newspaper the following day and indeed for the rest of the week. Diana's utterances included such personal statements as 'the enemy was my husband's department because I always got more publicity', 'who knows?' (when asked if Charles would be King), 'I would like to be queen in people's hearts but I don't see myself being Queen', 'yes, I adored him [Captain James Hewitt]', 'I had bulimia for a number of years, I was crying out for help' and (on Camilla Parker Bowles) 'there were three of us in this marriage, so it was a bit crowded'.

The Queen's role in the future King's divorce

It was almost universally felt within the establishment that such feuding and antagonism in the public eye had to end, because it was damaging the institution of the monarchy. It would be disastrous in terms of the public conduct, dignity and diplomacy of the head of state if this acrimonious relationship continued under a King Charles III and Queen Diana regime. This point of view was forcibly expressed by Lord Blake, the Oxford historian and adviser to the Palace, in a press article he wrote in response to receiving news of the impending BBC *Panorama* interview.

> I believe the lesson to be drawn from the fracas over Princess Diana's decision to give an interview to BBC's *Panorama* is that she and Prince Charles should divorce forthwith . . . I can see no constitutional problems in a divorce; and I see possible grave problems should it be long delayed . . . It seems to me that Diana should not become Queen. Her past conduct and the dreadful terms she is on with the man who would be King make that quite undesirable. To have a King and Queen on such

obviously bad terms would be unworkable as well as foolish: would there be two rival courts, as there are in embryo already?[15]

The Queen's response to the crisis, as it was generally perceived, was swift, with close attention paid to constitutional propriety. Advised by her senior household staff, especially her private secretary, Sir Robert Fellowes, Queen Elizabeth proceeded to speak with and consult the Prime Minister, John Major, and the Archbishop of Canterbury, Dr George Carey, on what could and should be done. The consensus of opinion was that divorce had now become a virtual necessity as the lesser of two evils, a divorced future King and head of the Church as opposed to a feuding King and Queen of the United Kingdom. And if, as now seemed clear, there was no prospect of the marriage being repaired, it was better Charles was divorced before he became King Charles III and Supreme Governor of the Church of England.

On 20 December 1995, exactly one month after the *Panorama* interview, Buckingham Palace made it known that Elizabeth II within the previous few days had written to both the Prince and the Princess of Wales. In her capacity as monarch, head of state and head of the royal family, she urged the couple to agree to 'an early divorce'. It was also made known that the Archbishop of Canterbury and Prime Minister agreed with this view. To assist matters, Mr Major had met both parties, Prince Charles the previous week, and Princess Diana for one hour earlier that day, to discuss the future arrangements. Everyone agreed that a public place should be retained for Diana, and indeed was unavoidable given her position as mother to the future William V. The key difference was that she would never, after divorce, become 'Queen Diana'.

This action by the Queen led directly to the divorce arrangements being negotiated, agreed and completed within a short space of time. Lawyers for each party, Farrer & Co for the Prince and Mishcon de Reya on behalf of the Princess, were immediately instructed. Within ten weeks the basic terms of the agreement to divorce had been negotiated and settled, with a public announcement being made on 28 February 1996. The financial arrangements and settlement on Princess Diana was concluded on 12 July and the decree nisi granted three days later. Finally, the royal divorce was made absolute on 28 August 1996.

The matters to resolve during the divorce negotiations had needed the Queen's involvement and concurrence on at least two major issues. First, there was the question of Diana's future title. It was agreed that she would lose the prefix 'Her Royal Highness', and be known after the divorce simply as Diana, Princess of Wales. This situation would remain when Charles III ascended the throne. A future title of 'Queen Mother' when William became King was not applicable, since this had been a title created specially for the widow of George VI arising from the special circumstances of her bearing the same name as the incoming monarch, her daughter Queen Elizabeth.

Second, there was the question of custody of and access to the children of the marriage, the Princes William and Harry. The normal legal principles of family law did not operate in this particular royal situation. This is because a monarch, in this case Elizabeth II, has an ancient common-law right and duty over matters relating to the upbringing of her close relatives, certainly those of her grandchildren and the future heir to the throne.* Princess Diana's public statement, in recognition of this, simply claimed that 'the Princess will continue to be involved in all decisions relating to the children'. The later statement by Buckingham Palace on 12 July 1996 expressed the situation in terms that the Prince and Princess 'will continue to share equal responsibility in the upbringing of their children'.

The precedent of Edward VIII

A young person today has difficulty imagining the huge social taboo that divorce represented down to the middle of the twentieth century. For a husband and wife to terminate their partnership and cause the break-up of their family unit was regarded in centuries past and until very recently as a serious abnegation of social and religious duty. As attitudes and the divorce laws have liberalised, so the rate of divorce has dramatically expanded, from 5,916 petitions being filed in 1936 to 166,700 divorces taking place in 2003. The Queen is a traditionalist in every sense. She belongs to the earlier era that seriously frowned upon divorce. But more than this, in the case of her own family, matters of divorce had created a huge ruction in her life and that of her parents.

It was the decision of her uncle, Edward VIII, to marry a divorcee, Mrs Wallis Simpson, that led to his abdication and a constitutional crisis in 1936. As a consequence, the relatively carefree life of Elizabeth's shy and retiring father, the then Duke of York, was shattered by his being required to take

---

* In 1717 King George I asked the judges to give a ruling on this matter: the opinion given by a ten to two majority was that the monarch's right of supervision extended to his grandchildren. See *Halsbury's Laws of England*, 4th edn (London: Butterworths, 1973–87), vol. 12(1), pp. 20–1.

over the burdens of office as head of state. It was only his overwhelming sense of duty that made him accept the crown, despite deep personal reluctance to have to perform this high-profile role for which he had had virtually no preparation. The impact on the charmed life of his family, his wife, then Duchess of York (subsequently Queen consort then Queen Elizabeth the Queen Mother), and his young daughters, Princesses Elizabeth and Margaret, was one of enormous personal strain. As the Duchess of York wrote in a letter, 'I don't think we could ever imagine a more incredible tragedy, and the agony of it has been beyond words'.[16]

It was a burden for George VI that many in his family believe took him to a premature death on 6 February 1952 at the age of only fifty-six, leaving behind his 25-year-old daughter to take over the work as head of state. Queen Elizabeth the Queen Mother voiced resentment and hatred towards Mrs Simpson from 1936 onwards for the rest of her life, adding to the doom-laden nature of divorce in the eyes of Elizabeth II. In his biography of George VI, the historian Robert Rhodes James described her feelings as follows:

> The Yorks blamed Mrs Simpson rather than the King [Edward VIII]. Indeed, the Duchess [later Elizabeth, Queen consort] could not abide Mrs Simpson personally, a dislike which was warmly reciprocated, and although the increasing coldness between the two brothers – or rather, coldness from the King towards the Duke – might have been transformed had the Duchess invited Mrs Simpson to their home, this she emphatically would not do. One of her great qualities was her refusal to dissimulate on really important matters, and the sanctity of marriage was something she took very seriously.[17]

It is unsurprising, therefore, that the Queen and the Royal Household did not welcome Camilla Parker Bowles with open arms as Charles's romantic partner. On 21 December 1995 Prince Charles had made a public statement that, if his intended divorce to Diana went through, then he would not re-marry. But whilst this might have reassured traditionalists in the Church, it hardly resolved the secular and diplomatic problems of state for the possible future situation where he was King Charles III with a live-in divorced lover.

Over the ten-year period from her son's divorce in 1995 to the royal engagement in 2005, Queen Elizabeth II had maintained a distance from Mrs Parker Bowles, meeting her only on a handful of occasions in the later few years. The first landmark came on 3 June 2000, when the two met socially at Highgrove for a sixtieth birthday party given by Prince Charles for his relative, the ex-King Constantine of Greece. A Buckingham Palace spokesman told the press, 'The question of Mrs Parker Bowles' attendance of private royal family functions will depend on circumstances.'[18] Two weeks later it was reported in the *Sunday Times* by the religious affairs correspondent that 'the Queen has let it be known that her decision to meet Parker Bowles at a lunch earlier this month, after years of refusing to do so, did not constitute "approval" of her son's relationship.'[19] Two years later, Camilla was invited by the Queen to sit in the royal box for the classical concert in Buckingham Palace Gardens to celebrate her 2002 Golden Jubilee. Throughout this period, whatever Queen Elizabeth's personal feelings on her son's relationship with Mrs Parker Bowles, there also remained numerous protocol and ceremonial considerations which would often preclude her from attending Palace functions as the partner of Prince Charles.

The Queen's formal consent under the Royal Marriages Act

Over Christmas 2004, Prince Charles discussed his wedding plans with the Queen, suggesting provisional dates be set for the announcement in February and the wedding in April. The principal concerns of his mother were then twofold. First, she needed to comply with her constitutional obligations to follow prime ministerial advice in exercising her decision under the Royal Marriages Act. This Act, whose provisions and possible reform are discussed in Chapter 5, prevents Prince Charles from marrying without the consent of the monarch, on the historical basis that marital unions of members of the royal family have political implications. After duly consulting the Prime Minister in early February, she was able to indicate to Charles that the royal consent would be forthcoming. This royal act was formalised by way of an order issued through the Privy Council:

Orders approved at the Privy Council held by The Queen at Buckingham Palace on 2 March 2005

Royal Marriages Act 1772	Declaration of Consent to the marriage of His Royal Highness The Prince of Wales, K.G., K.T., G.C.B., O.M., and Mrs Camilla Parker Bowles.
	Order directing that the Instrument signifying consent be entered in the Books of the Privy Council.

The Queen's religious duties and her involvement on the wedding day

The second obligation upon Queen Elizabeth as monarch was to ensure she complied with her religious and moral duties as head of the Church of England. This presented a parallel conundrum to that already wrestled with by the Archbishop of Canterbury. The well-known problem was that the Church of England takes a restrictive stance on conducting wedding ceremonies for second marriages where one or both parties are divorcees.[20] Clearly, as part of the arrangements that were agreed with Dr Rowan Williams, the Archbishop of Canterbury, the marriage of Prince Charles and Mrs Parker Bowles was not deemed appropriate for a church service.

Instead, as is discussed below, to provide a cloak of Anglican support, Dr Williams had agreed to conduct an Anglican service of blessing after the wedding. This formula – a civil registry marriage followed by an Anglican church blessing – has been adopted on many occasions by other couples over the past thirty years. The church blessing ceremony is formally called a service of prayer and dedication. As the Bishop of Hereford, Rt Rev. Anthony Priddis, chairman of the Church's group on marriage and family life, explained to the press, 'a blessing does not equate with condoning what has happened before but it does recognise a new beginning.'[21]

To be blunt, therefore, strictly speaking the religious attitude of the Church of England towards the re-marriage of Prince Charles and Mrs Parker Bowles did not formally condone or approve of the marriage. It was unable on religious grounds to recognise or offer the re-marriage as being appropriate. Furthermore, there were many Anglican priests on the hard-line, traditionalist wing of the Church who condemned the re-marriage on moral grounds. The Rev. David Phillips of the Church Society, for example, was quoted in the press as saying, 'I don't believe Charles should be remarrying, and if he is determined to go ahead, he shouldn't be in a position where he can become Supreme Governor of the Church of England.'[22] As the Church's General Synod happened to be meeting in London on 14 February, shortly after the engagement was announced, critics of the royal wedding attempted to call an emergency debate on it, but this was rejected. Rod Thomas, the spokesman for the Reform group of evangelicals, was quoted as saying the marriage would compromise Charles's 'moral authority' when he became King and Supreme Governor of the Church, and add to the pressures for disestablishment.[23]

In this sensitive religious and constitutional scenario the Queen declined to attend the civil wedding at the register office.[24] There then followed a wave of media comment misconstruing her action as a 'snub' to her son and prospective daughter-in-law, in response to which the Palace set the record straight through the means of an unattributable briefing to the press. According to a 'friend', the Queen had said, 'I am not able to go. I do not feel that my position [as Supreme Governor of the Church] permits it.'[25] In the same press report, a senior royal official added, 'The Queen takes her position as Supreme Governor of the Church of England incredibly seriously. She also has great personal faith.' Another aide added, 'The venue was never the issue for the Queen. The civil nature of the service is the issue. She did not feel it was appropriate for her to attend.' The Queen's absence from the royal marriage is significant in a number of different ways. Her conduct was typically meticulous, distinguishing clearly between her constitutional and personal roles – as Queen and as mother – in a manner that a great many, including a large section of the media and possibly even Prince Charles himself, did not seem to fully appreciate. As described in the narrative of the day's events below, once the civil marriage in the register office was over, the Queen joined the newly wed couple for the blessing service conducted by the Archbishop of Canterbury. She was then host at the warm, successful and large wedding reception held at Windsor Castle.

The attitude of the Archbishop of Canterbury and the Christian churches

Over the period since 1996 there had been a growing number of expressions of support from prominent Anglican clerics about the possibility of the future King Charles and Camilla Parker Bowles getting married if they wished to do so. To a large extent, this was driven by the realisation, already commented upon, that, if the Prince's partnership with Mrs Parker Bowles was going to be permanent, it was better (or less bad) that they be married rather than unmarried. With the Queen approaching her eightieth birthday and the prospect of King Charles III getting closer, the idea of the Supreme Governor of the Church being in a romantic liaison, possibly cohabitation, with a divorcee was not an attractive proposition. In a 1998 interview with the *Newcastle Journal*, the then Bishop of Durham, Rt Rev. Michael Turnbull, said it would be 'more desirable ethically and morally for Prince Charles to re-marry, rather than for the situation to remain as it is at present, in a state of flux'.

By the end of 2004, a consensus of encouragement and compassion had been reached among the leaders of the Church of England towards Prince Charles's marriage to Mrs Parker Bowles. A significant development had been the public support given by Dr George Carey, the former Archbishop of Canterbury, in his book *Know the Truth*. He wrote,

> He [Prince Charles] is the heir to the throne and he loves her. The natural thing is that they should get married. The Christian faith is all about forgiveness. We all make mistakes. Failure is part of the human condition and there is no doubt that there has been a strong loving relationship, probably since they were very young, that has endured over the years.[26]

Another significant voice of support in 2004 had been that of Rt Rev. Graham Dow, chairman of the evangelical group in the Church of England's House of Bishops. As a conservative traditionalist, his support represented a welcome boost for the future King and Mrs Parker Bowles's marital prospects from a quarter that that might be expected to offer a hard-line attitude against the marriage. 'I am in favour of Charles getting married. It is the best way to resolve a difficult situation.'[27]

In 2002 the Church had relaxed its previous rules against the re-marriage of divorcees whose previous partners were still alive. But this only extended to the situation where both parties to the re-marriage were innocent of causes such as adultery leading to the breakdown of the original marriage or marriages. In December 2004, Dr David Stancliffe, the Bishop of Salisbury, said, 'If the Prince of Wales and Mrs Parker Bowles expressed a wish to marry, the proper pastoral approach should be to advise them to seek a civil ceremony which may be followed by prayers of dedication in church.'[28] This had emerged at Lambeth Palace as the solution to the problem, which Dr Rowan Williams then offered to the future King Charles III in his personal meeting on the matter that winter. When the royal engagement was announced on 10 February, the archbishop's formal statement read as follows:

> *Rowan Williams, Archbishop of Canterbury: Statement on the marriage of HRH Prince of Wales and Mrs Camilla Parker Bowles, Thursday 10 February 2005*
> The Archbishop of Canterbury, Dr Rowan Williams, has welcomed the announcement that HRH Prince of Wales and Mrs Camilla Parker Bowles are to marry.
> In a statement from Lambeth Palace, Dr Williams said: 'I am pleased that Prince Charles and Mrs Camilla Parker Bowles have decided to take this important step. I

hope and pray that it will prove a source of comfort and strength to them and to those who are closest to them.'

Dr Williams has accepted an invitation to preside at a service of prayer and dedication following the civil ceremony. Dr Williams said: 'These arrangements have my strong support and are consistent with Church of England guidelines concerning remarriage which the Prince of Wales fully accepts as a committed Anglican and as prospective Supreme Governor of the Church of England.'

The statement lent Dr Williams's authority as Archbishop of Canterbury and leader of the Church to the proposition that the arrangements were legitimate under the Church's own rules and principles.

The two leaders of the Roman Catholic church in Great Britain both issued messages of personal support in response to the royal engagement announcement.[29] Cardinal Cormac Murphy-O'Connor, the Archbishop of Westminster, said,

> The Royal Family, with their unique role in our national life, are always assured of the goodwill and prayers of the Catholic community. I know that Catholics will join with me at this time in praying for the Prince of Wales and Mrs Parker Bowles and in wishing them every happiness.

Speaking for the Catholic church in Scotland, Cardinal Keith O'Brien, the Archbishop of St Andrews and Edinburgh, echoed these sentiments: 'I hope that the Prince of Wales and Mrs Parker Bowles will find future happiness together.' In his statement, Cardinal O'Brien took the opportunity to berate the continuing existence of the Act of Settlement's disqualification of Roman Catholics from the throne:[30]

> I am saddened to think that were Mrs Parker Bowles a Catholic, the Prince of Wales would, by marrying her, automatically lose his right to accede to the throne – as would his heirs. As the Scottish Executive currently is quite rightly focusing attention on eradicating the blight of sectarianism, the time may be opportune to assess the impact of existing blatant anti-Catholic legislation and the extent to which its existence hinders progress in this effort.

In both churches, Anglican and Catholic, therefore, the leaders were supportive. However, among the rank and file of the clergy there was a distinctly mixed response. A considerable number of Anglican priests disapproved of the marriage. The evangelical group Reform expressed the view that it would compromise the moral authority of the future King when he became head of the Church and add to pressures for disestablishment of the Church of England.[31] Demands for an emergency debate on the desirability of the royal marriage at a meeting of the General Synod in February had been quashed by officials. Allan Jones of the Liverpool diocese protested that time should have been found, adding, 'It has grave consequences for the future of this Church. It has grave consequences for the future of this nation.'[32] Later on, an attempt would be made to challenge the legitimacy of the civil marriage altogether.[33]

Religious opinion on the royal marriage mattered. In 1936 it had been fatal to Edward VIII's desire to marry the divorced Wallis Simpson and keep the throne. In 2005 it affected the Queen's behaviour in attending the events of the day. Most crucially, it was a factor to be taken into account by the Prime Minister, Tony Blair, in advising the Queen and future King Charles on the operation of the Royal Marriages Act and the constitutional implications of the royal marriage.

The constitution: political acceptance of the controversial marriage

The political establishment unites in support

Quite unlike the two well-known precedents of 1936 and 1955, when the wishes of Edward VIII and of Princess Margaret to marry divorcees caused great constitutional crisis and anguish, the announcement in 2005 of the royal marriage of the future King Charles to the divorcee Camilla Parker Bowles was immediately greeted warmly by all sections of the political establishment.

Giving his response to the engagement announcement on 10 February, the Prime Minister, Tony Blair, said, 'I am delighted for the Prince of Wales and Camilla Parker Bowles. It is very happy news and when the Cabinet heard it this morning they sent congratulations and good wishes on behalf of the whole government. We all wish them every happiness for their future together.'[34] At the No. 10 press briefing in the morning, the Prime Minister's official spokesman confirmed that the relevant government law officers had been consulted about the legal aspects. These would have been the Lord Chancellor, Lord Falconer, and the Attorney General, Lord Goldsmith. The Prime Minister's spokesman confirmed the constitutional position that 'it was established practice for the Queen to consult the Prime Minister' before the monarch exercised her power of consent or refusal under the Royal Marriage Act. A meeting of the Cabinet was not convened to discuss the matter in advance.

Curiously, the Prime Minister made no statement on the marriage to the House of Commons, on the rather specious ground that the wedding carried no constitutional implications. Instead, at 12.32 p.m., shortly after the engagement announcement, the Leader of the House offered his congratulations, which, in a rare display of vocal unity across all sides of the political spectrum, was supported by others who spoke after him:

The Leader of the House of Commons (Mr Peter Hain): The whole House will wish to send our warm congratulations to His Royal Highness the Prince of Wales and Mrs Parker Bowles. As Secretary of State for Wales, I am personally delighted, and the House wishes them every happiness for the future. . . .

Mr Oliver Heald (North-East Hertfordshire) (Con): May I associate myself and other Conservative Members with the congratulations extended to His Royal Highness the Prince of Wales and his bride to be? My right hon. and learned Friend the Leader of the Opposition has said today that he is also delighted at the news. . . .

Sir Stuart Bell (Middlesbrough) (Lab): Further to the congratulations and good wishes of the Leader of the House, supported by the shadow Leader of the House, following the announcement this morning that His Royal Highness the Prince of Wales will re-marry, may I, as Second Church Estates Commissioner, say that the Archbishop of Canterbury has warmly welcomed the statement? The arrangements have his strong support and are consistent with the Church of England guidelines on re-marriage, which the Prince of Wales fully accepts as a committed Anglican and as prospective Supreme Governor of the Church of England. As there are no constitutional implications, can I assume that there will be no statement next week?

Mr Hain: Well, the House is not sitting next week, so there will certainly be no statement. I am grateful for my hon. Friend's statement and we all echo his sentiments. The Archbishop of Canterbury has made clear his delight, as has the Prime Minister. We all share in that.

Mr Paul Tyler (North Cornwall) (LD): I very much welcome what the Leader of the House and the hon. Member for Middlesbrough (Sir Stuart Bell) said. Prince Charles is Duke of Cornwall which, as the Secretary of State for Wales will know, is his premier title. He has shared in our delights and disasters, most recently the floods in north Cornwall. I am sure that the people of Cornwall will be especially delighted by today's news. On their behalf and on behalf of my hon. Friends, I wish Prince Charles and his future wife every happiness for their marriage. We shall all celebrate with the Duke and Duchess of Cornwall on 8 April. . . .

Mr Hain: I note the hon. Gentleman's congratulations and I welcome the House's unity in supporting the Prince of Wales and Mrs Parker Bowles. As Secretary of State for Wales, I must dispute the hon. Gentleman's comment that the Cornish title is the premier title.

Mr Tyler: It is the older one.

Mr Hain: Well, 'Prince of Wales' is the premier title as far as I am concerned, but I grant that Mrs Parker Bowles will be known as the Duchess of Cornwall after the marriage.[35]

Outside the Commons, the leaders of the two opposition parties expressed their support and good wishes also. The Conservative Party leader, Michael Howard, said, 'I warmly congratulate the Prince of Wales and Mrs Parker Bowles,' and Charles Kennedy for the Liberal Democrats said, 'We wish them all future happiness.'[36]

The frequency of the future King's personal dealings with Labour ministers since 1997 may have assisted in gathering the support he needed over the royal marriage. For example, during the week commencing Monday 14 July 1997, shortly after the Blair administration took office, he met numerous ministers in addition to his regular communication with the Prime Minister.[37]

Utilising the media, some Labour MPs were more robust in their support for the marriage, using the occasion to score constitutional reform points more widely. For example, some warned the Church of England that if it opposed the Prince of Wales and Mrs Parker Bowles getting married, it would precipitate political pressure for disestablishment. Dr Tony Wright, then a parliamentary private secretary to the Lord Chancellor and now chairman of the House of Commons Public Administration Committee, told the BBC,

Either we can have a Supreme Governor who actually can manage his life in the way that other people manage it, and when they encounter difficulties have to solve them, or be told by this established Church that they can't do it, in which case we shall have a constitutional crisis and it will end in disestablishment.[38]

Meanwhile, the leading articles in the establishment-orientated press, notably the *Daily Telegraph* and the *Times*, which had condemned the royal association with divorce in 1936 and 1955, endorsed the royal marriage as the right way forward for the Prince and Mrs Parker Bowles. Some might have viewed the royal marriage as sufficiently controversial to be an opportunity to apply a wider judgement on the general suitability of the Prince of Wales to be King in due course. If that judgement was that he lacked the fundamental talents, skills and diplomacy of operation necessary to perform the role of monarch in the circumstances of the day, it could have influenced the interpretation of the legal and constitutional questions that some maintained posed obstacles to the marriage. In other words, judgement on the constitutionality of the marriage would be influenced by a broader personal judgement on the suitability of Charles to be King. The fact that 10 Downing Street and the political establishment did not raise any difficulties, and indeed could hardly have been more supportive of the royal marriage, would suggest that the future Charles III does indeed enjoy the body politic's constitutional blessing to ascend the throne.

Popular opinion: the democratic voice on the wedding
It is interesting that public opinion on the one hand, and the attitude of the political and religious establishment on the other, have historically been at some variance in their levels of support or criticism of the marital desires of the monarch or other senior figures in the royal family.

In 1936, public opinion disliked the idea of divorce but mostly supported Edward VIII, who had been an enormously popular Prince of Wales for many years. It would have almost certainly tolerated his marriage to Wallis Simpson, though she was divorced. In the press, the *Daily Express*, the *Daily Mail*, the *Western Morning News*, and the *News Chronicle* all spoke up for the King, who himself later calculated in his memoirs that the papers' combined readership represented 60 per cent of the population.[39] But the Prime Minister, Stanley Baldwin, and the Anglican establishment under Archbishop Cosmo Lang united in their moral condemnation of the suitability of the marriage to Mrs Simpson. Such a marriage could not, of course, take place in an Anglican Church, of which the King was Supreme Governor. Dr Lang later attributed the crisis to the King's failure to perform his public duties and his 'craving for private happiness'.[40] Soundings taken by 10 Downing Street from Canada, Australia and the dominions were also opposed to the marriage. As King Edward would not withdraw his intention to marry Mrs Simpson, he was forced to abdicate in favour of his younger brother, who became George

VI. Edward and Wallis were subsequently married in a private ceremony that took place in France.[41]

During the period 1953–5, once more it was popular opinion that was more sympathetic and supportive of a royal romance, this time that of Princess Margaret, the Queen's sister and then third in line to the throne, and her suitor, the dashing war hero Captain Peter Townsend, a divorcee. In a famous poll of over 70,000 people conducted in 1953 by the *Daily Mirror*, 67,907 thought Margaret and Captain Townsend should marry if they wished to do so, and a mere 2,235 thought they should not.[42] But as in 1936, the establishment united in its moral indignation. Two Prime Ministers on separate occasions, Sir Winston Churchill in 1953 and Anthony Eden in 1955, advised the Queen against the marriage, indicating that Princess Margaret would lose her royal privileges and right of succession to the throne if she went against the constitutional advice of the government. The final straw came with a leading article in the *Times* on 26 October 1955 opposing the marriage on grounds of the great symbolic importance of the monarchy and the damage this marriage would do to the institution of the family. A few days later, on 31 October, Princess Margaret issued a public statement terminating her relationship with Captain Townsend:

> I have been aware that, subject to my renouncing my rights of succession, it might have been possible for me to contract a civil marriage. But mindful of the Church's teaching that Christian marriage is indissoluble, and conscious of the Commonwealth, I have resolved to put these considerations before any other.

In the case of Prince Charles's re-marriage in 2005, the tilt of opinion has been rather different. Whilst, as seen, the political and religious establishment firmly closed ranks in its support for the future King's decision to marry Mrs Parker Bowles, such vocal criticism of the marriage as existed came from sections of the mass media and of public opinion. As Peter Riddell of the *Times* commented, 'public opinion is likely to prove a more severe test than any constitutional obstacles'.[43]

On the day of the wedding announcement, instant phone-ins by the media suggested that two-thirds of the public opposed the marriage.[44] However, scientific public opinion polling suggested that the earlier antagonism to the marriage at the end of the 1990s had moved towards a gradual acceptance of Mrs Parker Bowles and the idea of her being married to the future King. By 2005, more people were supportive of the wedding than were opposed. However, this picture is confused by the varied types of question posed by the professional opinion polling companies. So, for example, though a majority thought the Prince and Mrs Parker Bowles should marry if they wanted to, yet:

- a larger majority did not care whether they married or not;
- a majority were opposed the suggestion that Camilla become Queen;[45]
- a majority of people thought the marriage would weaken the monarchy.

Do you approve or disapprove of the recent marriage of Prince Charles to Camilla Parker Bowles, or do you not care either way?[46]

	All	Men	Women
Approve	24	20	27
Disapprove	13	10	17
Don't care	62	69	54
Don't know	1	1	2

Do you think that the monarchy as an institution will be stronger, weaker or unaffected by the marriage of Prince Charles to Camilla Parker Bowles?[47]

	All	Men	Women
Stronger	8	7	10
Unaffected	50	54	47
Weaker	33	31	34
Don't know	9	8	9

Part of a successful monarchy in the modern era has involved charming the nation and providing a feelgood factor among the general population. Since the creation of a royal family surrounding the royal head of state in Victorian times, monarchy has thrived on projecting a human interest story which ordinary families can enthuse at, identify with or dream about. It was this aspect of the glamorous and iconic Princess of Wales, of course, that proved so powerful, and explains the extraordinary scenes of spontaneous popular grief across the country at her death in 1997. In the performance of this incidental function of the monarchy, the first wedding ceremony of the future Charles III, on 29 July 1981, had of course been an absolute triumph with more than 600,000 people lining the streets of London to view the royal couple proceeding in an open horse-drawn carriage between Buckingham Palace and St Paul's Cathedral. It was a major national event, attended by statesmen or their representatives from across the world. Globally, more than 750 million people watched the wedding service on television, and another 250 million listened to it on the radio. 'Here is the stuff of which fairy tales are made,' as the Archbishop of Canterbury at the time, Dr Robert Runcie, pronounced.[48] It certainly fitted into the traditional description of monarchy as provided by Walter Bagehot in his 1867 classic account, *The English Constitution*:

> A family on the throne is an interesting idea also. It brings down the pride of sovereignty to the level of petty life. No feeling could seem more childish than the enthusiasm of the English at the marriage of the Prince of Wales. They treated as a great political event, what, looked at as a matter of pure business, was very small indeed. But no feeling could be more like common human nature as it is, and as it is likely to be . . . A princely marriage is the brilliant edition of a universal fact, and, as such, it rivets mankind . . . To state the matter shortly, royalty is a government in which the attention of the nation is concentrated on one person doing interesting actions. A Republic is a government in which that attention is divided between many, who are all doing uninteresting actions. Accordingly, so long as the human heart is strong and the human reason weak, royalty will be strong because it appeals to diffused feeling, and Republics weak because they appeal to the understanding.[49]

In these terms, of course, the royal wedding of the future King and Mrs Parker Bowles in 2005 could hardly compete, and never attempted to do so. For it raised the spectre of marital breakdown, a bulimic and unhappy Princess and a broken family.

Sections of the media occasionally made much of the historic precedents of 1936 and 1955, raising questions of constitutional crisis. But in reality, these were relevant only in the rarefied confines and collective memory of Cabinet Office archives and university common rooms. To the ordinary man and woman in the street, they had no relevance to their attitude to the re-marriage of the heir to the throne. Furthermore, there were no surviving victims of those earlier precedents to serve as a living reminder. In 1955, the predicament of Princess Margaret had suffered from the presence of the former Edward VIII, then Duke of Windsor, still very much alive and well, and living in Paris. If Princess Margaret was allowed to marry a divorcee, why had the former King been driven off the throne and why was he being treated like a social pariah, having to live in exile? By 2005, not only was the Duke of Windsor long since dead,* but the Queen Mother, a living testament to the trauma of 1936, and Princess Margaret herself had both passed away three years beforehand.

Did the register office wedding of Charles and Camilla constitute a legal marriage?

From a purely legal perspective, the most astonishing aspect of the royal events of spring 2005 was the decision for the Prince of Wales and Camilla Parker Bowles to get married in a civil register office in England. This flew in the face of any conventional reading of the statute book on marriage law, which expressly excludes members of the royal family from marriage by way of civil registration. It flew in the face of the standard legal textbooks and works of reference, which also clearly state that members of the royal family are excluded from marriage by way of civil registration. It flew in the face of two famous royal occasions in living memory, 1936 and 1955, when everyone accepted that members of the royal family could not marry by way of civil registration. This was, after all, an accepted legal position which had fuelled the abdication crisis and driven Edward VIII from the throne, and been a major factor in the painful termination of Princess Margaret's high-profile romance with a divorcee. The proposal put forward in spring 2005 directly contradicted the official legal advice that members of the royal family could not contract a legal marriage through a civil registry service, which had been given by previous Lord Chancellors to previous Prime Ministers and monarchs.

Exclusion of the royal family from the Marriage Acts
The legal position, succinctly stated, was as follows. Originally holy matrimony was recognised by Church and state alike in England as part of the natural order of human existence. It was controlled by ecclesiastical authority and celebrated in church by way of advance banns and a religious service. However, a divergence of clerical and secular provisions on matrimonial affairs started to emerge in the nineteenth century, largely through pressures to facilitate divorce. The provision for getting married by way of civil registration, commonly known as a civil marriage, instead of

---

* The duke died in 1972.

through a church service, arrived with the passage of the Marriage Act 1836. However, Section 45 of the Act specifically stated that the Act did not apply to the marriages of members of the royal family:

> This Act shall extend only to England, and shall not extend to the marriage of any of the Royal Family.

Subsequently, the Marriage Act 1949 was enacted by Parliament to modernise civil registry procedures. With regard to the royal family, this changed nothing. The general purpose of the 1949 Act was expressed in its preamble to be one of consolidation, not repeal or re-enactment. It was, as it stated, 'an Act to consolidate certain enactments relating to the solemnisation and registration of marriage in England'. It did not need to expressly re-iterate the exclusion of the royal family, because it did so in effect by way of its Section 79(5), which made it plain that the former law on royal marriages was to remain in place:

> Nothing in this Act shall affect any law or custom relating to the marriage of members of the Royal Family.

The other measure of relevance is the Registration Service Act 1953, which repealed such provisions of the original 1836 Act as were still in force. The removal of the 1836 Act's Section 45 from the statute book could be viewed as removing the royal family's exception from civil marriages. However, this would be wrong under the normal rules of statutory construction, whereby Section 79(5) of the 1949 Act, referred to above, makes it clear that the rules pre-existing its passage were applicable to royal marriages and remained in force. It seemed clear that members of the royal family were unable to contract matrimony by way of the statutory civil registry procedure.

The alternative options available to the future King and his fiancée
From an objective legal viewpoint, therefore, there were other routes to matrimony that would have seemed less fraught with difficulty. If they specifically wished a civil marriage, then because the apparent bar on the royal family in the Marriage Acts extended only to England and Wales, they could have conducted a civil marriage registration anywhere else in the world.

However, one might conjecture that the Prince of Wales and Mrs Parker Bowles, being religious minded, would have preferred a church wedding.

The problem here was the earlier respective marriages and divorces of the couple, but this was only really an issue with regard to the particular rules and canons of the Church of England. A church wedding could have taken place in Scotland, where there is a separate established church, or perhaps in Wales, where the Anglican Church has been disestablished. The future King Charles would then have been following in the footsteps of his sister, Princess Anne, the Princess Royal, who had earlier been divorced from her first husband, Captain Mark Phillips. In 1992, she chose to re-marry her present husband, Captain Timothy Laurence, in a religious service in the Church of Scotland, where opinion and canon law take a more relaxed stand on the re-marriage of divorcees than that of the Church of England.

No doubt careful consideration was given to presenting a case that the wedding take place in a Church of England service, in the light of the General Synod's relaxation of its earlier prohibition on the marriage of divorcees in 2002. Indeed many believed this liberalisation had been done specifically with the Prince in mind, though this was denied by those involved. Furthermore, Charles was no longer a divorcee, he was a widower. However, other factors weighed against the couple, especially Camilla's divorced husband being alive and Charles's public admission of adultery in 1994, shaping the eventual judgement of the Archbishop of Canterbury that opinion in the Church would not favour their re-marriage in the Church of England.

A very public controversy on a very personal matter

Given the state of the law and constitutional history on royal marriages, it was entirely predictable that a huge media fuss and public controversy would emerge around the civil marriage plans. This was launched on Sunday 13 February 2005, just three days after the public announcement of the engagement, with the BBC broadcasting a *Panorama* programme entitled 'Lawful Impediment?'. The *Panorama* team, led by reporter Steve Bradshaw, had had a special interest for some time in the future King's matrimonial prospects together with their constitutional implications. Thus it had earlier conjectured about a possible marriage between Prince Charles and Mrs Parker Bowles in its programme entitled 'Queen Camilla?'. The conclusions in that previous programme, broadcast on 27 October 2002, drew attention to the fact, which was supported by opinion polls, that a substantial majority of people did not want Mrs Parker Bowles to be called 'Queen Camilla' when Charles ascended the throne. It also drew attention to earlier official government views, especially from the time of the abdication crisis in 1936, that the wife of a King must be called 'Queen'. Therefore, the implication seemed to be, we were on target for another possible abdication crisis, or an unpopular King-and-Queen situation raising the spectre of whether the country 'would stand for it', and the monarchy itself might collapse.

The key figure relied on by *Panorama* in its discussion of the proposed civil royal marriage was Dr Stephen Cretney QC of Oxford University, a widely respected leading authority on family law. Interviewed on the subject by Mr Bradshaw, Dr Cretney said:

> I must say I was very surprised when I heard that this was what was proposed because the legislation which governs civil marriages in England and register office marriages is expressed not to apply to members of the royal family . . . there is no statutory procedure whereby members of the royal family can marry in register office ceremonies.

This view was backed up in the programme by a family law practitioner, Valentine le Grice QC.

The following day, other legal figures pitched into the public legal debate. Chief among them was Sir Nicholas Lyell QC, the former Conservative Attorney General. Querying how the legal advice being followed by Clarence House and Buckingham Palace could have been reached on a straightforward reading of the Marriage Acts, Sir Nicholas said:

> I do not think [the Queen] has been given enough advice. It is not really clear that this situation has been properly thought about. [I feel] some disquiet, because the last thing one wants is for the Prince of Wales and Mrs Parker Bowles, or the Queen herself, embarrassed by this question.[50]

The next day's newspapers contained headlines such as 'Camilla wedding is "not legal"'. According to the *Daily Express*, 'the marriage of Prince Charles and Camilla Parker Bowles was threatening to spark a constitutional crisis last night'.

On a personal level, it would be difficult to imagine a more upsetting scenario for a couple preparing for their wedding day. Prince Charles instructed his aides at Clarence House to contact the press and issue a rebuttal to the views of Dr Cretney and others, stating he had received starkly different advice on his position. The Prince's spokesman told the press,

'Legal advice was taken from four different sources and all agreed that it is legal for a member of the royal family to marry in a civil ceremony in England.' Unfortunately these legal opinions were never published, nor any source or identity for them.

To legislate or not to legislate?

One solution to the legal obstacle to the civil marriage, which would clear up the alleged uncertainty on what the law affecting the royal wedding arrangements was, would have been to pass a swift piece of legislation through Parliament on the matter. Whether this was ever seriously considered, and, if so, by whom and at what stage, is unclear. Curiously, a section of the press reported on 11 February, the day immediately following the announcement of the engagement, that a parliamentary Bill on the matter was expected. This was reported to be for 'settling the new constitutional arrangement . . . [and] to give the couple's wedding on 8 April full legal status'.[51] However, this may have been mistaken. Certainly, during the 10 Downing Street media lobby briefings on 10 February, the Prime Minister's official spokesman made reference to the subject of legislation on the royal marriage. But this was to deny such a Bill would be brought forward by the government. He said there were 'no plans for legislation at this stage', adding that legislation on royal marriages was 'a matter for the Palace' and that 'the Palace did not see a reason for any legislation to be made'.

Whilst an Act of Parliament specifically providing for a royal civil marriage would have been an attractive proposition from the point of view of clarifying the law, there would have been serious pitfalls of a political nature. It would, in fact, have potentially opened a can of legal worms, since it could have been argued that royal marriage was a matter that affected succession to the Crown. As such, the Statute of Westminster 1931 applied, so that all the countries of the Commonwealth which retain the Queen as their head of state had to be consulted and express their assent. The practical problems in legislating on matters relating to the royal succession are considered in some detail in Chapters 4 and 5. From the government's immediate point of view, it would have taken up valuable time in Parliament when it had a glut of other legislation it was anxious to push through onto the statute book before the general election in a few months' time.

Most unattractive of all for Buckingham Palace, there was the certainty that republicans and radical royal reformers in the House of Commons would have a field day in debating a far wider range of royal subjects. It would most likely lead to parliamentary calls for reform and changes in royalty law much further afield than were applicable to the future King's forthcoming marriage alone.

Law reform by ministerial decree

All earlier government legal advice, including that of former Lord Chancellors and Attorneys General, appears to have been unanimous that members of the royal family could not get married in a civil marriage ceremony in England.

The issue had been explored in depth most recently in the mid-1950s when Princess Margaret was famously considering marriage to the much respected and liked, but divorced, Captain Peter Townsend. Both the Lord Chancellor and the Attorney General at that time, Viscount Kilmuir and Sir Reginald Manningham-Buller respectively, clearly accepted the straightforward interpretation of the Marriage Acts, namely that members of the royal family could only be married in England in a church service. Thus, in a paper to the Cabinet dated 29 October 1955, Lord Kilmuir wrote, 'Marriages of members of the Royal Family are still not in the same position as marriages of other persons, for such marriages have always been expressly excluded from the statutes about marriage in England.' Sensibly, the New Labour administration, whether or not it had itself consulted the precedents before 10 February 2005, did not attempt to deny this in its eventual response to critics of how the royal marriage had been planned. The papers themselves were released under the Freedom of Information Act 2000 on 29 March 2005.

It is interesting, if purely academic, that the correspondence between the government lawyers in 1955 discloses an element of uncertainty about the conceptual nature and extent of the limitation upon royal marriages in England. This is revealed in a letter of 28 October from Sir Reginald to Lord Kilmuir, in which he said he was not 'not quite sure whether it is correct to say that exclusion from the Marriage Act 1949 means that marriage in England must be celebrated by a clergyman of the Church of England'. He went on to say, 'I feel that this must be the case, but it depends on the law and custom relating to Royal Marriages and not on the Marriage Act.' By this statement he can only have been thinking of the ancient practice of a common-law marriage, which in medieval times was widely recognised and accepted by church and state. Common-law marriages became an anachronism and were abolished by the Marriage Act 1753, but – ironically – this statute did not apply to members of the royal family. So, theoretically, the heir apparent could contract a common-law marriage.

The New Labour government had a powerful vested interest in Prince Charles's wedding plans not being treated or declared as unlawful. This is because it had been the constitutional duty of the Prime Minister to advise the Queen on how to exercise her power of permission under the Royal Marriages Act. If there were any legal or constitutional problems in the marital arrangements, which must have been discussed with the Prime Minister in advance of the marriage announcement, the Prime Minister would be seen as having been responsible for advising the Queen accordingly. By the same token, the government lawyers including the Lord Chancellor, Lord Falconer, and the Attorney General, Lord Goldsmith, were responsible for advising the Prime Minister on the law on royal marriages.

Some firm action was clearly needed by the government to stabilise the situation. The ongoing media speculation about the legality of a register office royal marriage was becoming a serious matter of concern, especially as there was a good prima facie case that the marriage would be unlawful and high-profile figures, such as Sir Nicholas Lyell, were suggesting it might be. To this, an added urgency was created by the emergence on the scene of a number of hard-line Anglican priests, who were deeply upset by the prospect of this particular marriage. Some of these priests were now seeking actively to challenge the legality of the register office ceremony and stop the marriage taking place altogether.

So far as the establishment was concerned, therefore, the simplest solution was for the government to take a stand on a particular interpretation of the law that would allow civil marriages for members of the royal family, and declare it to be so. It chose to do this by way of a ministerial statement to Parliament by the Lord Chancellor. This is worth reading in full:

> *The Secretary of State for Constitutional Affairs and Lord Chancellor (Lord Falconer of Thoroton):* In the light of recent interest in the law surrounding Royal marriages, I am making this Statement to set out in more detail the view that has been taken by the Government on the lawfulness of the proposed marriage between the Prince of Wales and Mrs Parker Bowles.
>
> The Government are satisfied that it is lawful for the Prince of Wales and Mrs Parker Bowles, like anyone else, to marry by a civil ceremony in accordance with Part III of the Marriage Act 1949.
>
> Civil marriages were introduced in England, by the Marriage Act 1836. Section 45 said that the Act ". . . shall not extend to the marriage of any of the Royal Family".

But the provisions on civil marriage in the 1836 Act were repealed by the Marriage Act 1949. All remaining parts of the 1836 Act, including Section 45, were repealed by the Registration Service Act 1953. No part of the 1836 Act therefore remains on the statute book.

The Marriage Act 1949 re-enacted and re-stated the law on marriage in England and Wales. The Act covered both marriage by Church of England rite, and civil marriage. It did not repeat the language of Section 45 of the 1836 Act. Instead, Section 79(5) of the 1949 Act says that "Nothing in this Act shall affect any law or custom relating to the marriage of members of the Royal Family".

The change of wording is important, and the significance is not undermined by the fact that the 1949 Act is described as a consolidation Act. The interpretation of any Act of Parliament, even when it consolidates previous legislation, must be based on the words used in the Act itself, not different words used in the previous legislation.

In our view, Section 79(5) of the 1949 Act preserves ancient procedures applying to Royal marriages; for example, the availability of customary forms of marriage and registration. It also preserves the effect of the Royal Marriages Act 1772, which requires the Sovereign's consent for certain marriages. But it does not have the effect of excluding Royal marriages from the scope of Part III, which provides for civil ceremonies. As the heading to Section 79 indicates ("Repeals and Savings") it is a saving, not an exclusion.

We are aware that different views have been taken in the past; but we consider that these were overcautious, and we are clear that the interpretation I have set out in this Statement is correct. We also note that the Human Rights Act has since 2000 required legislation to be interpreted wherever possible in a way that is compatible with the right to marry (Article 12) and with the right to enjoy that right without discrimination (Article 14). This, in our view, puts the modern meaning of the 1949 Act beyond doubt.[52]

Of particular interest to lawyers – and the source of some amusement in certain quarters – was the government's residual reliance upon the Human Rights Act 1998, which has incorporated the articles of the European Human Rights Convention into domestic British law. The relevant human rights articles set out more fully are as follows:

Article 12: Right to Marry. Men and women of marriageable age have the right to marry and to found a family, according to the national laws governing the exercise of this right.

Article 14: Prohibition of Discrimination. The enjoyment of the rights and freedoms set forth in this Convention shall be secured without discrimination on any ground such as sex, race, colour, language, religion, political or other opinion, national or social origin, association with a national minority, property, birth or other status.

So the view of the Lord Chancellor, a senior Cabinet member and Secretary of State for the Department for Constitutional Affairs, was that the wording in the Marriage Act did not mean what it appeared to most family lawyers and legal historians to say. In Lord Falconer's view, the future King Charles III has the fundamental human right to get married, and he has the fundamental human right to exercise and enjoy his right to marry without any discrimination on grounds of his 'birth or other status'.

More particularly, and technically, the government's legal argument was that the law on royal civil marriages was in fact uncertain, and as such, the Human Rights Act allows, indeed requires, uncertain or ambiguous statutory provisions to be interpreted in such a way as best promotes the fundamental human rights of a person affected – in this case, the future King Charles III. At section 3, the Human Rights Act stipulates, 'So far as it is possible to do so, primary legislation and subordinate legislation must be read and given effect in a way which is compatible with Convention rights.'

So according to the Lord Chancellor's declaration of what the law is, the Marriage Act 1949 should be construed to favour the future King's human right to get married 'like anyone else in a civil ceremony'.

Silencing the legal challenges from hard-line clerics and devotees of Princess Diana

The issuing of this ministerial statement proved a politically astute and largely successful tactic. Being a statement to Parliament, it provided the appearance of some quasi-constitutional process to what Lord Falconer had to say. Being delivered as a written, rather than oral, statement to Parliament, simply being printed in Hansard (the report of parliamentary proceedings), this procedure had the added advantage to the government of avoiding the prospect of the Lord Chancellor being challenged or examined too closely by the formidable legal brains, including former Lord Chancellors, Attorneys General, law lords and QCs, in the House of Lords.

Curiously, the media accepted what the Lord Chancellor said, as though he was the ultimate determinant of the law on the subject. They made light of the fact that he was a politician and Cabinet member, charged with sorting out a thorny problem for 10 Downing Street. This was one case in which the popular image of the Lord Chancellor – dressed in flowing black robes, wig and garter, the living embodiment of the Law, presiding over the House of Lords – worked a treat for the New Labour government, which otherwise rather resents the Victorian costume drama side of the political process. The next day's newspaper headlines reported the ministerial statement as though the legal controversy was over and had been laid to rest: 'Falconer rides to the rescue of a civil union' (*Daily Telegraph*). Lord Falconer's utilisation of the Human Rights Act was the feature most commented upon: 'Human Rights Act to the rescue of the wedding' (*Guardian*); 'Act that Prince despises is used to back his marriage' (*Independent*).

The Lord Chancellor's statement then came to serve as the shield with which the rather worried group of local government officials in the national and local register offices concerned could deal with the hard-line clerics and the devotees of the Princess of Wales. These objectors had been contacting the register office in Windsor to lodge their protests that the planned civil royal wedding between the Prince of Wales and Mrs Parker Bowles was not permissible in law.

The most high-profile objector was Father Paul Williamson, a large and imposing 56-year-old priest at St George's Church, Feltham, west London, where he had served for fifteen years. He told the media, 'I believe this wedding is an offence both in the eyes of God and the law. It is an abomination . . . I do not believe there is any provision in law for Charles to marry anywhere else other than in church and, as a divorcee, he cannot do that.'[53]

Another group reported as objecting was the Diana Circle, devoted to the memory of the Princess. Its joint secretary, Alan Berry, was reported in the media as saying, 'We do not think a wedding in a civil service for members of the royal family is legal, whatever the Lord Chancellor has to say'.[54]

The objectors were required to put their letters of complaint into the form of the proper statutory procedure as laid down in the Marriage Act 1949. The register office issues a caveat form under Section 29(1) of the Act for those maintaining that a lawful impediment to the marriage exists. Frivolous objections are punishable by a fine. The form requires the grounds for the objection to be set out, which, if considered legitimate, are then the subject of an inquiry. The forms should be delivered to the local register offices where bride and groom have homes, in this case Chippenham for Mrs Parker Bowles and Cirencester for Prince Charles. The deadline for receipt of these formal objections was 4 March 2005. By that date, eleven people had lodged caveats.

Under the Marriage Act, the superintendent registrar cannot issue a wedding certificate until 'he has satisfied himself that there is not sufficient evidence of the alleged impediment'. The matter was dealt with personally by the Registrar General for England and Wales, Mr Len Cook. In reaching his decision, he already had the benefit of the Lord Chancellor's statement of 24 February declaring the civil marriage lawful. As reported in the press, Mr Cook also informally consulted Dame Elizabeth Butler-Sloss, the senior judge and president of the Family Division of the High Court.

On 8 March, Mr Cook formally dismissed all the objections which had been lodged. He told the press, 'I am satisfied that none of these objections should obstruct the issue of a [marriage] certificate.'[55] By way of explanation, he said that for the 1949 Marriage Act to prevent the royal marriage would have been to 'interfere with their rights' under the European Convention on Human Rights. He issued the following written statement:

> The Superintendent Registrars for Chippenham and Cirencester have received and referred to me 11 caveats objecting to the marriage of the Prince of Wales and Mrs Parker Bowles. The principal grounds of objection are that the law does not allow the Prince of Wales to marry in a civil ceremony. I have examined this matter and I am satisfied that it ought not to obstruct the issue of a certificate.

Disappointed, some of the objectors then considered turning up personally at the registry service on the day of the civil registration to voice their objections. Unsurprisingly, this was overridden by security concerns. Nonetheless, the Windsor register office proceeded to make arrangements to receive objections on the day, with a specially arranged office opening at 10 a.m., two and a half hours before the marriage took place, which was attended by the deputy registrar general, Dennis Roberts.[56] In the event, three people attended to argue their objections, including Father Williamson, but these were all dismissed.

Some objectors will have considered the last remaining route for challenging the validity of the royal marriage, namely proceedings in the High Court by way of judicial review of the decision of the registrar general. However, an applicant for judicial review would have faced very formidable obstacles in even achieving a hearing in court. There are difficulties in establishing 'standing', entitling one to bring proceedings, in public interest cases where no direct personal connection exists. The time limit for bringing an application is just three months. Above all, however, judicial review proceedings are enormously expensive. It is not a practical remedy available to a poor vicar up against an army of senior government lawyers funded by the unlimited financial resources of the state.

The royal wedding ceremonies – 9 April 2005

The forced change of venue: from castle to town hall
The original plan was for the marriage to take place privately inside Windsor Castle. The announcement on 10 February said that 'it will comprise a civil ceremony in Windsor Castle'. However, a week later practical problems about this began to arise, leading to a further announcement on 17 February from Clarence House that the venue was to be switched to the Guildhall, Windsor's town hall.

The reason for the switch of venue was that the legal practicalities of holding a civil marriage in a place of Prince Charles's choosing had not been fully appreciated. Locations for a civil marriage service have to be licensed as suitable venues by the local authority, and once a licence is issued it remains in force for three years and allows not just the licence applicant to use the venue for a legal marriage service but others as well. As expressed in the Marriage (Approved Premises) Regulations 1995, 'the premises must be regularly available to the public for use for the solemnization of marriages'.[57] This was an important technicality, not easily overridden in the accustomed manner with which arrangements for normal people are routinely set aside because of the special status of the royal family. 'It would not be in the spirit of the law to prevent others marrying at the castle once a licence is granted,' commented an official at the General Register office.[58]

The idea of Windsor Castle becoming a venue for any ordinary members of the public to use for their weddings was obviously unacceptable from the Queen's and the Royal Household's points of view. They would have been inundated with applications for weddings to take place at what is, after all, the Queen's main domestic residence.

The Clarence House announcement of the change of venue on 17 February stated:

The Guildhall is a landmark building, designed by Sir Christopher Wren and adjacent to the castle. It has been Windsor's Town Hall since 1690. The venue will enable the public to see The Prince of Wales and Mrs Parker Bowles arrive and depart from the Guildhall and include the town of Windsor in the day's events.

This was a positive gloss being put on an unfortunate oversight, and a brave face on a forced change of location to a less desirable venue. It is true that the main chamber of the Guildhall is splendid and regal in design, but it was in fact the rather ordinary and business-like Ascot Room that was selected for the royal marriage. The Ascot Room was more intimate in that it was a much smaller size than the large 120-person capacity main chamber. Choosing the Ascot Room also perhaps had the advantage of being less intimidating for the heir apparent, avoiding any negative associations emanating from his ancestors' portraits hanging in the chamber, especially those of Elizabeth I – who promoted the early Anglican religious settlement – and Victoria, a strict moral puritan.

On the Clarence House announcement's point about enabling the public to view the comings and goings around the Guildhall, actually one of the key factors in the original decision to hold the marriage within the walls of Windsor Castle had been to keep the public at bay. Having the marriage within the castle would have avoided scope for public mischief or protests and made things much easier for security protection.

There was a strong public relations advantage in holding the marriage in Windsor Castle that now had to be abandoned. This was that in terms of media handling and the projection of powerful televised images of the occasion to the public and the world at large, television cameras could easily be prohibited within the castle from photographing anything to do with the civil marriage. If it was possible to televise and record only the subsequent church service with the Archbishop of Canterbury, then the only images of the day's events projected into the public mind would be those of the religious occasion. And many people would fail to appreciate the legal distinction between the short civil act of marriage and the longer religious service, viewing the marriage therefore as simply having taken place in an Anglican religious setting. This would have helped minimise the impact of the future Supreme Governor of the Church of England getting married in a civil register office instead of the Anglican Church.

The change of venue to a public place in Windsor town centre now meant that the world's press and television cameras could cover everything surrounding the civil register office event. Hoards of royal watchers and tourists would descend upon the town, wanting a glimpse of the royal couple. Most of the national and world television coverage throughout 9 April was indeed largely focused around the Guildhall, certainly all morning and down to 2 p.m.

Unlike the future King's first marriage, therefore, which was watched by 750 million people worldwide, no one except the twenty-eight family members present saw and witnessed the marriage. Requests by broadcasters, the press and members of the public, including those clerics who opposed the union as being illegal under canon and secular law, were turned down flat. A Clarence House spokesman said, 'It was never intended that the civil ceremony should be televised as it was always planned to be a relatively small, personal occasion.'[59]

Strictly speaking, under the terms of the Marriage (Approved Premises) Regulations 1995, members of the public are entitled to attend civil marriages and normally should have been. The regulations state that, 'public access to any ceremony of marriage solemnized in approved premises must be permitted without charge'.[60] However, all inquires from the media and other interested individuals that anyone except the invited twenty-eight family members might sit in and observe were understandably rejected out of hand by Clarence House, the royal protection officers and the registry officials. The legal basis of this restriction would have been the residual power of the registrar to impose restrictions on public attendance because of some overriding necessity,[61] coupled with the wide-ranging civil control powers that state officials and police now possess, both at common law and in numerous recent statutes.[62]

The forced change of wedding date: the Pope's death

As the Queen herself said in her speech at the eventual wedding ceremonies,[63] the married couple had to ride out all kinds of obstacles on their way to betrothal. After being beset by so many popular, legal and bureaucratic problems, what else could possibly stand in their way?

The unexpected answer was the death of the Pope. Following a very lengthy illness, John Paul II died on 2 April, six days before all the elaborate planning and detailed organisation for the royal wedding was due to come to fruition. When would the funeral be held? After an anxious forty-eight hours of uncertainty for the Prince of Wales and his fiancée, and the royal organisers, the Vatican announced that Pope John Paul's funeral would take place on Friday 8 April – the same date as the royal wedding.

The Pope's death was an event of global magnitude, and domestically within the United Kingdom it directly affected the British establishment in a way that was without precedent. John Paul II had been a charismatic Catholic leader, causing his presence to be felt across the world through his energetic missionary tours and visits, which no previous Pope had ever undertaken. This happened during a historic era in which the leading faiths of the world had reached an accord of mutual respect, and there were great ecumenical hopes for the Christian denominations to move closer towards unity. Around 100 heads of government or state across the world immediately expressed their wish to attend the Pope's funeral at the Vatican.

Included in this number was the British Prime Minister, Tony Blair, who immediately declared his intention to attend the Pope's funeral, and to his mind this almost certainly will have had primacy over attendance at the Prince of Wales's wedding. As a practising Christian, who had shortly beforehand had an audience at Rome with the Pope and is believed to have received holy communion from him, there was no way he was going to miss out what would have been for him a major life event. This was even more the case for the Prime Minister's wife, Cherie, a devout Catholic. The Archbishop of Canterbury was for a short while placed in a quandary, committed to giving the royal couple the blessing on 8 April, but now desperately desiring to attend the Vatican as an important mark of respect for himself personally and symbolically on behalf of the Church of England.

Any further royal controversy to add to the history of this marriage, however, was avoided by the Prince of Wales agreeing to postpone his wedding by twenty-four hours. The following statement was posted on the Prince's official website on 4 April, including an announcement that he would attend the Pope's funeral himself on behalf of the Queen:

HRH The Prince of Wales to attend funeral of Pope John Paul II
His Royal Highness The Prince of Wales will attend the funeral of Pope John Paul II in Rome on Friday 8th April.

As a mark of respect, His Royal Highness and Mrs Camilla Parker Bowles have decided to postpone their wedding until Saturday 9th April 2005.

It is expected that the arrangements will be largely the same as previously planned. Details will be announced as soon as possible.

This was first time in our history since the Church of England was established that a future monarch, or an Archbishop of Canterbury, or a

British Prime Minister had attended the Vatican funeral service of a Pope. Over 200 world leaders, from the US President, George W. Bush, to the United Nations Secretary General, Kofi Annan, travelled to Rome for this occasion, which is believed to have been viewed on television around the globe by more people than any other historic event.

A narrative of the day's ceremony

Finally, 9 April 2006 arrived, and with no more complications. The day commenced with crowds having formed overnight and in the early morning in the streets of Windsor around the Guildhall and the castle. Contrary to some weather forecasts suggesting it might snow, it was in fact sunny, blue-skied weather, perfect for the occasion. In the course of the morning, Mrs Parker Bowles travelled by chauffeur-driven car from Clarence House in London to Windsor Castle, the domestic home of the Queen. By midday, the crowds had swelled to around 15,000, and a jamboree atmosphere prevailed, with several bands playing music, including the Windsor Boys' School jazz band outside the Guildhall, and a large number of people waving the Union Jack and many foreign tourists with cameras.

Only a very few 'spoilers' were there, bemoaning Charles's treatment of Diana or propagating the end of the monarchy. A massive police presence of 1,000 officers ensured the crowd was contained within the erected barriers and behaved itself courteously. Two protesters at the front of one section of the barriers held up a banner reading 'Illegal, Immoral, Shameful: duty before pleasure', which the police then confiscated.[64] A gay rights activist was dissuaded from displaying his banner proclaiming 'Charles can marry twice; gays can't marry once'. A streaker leapt naked over the safety barriers opposite the Guildhall just as the newly wed royal couple left the register office but was seized by police before getting anywhere.

The civil marriage ceremony was scheduled for 12.30 p.m. and took just 25 minutes. As with any other registry marriage, there was no music, readings or speeches, just the legal registry procedures to be followed. In non-ceremonial fashion, the register office guests arrived at the Guildhall using the indecorous, but efficiently secure, transportation of two pristine white minibuses. A royal source commented to the press, 'The choice of transport symbolised the difference between the grandiose first wedding at St Paul's and the more low-key nature of the second. But it still looked very odd to see the Royals clambering off it.'[65] The first of these ferried Camilla's Shand relatives to the building's steps, and shortly afterwards the second arrived with the Windsor family contingent. Then at 12.25 p.m. precisely, the engaged couple together made the short journey out of the King George IV Gate, and from there through the Cambridge Gate, at the castle towards the register office at Guildhall, driven in the Queen's Rolls-Royce Phantom VI, presented to her at her Silver Jubilee in 1977.

Prince William and Tom Parker Bowles, the eldest respective sons from each partner's earlier marriage, acted as the formal witnesses to the civil marriage. Of the other twenty-eight guests attending the register office, sixteen were relatives of Prince Charles and twelve were relatives of Camilla Parker Bowles. Prominent among them was the two other children of the groom and the bride, Prince Harry and Laura Parker Bowles respectively. Charles's siblings all attended: the Princess Royal (Princess Anne) with her husband Rear Admiral Timothy Laurence, the Duke of York (Prince Andrew), and the Earl (Prince Edward) and Countess of Wessex, together with all their respective children except the Wessexes' infant daughter. Camilla's two children brought their respective girl- and boyfriend; and her brother Mark, and her sister Annabel with husband Simon, attended with nieces and nephews.

The bride's 88-year-old father, Major Bruce Shand,* was able to attend, but on Prince Charles's side, the Queen and the Prince Philip were noticeably absent, the planning and significance of which is discussed elsewhere.[66]

The civil wedding was conducted by the superintendent registrar of the borough, Claire Williams, assisted by the registrar, Claire Paterson. After exchanging wedding vows, Prince Charles and Mrs Parker Bowles exchanged rings made out of 22-carat gold from the Clogau St David's mine in Bontddu, Gwynedd. The two signatures of Prince William and Tom Parker Bowles as witnesses to the marriage were entered in the official register of marriages. Royal protocol then dictated that all sixteen members of the royal family present enter their signatures as witnesses for the special 'Royal Register', recording all marriages and baptisms taking place within the royal family.

Emerging from the Guildhall as the second wife of His Royal Highness the Prince of Wales and Duke of Cornwall, the former Mrs Camilla Parker Bowles was now formally entitled Her Royal Highness the Duchess of Cornwall. The newly married couple waved briefly to the crowds outside the

---

* Camilla Parker Bowles's mother, Rosalind, had died eleven years previously at the age of 73, after suffering for many years with osteoporosis.

Guildhall before getting back in the Rolls-Royce to return to Windsor Castle for the next stage of the day's proceedings.

The Anglican Church's blessing: the public spectacle

The Church's blessing of the royal marriage, by way of a service of prayer and dedication at St George's Chapel, Windsor Castle, constituted the primary public focus for the royal wedding's arrangements. It was designed to take place the same day, as quickly as practicable after the civil registry service. This was therefore timed for 2.30 p.m., about 90 minutes after the civil marriage, to allow for travelling, refreshment and, in the bride's case, a complete change of outfit.

The religious procedure for a service of prayer and dedication after a civil marriage has been available for thirty years. It is a service devoid of the normal symbols of marriage such as exchange of rings, but both parties formally resolve in turn to be faithful to their newly wedded spouse. In a significant part of the service, especially for Christian traditionalists who had reservations about the Prince's marriage to Mrs Parker Bowles, a prayer of penitence was selected from the 1662 Book of Common Prayer.* This, which was recited out loud by all those present, including the newly wedded couple, reads:

> We acknowledge and bewail our manifold sins and wickedness, which we, from time to time, most grievously have committed, by thought, word, and deed . . . We do earnestly repent, and are heartily sorry for these our misdoings; the remembrance of them is grievous unto us; the burden of them is intolerable. Have mercy upon us, have mercy upon us, most merciful Father . . . forgive us all that is past; and grant that we may ever hereafter serve and please thee in newness of life . . .

The church service was a large and grand occasion with almost 800 guests, clearly organised for public consumption, even if it lacked the more ostentatious features of a state occasion, as with Charles's first marriage to Diana. First, there were the leaders of the political establishment. These politicians, attending with their wives, were the Prime Minister, Tony Blair; the leader of the opposition, Michael Howard; the leader of the Liberal Democrats, Charles Kennedy; the Secretary of State for Northern

---

* This inclusion in the service was indeed taken by many as an appropriate act of contrition and repentance. 'Charles to say sorry for adultery' was the front page headline in the *Daily Mail* on 8 April 2005, the day before the service.

Ireland, Paul Murphy; and the First Ministers of Scotland (Jack McConnell) and Wales (Rhodri Morgan).

The official state representatives from various Commonwealth states where the Queen still serves as head of state attended, including the Governors General of Antigua & Barbuda, Australia, Barbados, Canada, the Cook Islands, Grenada, New Zealand, Papua New Guinea and St Christopher & Nevis. Kings or princes from eight foreign royal families, some ceremonial heads of state, some deposed heads of state and some still possessing real executive power, were invited and journeyed to Windsor specially for the occasion. These were the King of Bahrain, the King and Queen of the Hellenes, the Prince and Princess of the Netherlands, the Crown Prince and Princess of Norway, Prince Radu and Princess Margarita of Romania, Prince Turki Al-Faisal and Princess Nouf bint Fahad from Saudi Arabia, Prince Bandar bin Sultan from Saudi Arabia, and the Crown Prince and Princess of Yugoslavia.

The Third Estate of the realm, the Church of England, was represented in a carefully chosen and supportive small group of clergymen. Most prominent were the present and immediately previous Archbishops of Canterbury, respectively Dr Rowan Williams, who presided at the service, and Lord Carey, who had earlier privately and publicly endorsed the marriage. The other five clerics were personal friends of the Prince from those parishes where he lives at various times, including Windsor and Highgrove.

A careful decision was taken to allow the service to be televised and thus watched by hundreds of millions of people across the world. It was reported that Dr Williams originally wished the Anglican service not to be televised, in keeping with the union's quiet formalisation across the establishment; the Church could then be seen to be playing its part in supporting the monarchy despite its canonical opposition to the wedding.[67] If so, then at some point he was persuaded to give way. There were powerful secular reasons for televising the event, as it projected an image of pomp, circumstance and religion upon the future King's wedding, marriage and bride. And by sleight of hand, it was quite likely that a very large number of people would think the blessing *was* the marriage ceremony. Certainly, permanent memories of the heir apparent's wedding day, and the many photographs taken and recorded for posterity, would be of the Church service.

The remaining guests, some of whom participated in the celebrations by giving readings or musical recitals, were an eclectic mixture of artists, actors, musicians, environmental conservationists, charity directors, civil libertarians, broadcasters, writers, and garden designers. Among the thirty-nine names highlighted in Clarence House's guest list distributed to the media included those of Sir David Frost, Kenneth Branagh, Jilly Cooper, Sanjeev Bhaskar, Joanna Lumley, Sir John Mortimer, Prunella Scales, Robert Harris, Trudi Styler (wife of the pop star Sting), the Hon. Nicolas Soames and Lord Rees-Mogg. Other well-known figures included the actor Stephen Fry and comedian Barry Humphries. The great majority of guests were drawn from the social elite of Britain. There were some who stood out as representing the 'ordinary' people, however, such as Joe and Hazel Relph, proprietors of the Yew Tree Farm bed and breakfast in Borrowdale, Cumbria, and Barbara Fell, landlady of The Rose and Crown in Boylestone, Derbyshire, one of the Prince's favourite pubs.

Charles's style and tone for the marital celebrations: a foretaste of the court of King Charles?
'The wedding is as pleasantly idiosyncratic as some of the Prince's enthusiasms, and is intended to reflect them,' commented the *Daily Telegraph*. This was a fair summary of the service of prayer and dedication as a whole, and of the walkabout that followed to greet well-wishers invited to the grounds of the castle afterwards. It was indeed an interesting and intriguing gathering of diverse cultural contributions, peoples and interests. If one wants to contemplate what the future court of Charles III will be like in its style and tone, then one need look no further than at the gathering and ceremony attendant on this wedding.

Among the exotic touches at the service was the participation of a young Russian mezzo-soprano, Ekaterina Semenchuk. She had flown over to London and travelled to Windsor Castle especially to sing a Russian version of the Creed from Alexander Grechaninov's *Liturgy of St John Chrysostom*, one of the Prince's favourite pieces of music. The Prince had heard Ms Semenchuk sing at the Royal Opera House in 2000, when she performed in a production of *War and Peace* as part of the residency that year of the Mariinsky Theatre, of which the Prince is a patron and benefactor.* The Welsh composer Alun Hoddinott composed a special fanfare to commemorate the marriage, called 'Celebration Fanfare for Their Royal

---

* Prince Charles has a deep spiritual interest in the eastern European Orthodox faith, as witnessed the very next month when on 11 May Charles took himself on retreat for five days' virtual solitude to Romania, staying for three days at Horezu Monastery and visiting other Orthodox monastic sites.

Highnesses The Prince of Wales and The Duchess of Cornwall', which was performed after concluding the blessing. The second reading at the service was delivered by that most English of actors and a friend of the Prince, Timothy West, who read 'Ode on Intimations of Immortality' by that most English of poets, William Wordsworth.

Outside the occasion, in the environs of St George's Chapel, were a host of other people invited to the castle's grounds, waiting to either meet or gain a close view of the Prince and his new bride. At the end of the service, the couple and their guests appeared on the steps of the church, pausing for a few minutes for photographs. Then, whilst the guests made their way to the State Apartments for the reception, the future King and Duchess of Cornwall went for a short walkabout in the Horseshoe Cloister.

There, the royal newly-weds met with an enthusiastic host of representatives from charities and other organisations with which they are associated as patron or otherwise. These extraordinarily diverse bodies ranged from the Battle of Britain Fighter Association, Help the Aged, the Caithness Archaeological Trust and the Royal Agricultural College, to the Royal Opera House, the Royal Ballet, World Jewish Relief, the Suffolk Cathedral Millennium Project and the Scottish Wildlife Trust.

This was the new Duchess of Cornwall's first meet-the-people occasion as a now senior member of the royal family. She delighted several of those she met in the crowd, including David Dudley, a 72-year-old retired teacher, by greeting them with a kiss. Watching from the Parade Ground of the Lower Ward were more well-wishers from further organisations with whom the couple are connected in some way. These were equally diverse in character, from the Aberdeen Angus Cattle Society, the Actors' Benevolent Fund and the Royal Academy of Arts to Business in the Environment, the Flyfishers Club, the Gurkha Welfare Trust, the Soil Association and the Specialist Cheesemakers Association.

Social aspects of the royal wedding party
The reception party, at 4 p.m., was hosted by the Queen in the castle's magnificent state apartments. Musical background was provided by a young harpist from Ebbw Vale, Jemima Phillips, who has served as the 'royal harpist' since 2004. The large square wedding cake – an organic fruit cake – was made by Dawn Blundone and Mary Robinson from the shop at Highgrove. Refreshments included 16,500 canapés, sandwiches of roast venison with Balmoral redcurrant and port jelly, Cornish pasties, and scones

with Cornish cream and Duchy strawberry jam. A 74-year-old grandmother, Etta Richardson, baked a further twenty fruit cakes for the reception, specially ordered by the Prince, who had first tasted and enjoyed Mrs Richardson's cooking at an exhibition in Llansteffan, Carmarthenshire, a year earlier. Subsequently, she dubbed the recipe 'Etta's royal cake'.

By all accounts, the flavour of this social event, from which television cameras and the media were banned, was as informal as any major royal occasion gets. The Queen was reported by those present as giving a witty speech commencing with, 'I have an important announcement to make . . . Hedgehunter has won the Grand National!' Whatever jokes were made were greeted with great hilarity. The actor and friend of the Prince, Stephen Fry, said afterwards, 'The Queen's speech was very funny, as was Prince Charles's,' and Lord Bragg commented, 'Every time they said anything it was more like being a football hooligan at an Arsenal match – instead of clapping politely they just went "Yes!" '[68]

In her speech delivered to the assembled wedding party, the Queen memorably said, 'They have overcome Becher's Brook and The Chair and all kinds of other terrible obstacles. They have come through and I am very proud and wish them well. My son is home and dry with the woman he loves. Welcome to the winner's enclosure.'[69] In response, Prince Charles gave thanks and proposed toasts to his family, including his sons and his late grandmother, Queen Elizabeth the Queen Mother. He movingly gave praise to his new bride as 'my darling Camilla, who has stood by me through thick and thin – and whose precious optimism and honour have seen me through'.[70]

Some wounds of the past were evident in notable absences from the occasion. Unsurprisingly, the guest list did not include Earl Spencer, Princess Diana's brother, leader of the aristocratic Spencer dynasty (which has an ancient and blue-blooded pedigree to match that of the Windsors). Relations between him and Charles appear to have been deeply strained. During the wedding, he and his wife Caroline, with his son Edmund, were 130 miles away, staying with his sister, Lady Jane Fellowes, and her husband in west Norfolk. By way of some counter-balance, however, Camilla's first husband, Andrew Parker Bowles attended the service, though not the civil marriage. He and his new wife Rosemary prominently joined in the social celebrations. According to one newspaper report, he even chipped in during Prince Charles's eulogy to his new wife, calling out, 'Hear, hear. She's a good woman!'[71]

As a social event, even though this royal marriage was tinged with the surreal and the sense of a rather edgy nervousness, the personal show of support was impressive. As Charles and Camilla departed the reception, making for their Bentley, which was covered in balloons and daubed with 'Just Married' and 'Prince and Duchess', gestures of affection were much in evidence, and kisses were exchanged between Queen and new daughter-in-law, and between the royal Princes and new stepmother.[72] In the *Daily Mail*'s dramatic commentary, 'That moment symbolised the seismic shift in Camilla's fortunes – from one-time social outcast to the second-highest ranking woman in the land.'[73]

One aspect of the arrangements as promoted and publicised by Clarence House to the press was rather telling. This was the disparity in certain aspects of the treatment afforded to the groom's and bride's respective family and friends. For example, within the 47-page press pack of information which Clarence House carefully prepared about the event, Camilla Parker Bowles's side was far less prominent. This was an influential document, faithfully relied upon or re-produced in most papers.[74] Its 'selected guest list' was all about the great and the good associated with the monarchy, starting with a long list of 'Members of the British Royal Family'; in other words, Charles's relatives. Among those listed in the document as 'Other guests at the Service', the great majority comprised those friends of the Prince who shared some special personal interest of his: from the dramatic arts such as Edward Fox, the Prince's Trust such as its 'ambassador', Jools Holland, gardening design such as Martin Lane Fox, or the environment such as Sir Jonathon Porritt. Even for the core personal event of the civil marriage, the names of Camilla's father and sister appeared at the bottom in a short paragraph starting 'Also attending . . . .'.

In a sense, all this shows is that the monarchy can never operate in an entirely normal civic personal manner. Clarence House is institutionally inculcated with a culture of affording primacy based upon aristocratic title, bearing fine points of etiquette and rank in mind. But today what normal bride is content with inequalities of treatment for herself, her family and her relatives at her wedding? Rather like the traditional vow of obedience to one's husband, for most people this is a relic of a bygone social structure. This is certainly not to say that Camilla Parker Bowles appeared unhappy in any way about the day's plans. Completely to the contrary, she displayed her delight that her long-standing love affair with the future King Charles III was finally being consecrated by marriage. 'I just can't believe it,' friends reported her exclaiming at the reception.[75] Nonetheless, the organisers of this very English occasion clearly felt an institutional imperative to give public emphasis to the heir apparent's side of the union, especially in its projection of the event to the mass media. This was inevitably, despite the couple's best wishes, a public and, indeed, constitutional event.

Royal advisers and the wedding's strategic planning – a very English compromise

A prominent theme running throughout the media coverage over the period from engagement to wedding day was that the planning and organisation of the event was a 'fiasco' and 'a right royal shambles':[76] so many difficulties and questions, from the legality of the civil marriage to the location where it could be held, had arisen during the period of the engagement.

This was in fact far from the truth. Whatever the technicalities in fixing the arrangements, this was a carefully thought-out, sensitively fine-tuned occasion, comprising a series of inter-woven ceremonies. The day was designed to formalise a long-standing, 'non-negotiable', de facto partnership that would have posed considerable difficulties and embarrassment in the future King's performance of his public and diplomatic functions, both as heir apparent and representative of the Queen, and when he himself became head of state.

The arrangements for the wedding, whether one agreed with each decision or not, sought to accommodate and harmonise a considerable number of complex conflicting pressures, sensitivities and dogmas. Many of these touched on the issue of divorce and re-marriage within the body and membership of the Church of England, of which Prince Charles will one day be ex officio head and Supreme Governor. A decision was made to marry in England, with an Anglican Church blessing by the Archbishop of Canterbury, even if a wedding in the Church of England was accepted to be inappropriate.

As a social celebration, it sought to maintain a low profile, consistent with this being a personal occasion with no implications for future children and new successors to the throne. Respect for the public memory of the popular Diana, Princess of Wales, mother of Prince William and Prince Harry, was included in the low-key, discreet nature of the event. The occasion was as informal as it might be, especially the registry service and celebration party hosted by the Queen afterwards. As that veteran royal commentator and former Conservative Cabinet minister Lord St John of Fawsley was quoted the next day as saying, a lavish and ostentatious celebration would have been 'inappropriate'. 'If they had made a great public and state occasion of it, it would not have been appreciated at all. The Princess of Wales is still remembered with great affection.'[77]

It was not a state occasion but a personal and family affair – at least, so far as any marriage of the Prince of Wales can be. At the same time, ordinary members of the public – the public interest – were not excluded. Access to the occasion was provided by allowing television cameras into Windsor Castle, so that people could witness the most spectacular part of the day's events, the blessing of the marriage by the Archbishop in the service of prayer and dedication. This was a magnificent ceremony, incorporating performances of choral and orchestral music, and religious and literary readings.

The wedding served to illustrate the truth that monarchy is an intertwined mix of public and private. This is the perennial problem or difficulty in the analysis and organisation of most royal matters, 'where to draw a line between the public and private spheres'.[78] On this occasion, the royal planners struck the right balance. A difficult task completed, not without hitches of the most formidable kind, the Prince's private secretary, Sir Michael Peat, is reported to have said as he was leaving the reception, 'Thank God, it's all sorted.'[79]

3

The prerogative powers and constitutional duties of the future King

Monarchy and the royal prerogative

The subject of the monarch's prerogative powers, and how and when they are or might be exercised, is a corner of the constitution that is little understood and is routinely misinterpreted.

On the royal power to choose a Prime Minister, for example, what is the position if at the next general election, the Labour Party led by Gordon Brown slumps at the polls and loses its majority, gaining only 280 seats in the Commons, with David Cameron and the Conservatives winning 300 seats, and the Liberal Democrats under Menzies Campbell 60 seats?

The majority of people would answer that the Queen, or any future King, will, or should, send for Mr Cameron. But that is quite wrong, of course, as a proposition of existing constitutional law and practice. The situation is that Mr Brown as the incumbent Prime Minister would possess the first opportunity to consider whether he could remain in office. Given the Labour Party's close dealings with the Liberal Democrats at various times since 1996, particularly in Scotland, he would almost certainly attempt to negotiate a deal with that party. He could sustain Labour in office with himself remaining as Prime Minister, either through a pact with the Liberal Democrats on an agreed legislative programme or by way of a formal inter-party coalition in government.

A great deal of public confusion and ignorance surrounds the exercise of the royal political powers, yet the issues involved are of fundamental importance to the operation of our whole democratic system of government.

Not only does the monarch appoint our Prime Ministers, he or she gives his or her assent to new laws passed by Parliament, as well as agreeing the date when general elections are to be held by dissolving and summoning Parliament.

These three royal powers of state – (1) prime ministerial appointment, (2) Royal Assent to legislation, and (3) dissolution of Parliament – are best described as the monarch's 'direct' legal prerogatives. At common law they form part of what is known as 'the royal prerogative', being the term used to describe the network of inherent powers, privileges and immunities of the Crown which have existed since time immemorial by virtue of past de facto judicial recognition.[1] While the monarch's three direct legal prerogatives referred to above, together with the award of certain honours, can only be exercised by or under the express authority of the reigning King or Queen personally, all other prerogative acts are conducted by government ministers (including for example treaty making, the issue of passports, the deployment of military forces overseas, and the creation, merger or disbanding of departments of state).

The legal immunity of the monarch

The existence of the prerogative is inter-woven with the fact that the United Kingdom does not possess a written constitution.[2] In countries with a written constitution, the constitution itself is the ultimate source of legitimacy in the state, and it dictates the fundamentals and basic functions of government. But in the United Kingdom, many such fundamental functions of state have never been codified into statutory written form at all.[3] So we continue to rely upon the historical common-law acceptance of these Crown functions, as being basic to the very rationale and operation of central government, under the name of the 'prerogative'. Since these powers are derived from common law, not from any Act of Parliament, they are all exercisable without any formal requirement for ratification or consent by either House of Parliament.

An important point to realise about the direct prerogative powers of the monarch is that they are subject to no forms of legal control. If a delinquent King chose to appoint himself, or his wife, or even his dog, Prime Minister, that would be lawful. If he decided not to appoint a Prime Minister at all, there is nothing in law that could be done about it. If he refused to sign a government Bill that he heartily disliked, the government, Commons and Lords would have no legal redress. If, after Parliament was dissolved, he chose not to summon a new Parliament and call a general election at all, nothing in law could compel him to do so.

This is because, firstly, the conduct of the monarch is not justiciable; in other words, it is outside the scope of judicial review or any intervention of the courts. This is quite unlike, for example, the President of the United States of America, who is subject to the jurisdiction of the Constitution and the Supreme Court, and also to the law of impeachment. The common-law theory of the prerogative gives the person of the monarch immunity from legal suit or prosecution in the courts. Hence the famous definition of the prerogative as being the 'special pre-eminence which the King hath, over and above all other persons, and out of the ordinary courts of the common law in right of his royal dignity'.[4] And even if such immunity did not exist, the courts have regarded the important prerogative acts of state as being 'absolute'. This means that, whilst they will inquire into the existence and scope of a prerogative power, they will not entertain any legal challenges to the legitimacy of the way it is in fact used, or inquire into the reasoning, grounds, manner or purpose behind the exercise of the prerogative act.[5]

The other reason why the monarch is legally untouchable is that, remarkably, there is no alternative office or legal machinery in existence to carry out the direct legal prerogative acts of the monarch in default of him or her actually doing so. Long ago in Stuart times, parliamentarians were indeed troubled that the King might not cause election writs to be issued or a parliament summoned, and instead might choose to govern without it. Thus an elaborate statutory machinery was imposed upon Charles I under duress in 1641, enabling other officers of state to summon Parliament at least once every three years if the King defaulted to do so. But this was repealed in 1664, shortly after Charles II acceded to the throne following the Civil War and Cromwellian interregnum, as being 'in derogation of His Majesty's just rights and prerogative inherent to the imperial crown of this realm'.[6] Today, legal substitution to the reigning monarch can be made only by way of creating a regency to cover the situations of an infant or sick monarch under the terms of the Regency Acts 1937–53.[7]

The importance of political convention

What is crucial to the conduct of the monarch in exercising his or her direct prerogative duties, therefore, are the political conventions directing him or her. The guiding principles of constitutional monarchy are that the monarch must carry out all his or her public duties, and must exercise his or her legal powers of state, with strict political neutrality. He or she must accept and follow ' ministerial advice', taking his or her lead from the Prime Minister of the day, the head of government, who together with his or her Cabinet colleagues is accountable to Parliament and holds office subject to the confidence of the House of Commons. The monarch does not make public utterances on matters of partisan political dispute, unless it is on the advice or with the approval of the government.

It is imperatives of politics, therefore, and not law, that presently govern and control the monarchy, and will continue to do so under Charles III. The political imperative is that he will exercise his royal prerogative duties in accordance with prime ministerial advice, consistent with established constitutional law and practice. What supports this imperative is a combination of royal self-interest and respect for the primacy of the elected government and Parliament. The ultimate sanction is that if a King started to behave in an 'unconstitutional' manner, however lawful it might be in theory, the political system would remove the King or the institution of monarchy altogether. The lesson of Edward VIII's abdication in 1936 for us today has little to do with personal morality and the stigma of divorce. The lesson is that a monarch who will not comply with ministerial advice and the political understandings and expectations of the royal institution can and will be required to vacate the throne.

Royal activism: the terminology and thesis of 'personal prerogatives'

Difficulties will emerge if we allow uncertainties to exist over the parameters of the constitutional procedures to be followed by the future King. Likewise a crisis for the monarchy lies ahead if there is any ambiguity on the question of the legitimacy with which he might ever intervene to impose his own personal views in the performance of a royal duty.

It is foreseeable that problems could arise with regard to prime ministerial appointment, Royal Assent and dissolution of Parliament. These royal powers have been described by some influential theorists – inappropriately – as the 'personal prerogatives' of the monarch. Indeed, there has been a remarkable quantity of constitutional speculation and theorising generated on this whole subject. There has been a tide of opinion that has had the effect of promoting a royal interventionist mentality on the matter. And, worse, it appears to have had a practical impact on how Buckingham Palace, the Cabinet Office and 10 Downing Street view the legitimacy with which a monarch might intervene in the political process today.

Regrettably, the idea has been put forward by some theorists that a monarch is not, in fact, always bound to follow ministerial advice and established constitutional procedure. Instead it has been suggested by some that a monarch possesses a residual personal discretion in how his or her direct legal duties of state are exercised. It has been claimed that the monarch has a constitutional right to reject the Prime Minister's advice, even though no impropriety in that advice exists. This would extend, for example, to the actions of a monarch, and therefore the future Charles III, in giving or withholding Royal Assent to certain legislative measures, or to the question of the timing of a dissolution of Parliament and a general election. We are even told by some that a reigning monarch has a constitutional discretion allowing him or her to prefer alternative advice, such as from other Cabinet ministers or the leader of the opposition, to that which he receives from the Prime Minister.

Much of the contemporary advocacy of this view has been shaped by the writings of Sir Ivor Jennings. Sir Ivor was a prominent university legal scholar, working at various times as reader in English law at the London School of Economics, vice-chancellor at Ceylon University and latterly a college master and professor at Cambridge University. It was he who coined the expression 'personal prerogatives', in the following key passage on the royal powers from his influential book, *Cabinet Government*:

> While the King has in normal circumstances 'the right to be consulted, the right to encourage, the right to warn', he must, in the last resort, give way to the advice of the Cabinet. There are, however, certain prerogative powers which he exercises on his own responsibility, and which may fitly be called 'the personal prerogatives'.[8]

A half-century later, Sir Ivor's views were still alive and well, being propounded by leading academics at Oxford University who were widely believed to serve as advisers on constitutional affairs to Buckingham Palace. Lord Blake was one such dignitary, a distinguished Oxford historian of the Conservative Party and political biographer. In 1984, he made public his view, expressed in a letter to the *Times*, that 'there are, and long have been, matters (a few) on which the Crown does not need to take ministerial advice'.[9] A few months later, he delivered a Gresham College Special Lecture entitled 'Monarchy', setting forth his views that 'the monarch has the right to dismiss a Prime Minister, to dissolve Parliament, and to refuse to dissolve Parliament'.[10] More recently, in 1995, Vernon Bogdanor, the distinguished Oxford political scientist, published a monograph called *The Monarchy and the Constitution*, in which he maintained:

> When exercising the personal prerogatives, the sovereign acts in a personal capacity and not on the advice of ministers. The extent and scope of the personal prerogatives are, however, unclear. It is difficult if not impossible to circumscribe them accurately. It may, indeed, be inherent in the notion of constitutional monarchy that the personal prerogatives remain undefined in extent and scope.[11]

The terminology of this passage relies heavily on Sir Ivor's work. It even manages to exaggerate the implications of Sir Ivor's own account of the 'personal' nature of the monarch's prerogative powers,* by claiming a non-circumscribed legitimacy for the monarch to act free from ministerial advice and instead rely on his or her own personal decision.

The proper role and duties of the monarch today

This approach to the prerogative powers of the monarch is wrong, misconceived, and belongs to an earlier era. As statements of political reality and constitutional sense today, they are anachronisms.

When Sir Ivor Jennings was writing in the 1930s, there was still some semblance of accuracy in his description. Britain was still a class-dominated society where the aristocracy (with the monarchy at its apex) still wielded great social and therefore political power and influence. Sir Ivor was – as are we all – a creature of his time and he reflected the political and social mores and realities of his era. Only five years before the publication of *Cabinet Government*, the political and economic crisis of 1931 had taken place. This had witnessed the two major party leaders being content to collude in George V playing the role of broker in the re-appointment of

---

* A curiosity of Sir Ivor's interpretation of the 'personal prerogatives' is his failure to harmonise theory and practice so as to reach a coherent conclusion. Thus at page 428 (*Cabinet Government*, 3rd edn (Cambridge: Cambridge University Press, 1959)), he comes frustratingly close to accepting the reality of the situation when he writes, 'While the Queen's personal prerogative is maintained in theory, it can hardly be exercised in practice.'

Labour's leader, Ramsay MacDonald, as Prime Minister of a Conservative-dominated National Government.[12] Clearly, in the 1930s the monarchy still mattered in the game of politics, even though King George's actions were condemned within the Labour Party itself,[13] with Mr MacDonald being subsequently expelled from the Labour Party for his collusion. But even if Sir Ivor's conclusions are regarded as a fair description of the times in which they were published (still within living memory), they must also be viewed as coming at the tail end of the era of monarchical intervention in political affairs.

Elsewhere in his famous book, there are numerous examples of Sir Ivor's obvious datedness and loss of relevance concerning royal power and intervention for today's constitutional purposes. For instance, near the front of the book he says, 'It is a settled rule that the Prime Minister must be either a peer or a member of the House of Commons.'[14] But, as we all know today, it has in fact become a settled rule that the Prime Minister must sit in the House of Commons, and this was shown conclusively by the events of 1963.* Two years later, the Conservative Party adopted its own independent rules for selecting its leader, rendering Sir Ivor's account of the prerogative over prime ministerial appointment even less valid.

Another example of Sir Ivor's obvious datedness is his theorising of the role of the monarch as 'mediator', suggesting that 'the King may also use his prestige to settle political conflict or diminish the virulence of opposition'.[15] He then went on to discuss episodes of past monarchs interviewing opposition leaders in times of crisis so as to secure their agreement to various government policies or items of legislation. This is far-fetched from political reality in the twenty-first century. Today, whether the controversy be university top-up fees, foreign policy on Iraq, or UK adoption of the euro, no one can seriously maintain it is the place of a hereditary monarch to get proactively involved in political debate and seek to persuade one or more of the opposition parties to support the government line.

Certainly since the 1960s, if not earlier, talk of the 'personal prerogatives' as signifying personal discretionary constitutional rights of the sovereign, or of the monarch's freedom from ministerial responsibility in exercising the prerogative, has become redundant in practice and an arcane

---

* In 1963 two peers, Lord Home and Lord Hailsham, disclaimed their peerages under the newly enacted Peerage Act and took seats in the Commons in order to submit themselves for consideration as leader of the Conservative Party and Prime Minister; the former, as Sir Alec Douglas-Home, served as premier between 1963 and 1964.

academic red herring. The true constitutional position can be summarised as follows:

The duties of the monarch in the exercise of his or her direct prerogative powers as head of state

- A monarch exercises his or her prerogative powers on the advice and direction of the Prime Minister of the day.
- A monarch is duty bound to reject prime ministerial advice, and dismiss the Prime Minister from office, when the Prime Minister is acting in manifest breach of convention.*
- For the avoidance of doubt, the monarch exercises his or her legal powers exclusively in accordance with established procedures.[†]

The appointment of a Prime Minister

Generally, there is no issue of royal intervention in prime ministerial appointment. The leader of the party with an overall majority in the Commons is appointed (or remains) Prime Minister.

The most recent constitutional example of the monarch appointing a new Prime Minister at a general election occurred on 1 May 1997. Labour won 419 seats in the Commons, the Conservatives 165, the Liberal Democrats 46, and others 29. Labour had a large overall majority of 179. Even before the polls closed at 10.00 p.m. that day, it was clear from opinion polling that the incumbent Conservative Prime Minister, John Major, would be defeated and Tony Blair's New Labour party would win a landslide victory, sweeping him into 10 Downing Street.

---

* In other words, where the advice itself is unconstitutional. For example, if a motion of no confidence in the government is carried in the House of Commons, there is a constitutional requirement for the Prime Minister to resign or call a general election: see further below. If the Prime Minister refuses or fails to do so, then the monarch has no choice in the matter and is duty bound to exercise his or her legal power to dismiss the Prime Minister from office and appoint the leader of the opposition instead.

† In other words, with no element of personal discretion or private preference. Instead, with respect to the second obligation above, it is best to speak of a 'judgement' being required, in the sense that the monarch will need to consider, recognise and declare that a breach of convention has taken place.

The count of ballot papers in the great majority of constituencies these days is conducted with remarkable speed. At about 2.00 the next morning, even before daylight, Mr Major telephoned Mr Blair to concede defeat.* While the defeated premier snatched a few hours' sleep, packing and removals of his belongings was quickly carried out so his departure from the building could be completed before his successor moved in the same day. Mid-morning, the permanent staff at 10 Downing Street lined the hall to bid farewell to the outgoing Prime Minister, according to custom, as he and his wife Norma made their exit, only to re-assemble there an hour later to greet the newcomer.

The defeated, outgoing Prime Minister was then driven with his wife the half-mile to Buckingham Palace, where he met Queen Elizabeth to formally tender his resignation and relinquish the premiership. Only a few minutes later, Mr Blair arrived at the Palace to meet the Queen and, after exchanging a few short pleasantries, was formally invited by her to form an administration. On acceptance, Mr Blair immediately became Prime Minister. Traditionally, this meeting to formalise the appointment of a new Prime Minister is known as 'kissing hands', but – in case anyone thought this still happens – it is a ceremony that is no longer followed. Returning to the entrance to Downing Street, Tony and Cherie Blair then made a slow triumphal walk towards No. 10, shaking hands along the way to crowds of well-orchestrated New Labour supporters waving Union Jack flags, culminating in a speech by Mr Blair to the press and waiting television crews.

It is 'hung' Parliament situations – or a 'balanced' House of Commons, as some prefer to call the position, where no single party has an overall majority in the Commons – which have generated much academic speculation and encouragement of royal intervention. In this matter, according to Sir Ivor Jennings, 'the King need not accept advice as to the appointment of a Prime Minister'.[16] A constitutional authority today who propounds a thesis of 'reserve powers' for the monarch to intervene in such situations is Rodney Brazier, Professor of Constitutional Law at Manchester University and the

---

* In his memoirs, John Major wrote, 'At about 2 a.m. I asked Alex Allan to get Tony Blair on the telephone, so that I could congratulate him on his success. I spoke to the new Prime Minister from my study . . . I can remember little of what I said, I was so exhausted, but we were both friendly enough.' Elsewhere he recounts that on leaving the Prime Minister's flat at 10 Downing Street later that morning, he left a bottle of champagne behind for Tony and Cherie Blair, with a note saying, 'It's a great job – enjoy it.' *John Major: The Autobiography* (London: HarperCollins 2000), pp. 723, 726.

author of several leading works on the constitution. In his book *Constitutional Practice*, Professor Brazier says, 'There are no rules about government formation from a hung Parliament.'[17] Elsewhere he maintains, echoing Sir Ivor's theorising about the monarch as mediator, that if the party leaders disagree as to who should be Prime Minister, then the monarch 'is ideally placed to moderate between any competing wishes of party leaders in a hung Parliament'.[18] As to the political setting in which such mediation/moderation would occur, Professor Brazier's opinion is that the monarch 'should hear the views in audience of each party leader in turn'.[19] In the future, according to this view, it would be Charles III who was entertaining each party leader in turn, in order to oversee the formation of a government.*

But it is unreal politically and inappropriate constitutionally to acknowledge – and indeed advocate – a personal discretionary power for a hereditary monarch to operate as the means for determining the outcome of a general election. There needs to be, and is already in existence, an established procedure and basis for the resolution of who will be Prime Minister after a general election that produces a House of Commons with no overall majority for a single party.

The true position is as follows:

Procedure for prime ministerial appointment under hung Parliaments
- The incumbent Prime Minister has the first opportunity to continue in office and form an administration.
- If he or she is unable to do so (and resigns, or is defeated on the Address at the meeting of Parliament), then the leader of the largest opposition party is appointed Prime Minister.

There is really no problem in establishing the constitutional answer to the question of who is appointed Prime Minister under a hung Parliament. Yet reams of academic speculative theorising[20] and much exaggerated comment about 'grey areas' have been generated on the subject, misleadingly suggesting that the Queen and the future King will/should/must somehow

---

* Professor Brazier defends his thesis of 'reserve powers' by saying 'the guiding light ought to be that the political crisis should if possible be resolved by politicians'. But if opposition party leaders are encouraged to believe they are in with a chance of King Charles preferring their claim to hold office to that of the incumbent, they may well think it worthwhile publicly disputing the Prime Minister's (legitimate) prior claim.

get involved to mediate or moderate competing claims from party leaders. This is removed from political actuality, and indeed convention.

The above procedure for prime ministerial appointment was followed in each of the real hung Parliament situations arising from the general elections in 1923, 1929 and February 1974. On the first of these, the Labour Party was in the process of eclipsing the Liberal Party as the second major party of state. The result of the election was that the Conservative Party won 258 seats, the Labour Party 191 and the Liberal Party 159. When the results were known, the incumbent Prime Minister, Stanley Baldwin, did not resign but sought to remain in office, which he was entitled to do. However, when the new House of Commons met five weeks later, a resolution expressing no confidence in the government was passed by dint of Labour and Liberal MPs voting together. It was only the effect of this censure vote that obliged Mr Baldwin to resign, not the result of the general election itself. Subsequently, Ramsay MacDonald, the leader of the Labour Party, being the largest opposition party in the House of Commons, was invited to form an administration and appointed Prime Minister by George V.

The next hung Parliament to be produced at a general election was in 1929, when the Conservative Party won 260 seats, the Labour Party 288 and the Liberal Party 59. On this occasion, the incumbent Prime Minister, once again Stanley Baldwin, as soon as the results were known tendered his resignation to the King. This was in the certain knowledge that the Labour and Liberal MPs would unite once more to pass a no-confidence motion in his govern-ment if he attempted to stay on. The Labour leader, Ramsay MacDonald, visited the Palace a second time to be appointed Prime Minister.

The third and most recent time a general election produced such a situation was in February 1974. Here, the Conservative governing party obtained 296 seats to Labour's 301, but with the Liberals gaining 14, the Ulster unionist parties 11, the Scottish Nationalists 7, Plaid Cymru 2 and the Ulster republican parties 2. Polling day had been Thursday 28 February, and into the morning of the next day the closeness of the contest made it uncertain whether either of the two major parties had won a narrow overall majority. By the afternoon of the next day, however, it became clear that not only the Conservative Party but also Labour were short of a majority. The Prime Minister, Edward Heath, responded by choosing not to tender his resignation to Queen Elizabeth immediately. Instead, he entered into negotiations with the Liberal Party leader, Jeremy Thorpe, on the possibility of a governing coalition composed of the two parties. Only when these talks failed four days later did Mr Heath conclude he was unable to continue in office and form an administration. He was driven to Buckingham Palace to meet the Queen at 6.30 p.m. on Monday 4 March, where he resigned office. The Labour leader, Harold Wilson, met the Queen shortly afterwards at 7.30 p.m., to be appointed Prime Minister and invited to form the next government.

Some, of course, will say that the incumbent Prime Minister should not have the first claim on forming a government and that it should be the leader of the party with the largest number of seats in the House of Commons. But this is an argument for reform, not an elucidation of UK constitutional law as it currently exists.[21]

Royal Assent to legislation

In our constitutional law, Parliament is shorthand for 'the Queen-in-Parliament'. Parliament comprises three bodies – the House of Commons, the House of Lords, and the Sovereign. The consent of each (subject to the Parliament Acts in the case of the House of Lords) is required before a Bill becomes an enforceable Act of Parliament.[22] The consent of the monarch takes place at the end of the legislative process, after the Bill has gone through its various readings and procedural stages in both Houses of Parliament.

Today, the monarch's role and act in giving Royal Assent is as constitutionally routine as the Queen's or King's Speech at the ceremonial opening of Parliament. As a matter of political reality, there has been no royal veto – as it was once called – for three centuries. The last occasion was when Queen Anne refused to sign the Scotch Militia Bill in 1707.

Legally, Royal Assent can be effected by the monarch through any means of communication he or she wishes. However, the last occasion a reigning monarch declared assent personally in the House of Lords was when Victoria did so on 12 August 1854. One method for giving Royal Assent is by way of notification in the House of Lords by Lords Commissioners appointed for the purpose by the King or Queen.[23] The commission usually comprises the Lord Chancellor and four other peers who must be members of the Privy Council. They are empowered to give Royal Assent by letters patent signed by the King or Queen, with the Great Seal attached. These letters patent specifically refer to the Bills to be assented to, and the commissioners are authorised 'to do all things in Her Majesty's name which are to be done on her part in this Parliament, as by the letters patent will more fully appear'.

Since 1967, however, this commission ceremony has been superseded by a new procedure whereby the speaker of each House simply notifies the two chambers that 'the Queen has signified her Royal Assent' to the list of measures read out. The commission ceremony only now takes place at the end of a session, and only then if a prorogation ceremony is taking place to bring the annual session to a close. This remains the most colourful and theatrical method of communicating Royal Assent. As an apparition, it involves the Lords Commissioners dressing up in dark robes and hats, a reading clerk reading out the terms of the commission, the Clerk of the Crown reading out the Acts in turn and the Clerk of the Parliaments pronouncing Royal Assent in Norman French.

But are there circumstances in which the Queen or the future King can legitimately withhold or refuse Royal Assent? Here again, some have 'talked up' a discretionary and personal element in the exercise of this ancient monarchical prerogative power to formalise an Act of Parliament. Proponents of this theory have suggested that the monarch possesses some residual personal discretion in the matter, and is not always bound to sign the letters patent authorising that the parliamentary Bill pass into law.

Sir Ivor Jennings and like-minded writers expressing this theory in recent times have drawn up lists of situations or general categories of scenarios in which they speculate or suggest that the monarch could legitimately exercise a royal veto over the legislation. Thus, Sir Ivor in *Cabinet Government* wrote:

> He [the King] would be justified in refusing to assent to a policy which subverted the democratic basis of the Constitution, by unnecessary or indefinite prolongations of the life of Parliament, by a gerrymandering of the constituencies in the interests of one party, or by fundamental modification of the electoral system to the same end.[24]

This theoretical recognition of royal activism in legislative affairs is still perpetuated by some academics today. The most notable among them is Professor Rodney Brazier, who, in *Constitutional Practice*, has similarly drawn up lists of situations where it is stated that a monarch can and, he implies, should refuse Royal Assent to a government Bill. For instance, borrowing Sir Ivor's phrase, Professor Brazier says, 'A government Bill designed to achieve a permanent subversion of the democratic basis of the constitution could be appropriately vetoed.'[25]

The problems inherent in such a view are various. How does one determine if, when and whether a Bill is 'subverting the democratic basis of the constitution'? Some maintain that a number of authoritarian measures in recent years have been doing just that. Many have condemned the effective restrictions on personal liberty and the ancient remedy of habeas corpus by the anti-terrorism legislation since 2000.[26] Others were outraged by the government's removal of two-thirds of the House of Lords' membership in 1999 (the great majority of whom belonged to the opposition party), without securing agreement beforehand on what the permanent constitution of the upper House would be.[27] So could the Queen have intervened and blocked the legislation to make the government think again? The answer is, clearly, no. If any such ground for vetoing legislation did exist, such a weighty matter should be for a constitutional court to determine, not a politically neutral, hereditary monarch.

Furthermore, if Royal Assent is regarded as a discretionary act allowing some residual personal element in its exercise, then it opens the possibility for a future Charles III, William V or Henry IX to claim personal factors in refusing assent to a Bill. What if, after the future accession of Charles III, the new King is given a Bill to sign by the government that he finds funda-mentally at odds with his own personal conscience and core beliefs?[28] What if, for example, he was presented with a Bill to require all farmers, including organic growers, to make government-directed genetic modifications to all crops sold to the public? What if he was asked to sign a Bill that sought to ban homeopathic medicine as being dangerous to health? Or how would he respond if asked to sign a Bill to enable scientific cloning of humans subject only to individual applications to the Home Office and payment of a processing fee? It is possible that with legislative measures such as these, Charles III might agonise over the moral issues involved – and it is not difficult to imagine him doing so.* He might find himself morally and emotionally incapable of putting his signature to a law that in his heart and soul he opposed and despised.

Indeed in the light of the Human Rights Act – especially given its utilisation for effectively re-writing the Marriage Acts to enable Prince Charles to marry in a civil register office[29] – perhaps once more, as King, he

---

* The philosophically inquiring and soul-searching nature of Prince Charles's personality is well known and he is certainly no stranger to controversy in expressing his own ideological views on a range of matters outside the mainstream of party politics, including in his public speeches and in correspondence or meetings with government ministers: see generally Jonathan Dimbleby, *The Prince of Wales: A Biography* (London: Little, Brown, 1994).

might claim his fundamental human rights were at stake. He might seek to argue that, as a private citizen even when performing a public duty, he should not be compelled, by constitutional convention or otherwise, to act in a manner which violated the freedom and integrity of his conscience.

These may seem hypothetical situations. But as human-rights thinking gathers momentum, and when in the future a more assertive individual than Elizabeth II comes to the throne, the situation of a future King wishing to avoid the task of putting his personal signature to a law he regards as debasing his conscience or soul will become increasingly likely. Furthermore, this type of situation has arisen in practice in other countries in modern times.

The most famous occasion of a royal intervention was in Belgium in 1990, when King Baudouin refused to sign a Bill passed by the Belgian Parliament which legalised abortion, on the grounds that he was a devout Catholic. In the King's letter to the Prime Minister he explained that his conscience forbade him from giving his assent to it. The government and the King found a way out of the crisis through deft use of the provisions in their written constitution of state. King Baudouin was declared 'unable to reign' for a day and a half, during which time the Council of Ministers signed the law on his behalf as permitted under a provision in the Belgian written constitution.*

The possibility of such constitutional difficulties arising in the United Kingdom will be exacerbated if the monarch of the day believes he or she has a personal discretion in the exercise of Royal Assent, as he or she is being encouraged to think by those who continue to talk up the 'personal prerogatives'. But if established practice and political reality are accepted and followed, there will be no crisis or problem. The following is the true position:

---

* The chronology and constitutional law of this interesting event is as follows. On 30 March 1990 King Baudouin wrote a letter to the Prime Minister communicating his refusal to sign the abortion law reform Bill on grounds of conscience. On 3 April the King abdicated, relying on an article (now Article 93) in Chapter III of the Belgian constitution which provides that, 'should the King find himself unable to reign, the ministers, having observed this inability, immediately summon the Houses [of the Belgian federal legislature, i.e. the House of Representatives and the Senate]. Regency and guardianship are to be provided by the united Houses.' No regency was made at this stage, nor was one ever intended as part of this scheme of arrangement, which then allowed the Council of Ministers to adopt the powers of the King and sign the Bill, enabling it to pass into law under the authority of another article (now Article 90) of the constitution, which provides that 'until the taking of oath by his [the King's] successor to the throne or by the Regent, the King's constitutional powers are exercised, in the name of the Belgian people, by the Council of Ministers, and under their responsibility'. On 5 April the assembled Houses recognised that King Baudouin's 'inability to reign' had terminated and his position as King was restored.

> *The role and duties of the monarch with regard to the Royal Assent*
> - The monarch's duty is limited to one of due process in the passage of the Bill.
> - The royal act of Assent is in the nature of a certificate that the Bill has passed through all its established parliamentary procedures.
> - There is no royal veto on grounds of the personal views or beliefs of the monarch.

In view of all the emphasis on the personal prerogatives by Sir Ivor Jennings and others even today, it would be desirable for an agreed written statement to be issued from Buckingham Palace or a Conference on Royal Affairs initiated by the Palace. This should confirm the position that the constitutional basis on which the monarch exercises Royal Assent, now and in the future, is limited to one of certification of due process. A suitable timing for this announcement might be shortly after the accession of the next monarch, Charles III.

The dissolution of Parliament and the timing of general elections

The constitutional procedure whereby Parliament – our national representative assembly – is dissolved and summoned is of fundamental importance to our democratic system of government. It determines the date of a general election.

Archaic law and the form of royal acts

The law governing the life of Parliament today is a mixture of common-law royal prerogative and parliamentary statute. The Parliament Act 1911 lays down a five-year maximum duration for a parliament, calculated from the date of its first actual meeting.[30] Within each five-year period Parliament is dissolved and a general election called under the legal authority of the reigning monarch's prerogative powers to dissolve and summon Parliaments. This legal regime is a direct inheritance from Parliament's origins in medieval times, when it was simply a royal council of state to be called into existence at the monarch's pleasure and for his own purposes, such as obtaining consent to some extraordinary action or new levy of taxation.

The legal theory is still that the Queen or the future King could dissolve

Parliament by any means of communication, including personal attendance in the House of Lords to declare her or his intention and command that Parliament is no more. In his popular treatise on the English system of government two centuries ago, the Swiss advocate Jean-Louis de Lolme colourfully described the marvels of English royal law on this subject as follows:

> The person who is invested with the kingly office, in England, has need of no other weapon, no other artillery, than the civil insignia of his dignity, to effect a dissolution of the Parliament. He steps into the middle of them, telling them they are dissolved, and they are dissolved; he tells them they are no longer a Parliament, and they are no longer so. Like Popilius's wand a dissolution instantly puts a stop to their warmest debates and most violent proceedings. The wonderful words by which it is expressed have no sooner met their ears, than all their legislative faculties are benumbed: though they may still be sitting on the same benches, they look no longer upon themselves as forming an assembly; they no longer consider each other in the light of associates or of colleagues. As if some strange kind of weapon, or a sudden magical effort, had been exerted in the midst of them, all the bonds of their union are cut off: and they hasten away, without having so much as the thought of continuing for a single minute the duration of their assembly.[31]

However, the last two occasions Parliament was dissolved by a monarch in person was on 28 March 1681 by Charles II and, most recently, on 10 June 1818 by the high-handed Prince Regent, later George III. Ever since then, a royal proclamation, declaring and making public the dissolution of Parliament, has been the invariable modern practice for performing the King's direct legal duty in the matter.

Set out in flowery royal legalese, the royal proclamation contains several essential legal ingredients. Firstly, it dissolves Parliament with immediate effect. It will have been preceded by a prorogation or adjournment of parliamentary business, usually on the previous working day, so as not to peremptorily terminate business or debate still being carried on in either chamber. Second, it summons a new Parliament, and directs election writs to be sent out for the purpose of electing members of the Commons.[172] Though unnecessary to its legal force, it is customary for the proclamation to be published in the *London Gazette*, and to be read out from the steps of the Royal Exchange in the City of London by the Common Cryer and Serjeant-at-Arms.

The Royal Proclamation in 2005

BY THE QUEEN: A PROCLAMATION for Dissolving the Present Parliament and Declaring the Calling of Another. ELIZABETH R.

Whereas We have thought fit, by and with the advice of Our Privy Council, to dissolve this present Parliament, which stands prorogued to Thursday, the fourteenth day of April: We do, for that End, publish this Our Royal Proclamation, and do hereby dissolve the said Parliament accordingly: And the Lords Spiritual and Temporal, and the Members of the House of Commons, are discharged from further Attendance thereat: And We being desirous and resolved, as soon as may be, to meet Our People, and to have their Advice in Parliament, do hereby make known to all Our loving Subjects Our Royal Will and Pleasure to call a new Parliament: and do hereby further declare, that, by and with the advice of Our Privy Council, We have given Order that Our Chancellor of Great Britain and Our Secretary of State for Northern Ireland do respectively, upon Notice thereof, forthwith issue our Writs, in due Form and according to Law, for calling a new Parliament: And We do hereby also, by this Our Royal Proclamation under Our Great Seal of Our Realm, require Writs forthwith to be issued accordingly by Our said Chancellor and Secretary of State respectively, for causing the Lords Spiritual and Temporal and Commons who are to serve in the said Parliament to be duly returned to, and give their Attendance in, Our said Parliament on Wednesday, the eleventh day of May next, which Writs are to be returnable in due course of Law.

Given at Our Court at Windsor Castle, this eleventh day of April in the Year of our Lord two thousand and five and in the fifty-fourth year of Our Reign.

GOD SAVE THE QUEEN

Constitutional conventions

As with each of a modern monarch's acts of state, the exercise of this royal power of dissolution of Parliament is circumscribed by certain established constitutional principles and procedure. The first of these political expectations is that the royal acts of dissolving and summoning parliaments are, and must be, simultaneous events. This is to minimise the period in which no parliament is in existence at all, which for democratic reasons is best kept in continuous existence so far as possible. Thus the two acts are recited in the same proclamation. This convention is in fact the only regulation preventing there being not five- but eight-year periods between general elections. This intriguing fact is a historical curiosity arising from the Meeting of Parliament Act 1694 still being the governing law on the summoning of Parliament. This statute, formerly known as the Triennial Act, simply stipulates that a parliament should be called into existence within three years of its predecessor's termination.

The second controlling principle is that it is the constitutional right of the Prime Minister alone to determine the timing of a dissolution and general election and to advise the monarch accordingly.[33] From the monarch's perspective, it is from the Prime Minister alone and personally, that he or she receives the formal request to put into effect the legal procedure for dissolution. Prior to this taking place, it is for the Prime Minister to decide whether and to what extent he or she consults Cabinet and party colleagues. The normal practice in recent decades has been for the Prime Minister to share this important tactical decision with only a handful of his or her closest and most trusted colleagues in 10 Downing Street. A Cabinet meeting is then usually convened the morning before he or she visits the Palace to tender the request for a dissolution. But, as the former Labour leader Harold Wilson wrote in his memoirs, 'there is no obligation of the Prime Minister to consult'.[34]

The announcement of news of the pending dissolution and general election dates – a sensational piece of political news, of course – is made not by Buckingham Palace, but by 10 Downing Street. Until 1935 the announcement was made in Parliament. In 1951 and 1955, the Prime Minister made the announcement over the radio. For the next four decades, the rather cursory practice was for a simple press notice to be issued by a 10 Downing Street official direct to journalists, for them to relay on television and in the next day's newspapers. This would be preceded, an hour or two earlier, by personal letters from the Prime Minister setting out the news being delivered to the leaders of the two main opposition parties and to the Speaker of the Commons.

Then in 1997, John Major made the public announcement of the news by way of a personal statement to an assembled gathering of television cameramen and journalists outside 10 Downing Street, capitalising on the occasion to give a short speech on why the country should vote Conservative. In 2001 and 2005, Tony Blair similarly used the occasion to make what was, in effect, a free party political broadcast. In 2001, Mr Blair moved the location away from Downing Street to what he hoped would be a more electorally advantageous setting. This was a school assembly he was attending in south London, to which journalists and cameramen had been groomed to come along. This occasion was widely ridiculed and regarded as a counter-productive public relations mistake (many of the children he was shown speaking to looked bored and all of them were obviously too young to vote). In 2005, Mr Blair reverted to Mr Major's earlier tactic of a speech from outside 10 Downing Street. However, in a departure from earlier practice, Mr Blair made the announcement immediately on his return from seeing Queen Elizabeth at Buckingham Palace, stepping out of the car and speaking without prepared notes. For the first time also, no courtesy letters were issued in advance to the other political leaders.

Hung Parliaments and alleged grey areas

The third political imperative guiding a monarch's direct legal duties with respect to dissolution is to be clear about the procedures in situations of a hung Parliament. The conventions on dissolution in such circumstances have been much muddied by more talk of the 'personal prerogatives' of the monarch and a great deal of nonsense about 'grey areas' of uncertainty.

Indeed, Sir Ivor Jennings and others over half a century after him have maintained that the monarch has a personal discretion over dissolution matters as a whole, and acts free from ministerial advice and responsibility. According to Jennings, the dissolution of Parliament is one of 'certain prerogative powers which he exercises on his own responsibility'.[35] His book relates stories stretching back to the beginning of the nineteenth century, citing supporting opinions of various aristocratic figures and parliamentarians of 100 or more years ago, such as the Duke of Devonshire, Lord Salisbury, Sir Robert Peel, and Queen Victoria herself. Today, the distinguished constitutional historian Professor Peter Hennessy writes that 'a Prime Minister can request but not demand a dissolution. The monarch can refuse this.'[36]

And as has so often been the case in the academic exposition of the 'personal prerogatives', many lists of situations and political scenarios have been drawn up in which it is speculated that the monarch might intervene. During the heady days of the SDP–Liberal Alliance in the mid-1980s, for example, when there was much conjecture on the possibility of a hung Parliament at the then forthcoming general election, Vernon Bogdanor of Oxford University wrote a pamphlet entitled *No Overall Majority*.[37] In it, he set out a list of circumstances in which 'it is suggested that the Queen would be entitled to refuse a dissolution'. These started with 'war or national emergency'. Later on, he said, 'no Prime Minister can be entitled to a series of dissolutions', in which case 'the Queen might reasonably take the view' that she should veto a Prime Minister's decision to hold a further election.

She can, or should, also intervene, Professor Bogdanor said, when Cabinet colleagues disagree with the Prime Minister's decision to hold an election.

This list of hypothetical situations (indeed any such list) is both vague and inadequate. We have just been at 'war' in Iraq – so would it have been legitimate for the Queen to have vetoed Mr Blair if he had sought a mandate from the electorate during the conflict? Between 2001 and 2005 the UK was formally in a state of 'public emergency' under international law. It was upon this basis that the United Kingdom derogated from its human rights obligations under Article 5 (Right to liberty and security) of the European Convention on Human Rights. So did this mean the Queen had the constitutional right to refuse an election until the public emergency was declared to be over? Professor Bogdanor's scenario of a Prime Minister who sought a third election shortly after two previous ones within the previous year is highly improbable. But in such a situation, if neither the Prime Minister nor the leader of the opposition could muster the parliamentary strength respectively to govern or to censure the government on the Address so as to replace it,[38] then there has to be an election to clear up the stalemate. And how does the Queen, and the future King Charles, go about soliciting the views of individual Cabinet members over whether they want a dissolution or not and/or whether they agree with the Prime Minister? If the Prime Minister as trustee of the party's electoral fortunes has lost the confidence of his party colleagues to make such a decision, there are party leadership rules whereby he or she can be challenged and replaced.

Reality, principles and practice
The fact is that there has been no refusal of a dissolution request by a Prime Minister in modern times. The last case of a monarch overruling the government on a dissolution matter was in 1834. The true situation is that all the academic theorising which has promoted the personal prerogative or discretionary power of the monarch to decide dissolution affairs and general election timing is an anachronism, and as political reality is defunct. Today, the monarch is obliged to act upon the advice and direction of the Prime Minister in all questions of dissolution, except where that advice is manifestly unconstitutional and in breach of convention. For example, if the Prime Minister lost the general election and the opposition gained an overall majority, any request of the incumbent for a re-run of the general election would be manifestly unconstitutional, and the monarch would reject the request and dismiss him or her from office. Furthermore, where the advice of

the Prime Minister is unconstitutional, the monarch is duty bound – there is no personal discretion – to reject it.

There are four key constitutional principles and procedures here:

Procedures governing the monarch's exercise of the legal power of dissolution of Parliament

- A Prime Minister who has lost a general election cannot request a dissolution. 'Lost' here includes the government being defeated on an amendment to the Address (in reply to the Queen's Speech) expressing no confidence in the government, taking place at the first meeting of the newly elected House of Commons.

- In a hung Parliament, where the Prime Minister's government wins or survives the debate on the Address, his or her advice to the monarch on dissolution affairs must thereafter be followed during his or her tenure in office.*

- A Prime Minister who loses a no-confidence vote in the Commons must request a dissolution of Parliament from the monarch, who will grant it. The Prime Minister is entitled to resign office (together with his or her government) instead, in which case the monarch will appoint the leader of the opposition as the new premier, who will advise on dissolution matters thereafter.

- Deselection of a Prime Minister as leader of the governing party causes him or her to lose his or her political authority to advise the monarch on dissolution affairs (or any other prerogative powers).† A monarch is duty bound to reject any request by a Prime Minister for a dissolution during a leadership contest.

---

* In political substance, passage of the Address in reply to the Queen's Speech in the opening session of a new parliament is a confirmatory resolution of the House of Commons in the Prime Minister remaining in, or taking, office.

† He or she must resign office as Prime Minister in favour of his or her successor as party leader, as occurred in 1990 when Margaret Thatcher was removed as Conservative leader. Any meaningful distinction between a Prime Minister's constitutional authority (dependent on the monarch's appointment) and his or her political authority (dependent on his or her leadership of the political party gaining an electoral mandate) has been eclipsed by the establishment of party leadership rules for all the major political parties. Furthermore, the institution of the political party, previously regarded as a private voluntary body, has now entered the domain of UK public law and the constitution, as is common in other countries, especially since passage of the Political Parties, Elections and Referendum Act 2000.

Repercussions of 'talking up' the idea of 'personal' prerogatives

There are real and serious dangers, both to the integrity of our parliamentary democracy and to the future of the monarchy, in the effects which may occur through academic theorists 'talking up' the personal discretion and moderating role of the monarch. Regarded as authorities on constitutional law, these professors are giving licence and encouragement to the monarch of today and of tomorrow (and to her or his Palace officials) to intervene in difficult, sensitive and highly charged political situations. They are, in effect, inciting royal activism when none is necessary, appropriate or desirable.

There will be no problem during the reign of the present monarch, Elizabeth II. Contrary to the perception of some, Queen Elizabeth has been the model of a 'modern' monarch. She may have, and indeed has, offered views on government affairs to Prime Ministers in private during their regular meetings.* But she has never come close to using her personal prerogatives in order to challenge the Prime Minister's legitimacy to govern and control the prerogative acts of state. Her tightly drawn interpretation of her constitutional role in practice, inhibited in its sphere of interference in politics, has been in tune with the changing nature of society and politics since the 1960s – and indeed is consistent with Labour's government-modernising agenda since 1997.†

However, the crucial point about constitutional arrangements for a hereditary monarchy is that one never knows what the accidents of birth will

---

* Nothing in this book suggests it is inappropriate for a monarch privately to speak their mind and express a personal opinion to the Prime Minister as head of government. Monarchs are human beings and have views like anyone else, and a Prime Minister hears and solicits views from a wide number of important people. The quality of opinion proffered obviously depends upon the mind and experience of the particular individual. Of Elizabeth II, her former Prime Ministers have spoken highly of the views and quality of advice she has given them. John Major refers to the Queen's 'encyclopaedic knowledge' of Commonwealth member states, commenting, 'I hope Tony Blair seeks her advice and heeds her response. I found them invaluable on many occasions' (*John Major: The Autobiography*, London: HarperCollins, 1999, p. 508). In his speech to the Queen at her golden wedding anniversary banquet on November 20, 1997, the present Prime Minister, Tony Blair, said, 'She is an extraordinarily shrewd and perceptive observer of the world. Hers is advice worth having.'

† The New Labour government's attack on the hereditary principle in the House of Lords, removing all but ninety-two hereditary peers by its House of Lords Act 1999, would imply a view of modern monarchy that was tightly drawn and restrictive in its sphere of royal power and intervention. Conversely, any notion that a 'modern' monarch should be more involved and energetic in political affairs would be misconceived.

produce.[39] In popular attitudes towards the monarchy, people very often equate the personage of the monarch of the day with the institution itself, but of course they are two quite separate things. If a King or Queen's personal discretion and preferences are to play an active role in decisions of a deeply political nature, such as prime ministerial appointment, Royal Assent, and general election timing, there is no guarantee that one monarch will behave in the same way as another. What is required is a constitutional framework of procedures into which the monarchic personality of the day is harnessed. Such a constitutional framework already exists. The trouble, emanating largely from academia, is that the reality of its existence is being muddied by continuing theories and constitutional talk of 'personal' prerogatives, 'reserve' powers and the like.

The repercussion might well be that a future Charles III, William V or Henry IX is misguidedly persuaded to believe that it is he personally who is best placed to resolve a political crisis, rather than leaving it to the normal constitutional and political processes. A monarch today who acted in such a way, rejecting prime ministerial advice and instructing the Prime Minister how to proceed over a decision requiring the monarch's prerogative authority, would be tempting political suicide. There would be outrage among members of the governing party,* and whether or not the Prime Minister resigned in protest (which is likely) or the incident led to an enforced abdication of the monarch, the crisis would galvanise proposals for radical reform or abolition of the monarchy. Lord Hailsham, the former Conservative Lord Chancellor, once commented that the monarch 'who ventured to use the prerogative against either of the two major parties of the state would risk either enforced abdication or republicanism'.[40] Or, in the words of Lord St John of Fawsley, a former Leader of the House of Commons, 'The modern monarchy must be and be seen to be above party political strife; partisanship of any kind would not only be self-defeating but could end in the abolition of the monarchy itself.'[41] From a monarch's self-interested perspective, it is always preferable to follow a Prime Minister's advice, especially if it is a dissolution request, for it is then up to the electorate to cast judgement on the Prime Minister and his choice of timing.

---

* This is against a political background in which there are already widespread reformist sentiments towards the monarchy within the Labour Party (see pp. 141–3) and the Liberal Democrats. In 1994, a poll of Labour MPs showed that 44 per cent wanted to replace the monarchy with a republic (*Independent on Sunday*, 23 October 1994); and another in 1996 found that only eleven Labour MPs supported the monarchy 'without serious reservation' (*Independent*, 18 February 1996).

The influence of academic theorising about 'personal' prerogatives at the Palace and the Cabinet Office, and in party political debate

The formidable battery of academic opinion emanating from Sir Ivor Jennings and more recent theorists, notably Blake, Bogdanor and Brazier, emphasising or elaborating upon the personal discretionary element in the monarch's prerogatives, has had, and continues to have, a powerful impact on the constitutional thinking on the monarch's role at the Palace and the Cabinet Office.

There is the famous episode of Sir Alan Lascelles, the then private secretary to the monarch, George VI, setting out the view from the Palace in a letter he wrote to the *Times* on 2 May 1950:*

> It is surely indisputable (and common sense) that a Prime Minister may ask – not demand – that his Sovereign will grant him a dissolution of Parliament; and that the Sovereign, if he so chooses, may refuse to grant this request. The problem of such a choice is entirely personal to the Sovereign, though he is, of course, free to ask informal advice from anybody whom he thinks fit to consult.†

This robust pronouncement of royal autonomy drew great strength from the academic testimony of Sir Ivor and the respectability that his theory of

---

* The letter of 2 May 1950 was written secretly by Sir Alan under the pseudonym of 'Senex'. Many saw through the deception, and his identity was formally revealed in 1958 by John Wheeler-Bennett in his official biography of George VI. The issue prompting the letter was whether the Labour Prime Minister, Clement Attlee, who had won the 1950 general election by a small margin, could call a second election simply to increase his majority or if defeated on a no-confidence motion, and in either case whether the King could reject the Prime Minister's request. In the event, after eighteen months in office, Mr Attlee requested and was granted a dissolution.

† Sir Alan then referred to three conditions that a monarch would take into account when deciding whether or not to grant a dissolution. Much has been made of this list, but it was far from being a coherent statement of constitutional procedure. It was a reference to the political and financial crisis of 1931 and was in the nature of a justification for what George V had done (persuading Ramsay MacDonald against resignation and dissolution, and to be re-appointed Prime Minister in a coalition with the Conservatives). He wrote, 'It can be properly assumed that no wise Sovereign – that is, one who has at heart the true interest of the country, the constitution, and the Monarchy – would deny a dissolution to his Prime Minister unless he were satisfied that: (1) the existing Parliament was still vital, viable, and capable of doing its job; (2) a general election would be detrimental to the national economy; (3) he could rely on finding another Prime Minister who could carry on his government, for a reasonable period, with a working majority in the House of Commons.'

the personal prerogatives provided in his 1936 book *Cabinet Government.**
But such sentiments from Palace officials were unsurprising for the social
circumstances of the 1950s. Much more surprising is that little seemed to
change over the course of the next five decades.† In another rare public
utterance on the subject from a key player in such a situation, the former
Cabinet Secretary Lord Armstrong told the historian Professor Peter
Hennessy in an interview in 1991, 'It is not just theoretically correct, but
common sense, that the Sovereign should have the right to withhold consent
to a request for a dissolution.'[42] Note the use of the expression 'common
sense' here, identical to the phrase used by Sir Alan in 1950. This suggests
rather clearly how constitutional opinions and phraseology on the monarch's
prerogatives at the Palace and the Cabinet Office have simply been repeated
from one generation of official to the next. Also elicited by Professor
Hennessy in 1994 was the public statement from Sir Robin Butler, the then
serving Cabinet Secretary, that Lord Armstrong's views reflected the latest
insider thinking on the monarch's prerogative powers at the Palace and the
Cabinet Office.[43]

Throughout, 'authoritative' advice has continued to be taken from
academics, mainly chosen from Oxford University, who have similarly
espoused and reiterated the interventionist mentality of Sir Ivor and his
Victorian predecessors. Another occurrence of this was early in 1974, when
the Labour government was looking to increase its strength in the Commons,
having taken office at the 28 February election with only 301 seats to the
Conservatives' 297. Could the Queen veto a decision by Harold Wilson, the
Prime Minister, to ask for a dissolution after a few months and hold a second

---

* Earlier constitutional writings on the subject were consulted as well, including those of
A. V. Dicey and Sir William Anson, who were even more emphatic than Sir Ivor on the
autonomy and personal role of the monarch in matters of dissolution of Parliament and prime
ministerial appointment. See the historical accounts of this episode in Basil Markesinis, *The
Theory and Practice of the Dissolution: A Comparative Study with Special Reference to the United
Kingdom and Greek Experience* (Cambridge: Cambridge University Press, 1972) and Peter
Hennessy, *The Hidden Wiring: Unearthing the British Constitution* (London: Victor Gollancz,
1995).
† The personnel or human resources issue of recruiting and appointing members of the office or
department of state that gives legal and constitutional advice to the monarch of the day is not a
subject for this book, but is a question raising matters of possible future reform. In practice, the
private secretary to the sovereign solicits constitutional advice informally and confidentially from
unpublicised and unknown quarters. This method was described by Sir Ivor in a section entitled
'Irresponsible Advisers' in *Cabinet Government* (Cambridge: Cambridge University Press, 1936),
Chapter XII:2.

general election later the same year? The view as expressed by Edward Short, then Lord President of the Privy Council and Leader of the Commons, was, 'Constitutional lawyers of the highest authority are of the clear opinion that the Sovereign is not in all circumstances bound to grant a Prime Minister's request for a dissolution of Parliament.'[44]

But the political reality was, as the earlier precedent of 1951 had already indicated, that there would be no attempt by the Palace to reject Mr Wilson's advice for a dissolution or to mediate between the parties on whether an alternative administration should be appointed and/or a coalition formed. The Queen quite properly simply accepted Mr Wilson's request and a second general election duly took place shortly afterwards on 10 October.

Even more damaging perhaps is that this whole idea that the monarch can, or should, intervene in the political process as an independent force dispensing constitutional justice risks leading party politicians astray, particularly since most MPs have only a rudimentary understanding of constitutional law. This danger most commonly occurs when politicians want to compel or stop government action over some issue, and so seek to recruit the prerogatives of the monarch on their side to interfere with Cabinet decisions.

To take one example, in the period before the 1987 election the SDP–Liberal Alliance was hoping to hold the balance of power in a hung Parliament. However, the Conservative government and Labour opposition, who regarded the SDP defectors as traitors, publicly declared in the years before the election that under no circumstances would they enter into a coalition with the Alliance. The response of the Alliance leaders was to claim that, if there were a hung Parliament, the Queen should intervene and use her prerogative powers to compel the two main parties to negotiate with them on a pact of support in the Commons or participation in a coalition government. At the Liberal annual party conference in 1985, the Liberal leader, David Steel, stated that 'no request for a dissolution and a second election should be made until the possibilities of negotiation for a majority have been exhausted'.[45] Meanwhile at the SDP conference, its leader, Dr David Owen, claimed the Queen should reject a Prime Minister's request for any such dissolution. He maintained it would be 'proper' for her to do so, unless and until the Prime Minister and leader of the opposition had exhaustively negotiated with the Alliance to see if a coalition could be formed.[46] But there is no legal or constitutional requirement to compel a government or opposition to negotiate with third parties against their will, and there would have been no basis in 1987 for the monarch to enter into conflict with the Prime Minister in the way that was being suggested.*

To take another more topical example, throughout 2003 there were claims made that the Queen should deploy her prerogative powers to intervene in the controversy over the draft EU constitution. According to reports in the press, one UK member of the European Parliament, Nigel Farage, believed that 'the Queen has the constitutional powers to prevent the government imposing foreign law on the UK. She should use them by either withholding the Royal Assent or dissolving Parliament and calling a general election.'[47] Many politicians at that time were demanding that the government hold a referendum on the EU constitution, especially those who opposed its adoption, who thought they could win a referendum, or at least had nothing to lose and everything to gain by one being held. It was being commonly claimed that the EU constitution would affect the national sovereign powers of Parliament and the monarchy, so it was the duty of the Queen as head of state to intervene and tell the Prime Minister what to do. As reported in the press,[48] this view had the authoritative support of the well-known television historian, Dr David Starkey: 'If the Prime Minister refuses to give the people a say [by holding a referendum], it would be her duty to act.'

This would be to expand the realm of the monarch's public acts of state far beyond the boundaries of constitutional legitimacy today.† It is time to bid

---

* A surprising feature of this episode was that two such senior parliamentarians, whose views in themselves could carry some authority, should be egging on the Queen to get embroiled in party political controversy simply for their own vested political interests. It is likely that they themselves had become emboldened by misconceived academic advice they had received.

† Further instances of the potentially damaging effects of academic theorising about the personal nature of the sovereign's prerogative powers can be gleaned from other countries where the UK monarch serves as head of state and is represented by a governor general. For an old study of dissolution in the Commonwealth shortly after *Cabinet Government*, see Eugene A. Forsey, *The Royal Power of Dissolution in the British Commonwealth* (Toronto: Oxford University Press, 1943). The practice and conventions governing the exercise of the powers of prime ministerial appointment, Royal Assent and dissolution of Parliament within the constitutions of those countries are a matter for their own indigenous political system. A famously regrettable incident was in Australia in 1975, when the then governor general, Sir John Kerr, personally decided to intervene in party politics and dismiss the ruling Prime Minister, Gough Whitlam, after the Senate had rejected a government supply Bill, despite Mr Whitlam possessing a large majority in the House of Representatives. The authority claimed by the governor general for his independence of action in the matter was the theory of the personal prerogatives as was said to exist and apply in the UK. This incident was widely condemned by Australian public opinion and precipitated a backlash of anti-monarchist and pro-republican feeling, sufficient to prevent Prince Charles being appointed governor general there in 1982 (*Times*, 4 May 1981).

farewell to theories of royal activism and the use of unfortunate terms such as the 'personal prerogatives' of the monarch that clearly belong to a bygone era.

Conclusion

This chapter has sought to explain the true constitutional position of a British monarch's direct legal acts of state in a manner that accords with political realities today. It has explained constitutional procedures that do, and should, determine the exercise of the monarch's legal powers over prime ministerial appointment, Royal Assent to legislation and the dissolution of Parliament.

Today, these prerogatives should be understood not as personal discretionary powers of the monarch, nor as matters over which the monarch has any independent personal rights, but as clearly circumscribed constitutional duties to be carried out on the advice of the Prime Minister. Any royal intervention is limited to situations where the Prime Minister himself has behaved in manifest breach of a convention, such as a failure to respond to a Commons' vote of no confidence or failure to resign after a general election defeat.

Only in this way will the political neutrality of the monarch be kept inviolate; and maintaining this political neutrality must be the golden rule for the continuity of the monarchy. Our royal head of state still has an important role and duty to perform as guardian of the constitution, which is to ensure that the Prime Minister acts and advises her or him in accordance with established constitutional law.

4

The religious requirements of a King and the Catholic disqualification

How appropriate is it for a modern monarch to be constrained in his or her religious faith and spiritual beliefs, habits and outlook by the legal restrictions, social values and political concerns of three centuries ago? The law on succession demands of a monarch active participation in the Anglican Protestant faith, of which he or she is ex officio Supreme Governor and head, and it disqualifies from the royal office of head of state anyone who is a Roman Catholic or who marries a Roman Catholic.

Succinctly stated, the provisions imposed by law on the person who would be monarch are that he or she

- cannot be a Roman Catholic;
- cannot marry a Roman Catholic;
- must make a public declaration that he or she is a Protestant;
- must join in communion with the Church of England;
- must swear to maintain the established Churches of England and Scotland.

The sources of these limitations lie in a number of ancient statutes, the most important of which are the Bill of Rights 1689, the Act of Settlement 1701, the Act of Union 1707 and the Accession Declaration Act 1910.

The disqualification of Catholics

The exclusion of Roman Catholics from the throne was first laid down in the Bill of Rights in the following terms:

> Whereas it hath beene found by experience that it is inconsistent with the safety and welfaire of this protestant kingdome to be governed by a popish prince or by any King or Queene marrying a papist the said lords spirituall and temporall and commons doe further pray that it may be eneacted that all and every person and persons that is are or shall be reconciled to or shall hold communion with the see or church of Rome or shall profess the popish religion or shall marry a papist shall be excluded and be for ever uncapeable to inherit possesse or enjoy the crowne and government of this realme and Ireland and the dominions thereunto belonging or any part of the same or to have use or exercise any regall power authoritie or jurisdiction within the same [And in all and every such case or cases the people of these realmes shall be and are hereby absolved of their allegiance.][1] and the said crowne and government shall from time to time descend to and be enjoyed by such person or persons being protestants . . .

The same disqualification was reiterated twelve years later in the Act of Settlement 1701, a statute with a generally much wider remit over the succession.

The principal purposes of the Act of Settlement were to combat the claims of the Catholic Jacobites* to the throne and to secure a long-term Protestant succession. The problem Parliament faced was that neither William III and Mary II, nor their prospective successor, Princess Anne of Denmark, who subsequently became Queen Anne, had any heirs. In the 1701 Act, therefore, Parliament re-routed the prospective succession back through James I's daughter Elizabeth, who had married Elector Palatine Frederick V, then through Elizabeth and Frederick's daughter Sophia, who had married Ernest Augustus, first Elector of Hanover.[2] In 1714, on Anne's demise, Sophia and Ernest Augustus's son duly became King George I.

Were it not for the Act of Settlement, there would naturally have been a very different line of succession, ending up today very far removed from Elizabeth, Charles and William Windsor. After Queen Anne would have

---

* Those who supported the restoration of James II to the throne, then his son and grandson (the Old and Young Pretender).

come James II's son the Old Pretender, as 'James III', then Bonnie Prince Charlie as 'Charles III', not Charles Windsor. The line of descent, laid out in the table on p. 111,* would eventually have merged with the aristocratic rulers of Saxony and the doomed twentieth-century Italian monarchy. Research conducted last year by Hugh Peskett of *Burke's Peerage* shows that the present monarch of the United Kingdom would be 'Queen Mary III', an Italian countess. Her son and heir to the throne, in Prince Charles's place, would succeed her as 'King Uberto I', whose actual name is Uberto Omar Gasche; he was born in 1951 and works in Rome as a dog breeder and photographer.[3]

The exclusion of those marrying a 'papist': Camilla's Catholic connection

One issue of great potential constitutional interest arising out the royal engagement in early 2005 went completely unnoticed and unreported. Indeed, the total silence on the issue was especially odd given the otherwise voluminous public and media discussion of just about every other conceivable nook and cranny of the royal wedding's constitutional implications. This was the question whether Camilla Parker Bowles might be regarded as 'papist' – in other words, a Roman Catholic – for the purposes of the Bill of Rights 1689 and Act of Settlement 1701. If this were the case, it would disqualify Prince Charles from ever becoming King.

The Bill of Rights 1689, as cited above, declares that 'all and every person and persons that is are or shall be reconciled to or shall hold communion with the see or church of Rome or shall professe the popish religion *or shall marry a papist* shall be excluded' (emphasis added). The Act of Settlement 1701 repeated the same Catholic disqualification in broadly similar terms:

> All and every person and persons, who shall or may take or inherit the said Crown, by virtue of the limitation of this present act, and is, are or shall be reconciled to, or shall hold communion with, the See or Church of Rome, or shall profess the popish religion, *or shall marry a papist,* shall be subject to such incapacities . . . (emphasis added)

---

* This table is also calculated on the basis of the royal succession passing through the monarch's eldest legitimate child, whether male or female: in other words, ignoring male primogeniture, on which see Chapter 5.

What the British royal succession would have been, if not for the Act of Settlement

QUEEN ANNE	Ruled 1702–1714
	Succeeded by her brother
King James III	'The Old Pretender'
	Ruled 1714–1766
King Charles III	'Bonnie Prince Charlie'
	Ruled 1766–1788
King Henry IX	Cardinal York
	Ruled 1788–1807
	Cardinal York had no children so the line ended there. The next monarch would have been a descendant of Charles I
Queen Amalia	Princess of Saxony
	Ruled 1807–1870
	Succeeded by her brother
King John II	King of Saxony
	Ruled 1870–1873
King Albert	King of Saxony
	Ruled 1873–1902
Queen Elizabeth II	Duchess of Genoa
	Ruled 1902–1912
Queen Margaret	also Queen of Italy
	Ruled 1912–1926
King Victor Emmanuel	also King of Italy, supporter of Mussolini
	Ruled 1926–1947
Queen Yolanda	Exiled countess and family beauty
	Ruled 1947–1986
Queen Mary III	b. 1924
	Exiled countess who married Robert Gasche in Egypt

The question of the possible application of these provisions to the royal marriage on 9 April 2005 arose from the Duchess of Cornwall's first marriage to Brigadier Andrew Parker Bowles, a Roman Catholic. Many thought therefore that the two children of this marriage were brought up in the Roman Catholic faith, and that as a family the Parker Bowleses often participated in Catholic church services together. Indeed, many seemed to think, or simply assume, that Mrs Parker Bowles was herself a Catholic. For example, in December 2004 a leading article in the *Spectator*, under the editorship of Boris Johnson MP at that time, now a Conservative frontbench spokesman in the Commons, baldly stated as a matter of fact that 'Camilla is a Catholic'.[4]

However, it is important to note that the only exclusionary provision is whether the monarch's spouse is a Catholic. She or he does not have to satisfy the other various requirements that apply to the monarch, considered below. In particular, she or he does not have to profess her or his Protestant faith, she or he does not have to join in communion with the Anglican Church, and she or he does not have to swear to uphold the established churches. The sole exclusion is that she or he must not be a 'papist'.

The issue then is how one ever determines what faith a particular person subscribes to, or to what church they belong as a member. There are no general legal tests or criteria by which to ascertain a person's religious affiliation under British civil law. Arguably an individual can nominate his faith perfectly freely, be it Anglican, Muslim, Catholic or Buddhist, from one day to the next. On this basis, national survey questionnaires often simply ask people what their religion is, without verifying it against any external legal test. And, more important, the Bill of Rights and Act of Settlement themselves fail to define or set any test for determining who is, and who is not, to be regarded as a 'papist'.

The official position is that the former Mrs Parker Bowles, now the Duchess of Cornwall, is a member of the Church of England. This was clearly pronounced by Buckingham Palace when asked to clarify the issue.[5] The Archbishop of Canterbury must have established this, having agreed to give the royal union his blessing in an Anglican church service. The Prime Minister, the custodian of constitutional advice on the matter, must have done so too. All four quarters of the rectangle concerned, therefore – Clarence House, Buckingham Palace, Lambeth Palace, and 10 Downing Street – have concurred that there is no problem arising from Mrs Parker Bowles's earlier marriage to a Roman Catholic.

This, then, now appears a closed question. Given the united support by the establishment for the wedding, it seems certain that any legal pretence or challenge to Prince Charles's claim to the throne on the basis of dis-qualification under the Bill of Rights and the Act of Settlement would fail. A remaining issue, discussed later in the chapter, is whether the law itself, discriminating as it does against Catholic spouses, is in need of replacement. The religious restriction on the spouse is limited only, it should be observed, to the Roman Catholic faith. No such bar exists if the monarch marries a believer in any other faith, such as Islam or Buddhism.

The royal declaration of Protestant faith

The Bill of Rights in 1689, in addition to its prohibition of Catholics from the throne, also laid down the requirement for a solemn public declaration of non-belief in the Roman Catholic faith to be made by a new King. This could be on the first day of the meeting of the first Parliament of his reign, the King speaking from his throne in the chamber of the House of Lords, with members of the Commons and Lords assembled there. Or alternatively, it could be during the new King's coronation ceremony, traditionally held in Westminster Abbey. The form of the declaration was an express rejection of the central tenets and practices of the Catholic faith, notably tran-substantiation, the adoration of the Virgin Mary, and the holding of mass.*

However, in 1910 this royal declaration of faith was re-phrased by the Liberal government under Herbert Asquith, in preparation for George V's coronation. The object was to remove unnecessary offence given to Catholics by the phraseology of the 1689 declaration, and to put the question of the King's faith in positive terms by simply expressing adherence to the established Protestant religion. As now required by the Accession Declaration Act 1910, the royal declaration reads:

> I [monarch's name] do solemnly and sincerely in the presence of God profess, testify and declare that I am a faithful Protestant, and that I will, according to the true intent

---

* The wording of this statutory declaration demanded of monarchs from 1689 to 1910 was: 'I [name of monarch], by the grace of God King [or Queen] of England, Scotland and Ireland, Defender of the Faith, do solemnly and sincerely in the presence of God, profess, testify, and declare, that I do believe that in the Sacrament of the Lord's Supper there is not any Transubstantiation of the elements of bread and wine into the Body and Blood of Christ at or after the consecration thereof by any person whatsoever: and that the invocation or adoration of the Virgin Mary or any other Saint, and the Sacrifice of the Mass, as they are now used in the Church of Rome, are superstitious and idolatrous. And I do solemnly in the presence of God profess, testify, and declare that I do make this declaration, and every part thereof, in the plain and ordinary sense of the words read unto me, as they are commonly understood by English Protestants, without any such dispensation from any person or authority or person whatsoever, or without thinking that I am or can be acquitted before God or man, or absolved of this declaration or any part thereof, although the Pope, or any other person or persons, or power whatsoever, should dispense with or annul the same or declare that it was null and void from the beginning.'

of the enactments which secure the Protestant succession to the Throne of my Realm, uphold and maintain the said enactments to the best of my powers according to law.

Elizabeth II duly made and signed this declaration from the throne in the House of Lords, attended by both Houses of Parliament, on Tuesday 4 November 1952, in the period between her accession and her coronation. In due course, under the existing legislation, the future King Charles III will in similar manner have to testify and declare before Parliament that he too is 'a faithful Protestant'.

The monarch must be in communion with the Church of England

It is a requirement of the Act of Settlement 1701 'that whosoever shall hereafter come to the possession of this crown shall joyn in communion with the Church of England as by law established'.[6] This means that the King must not only profess the Protestant faith (as required by the Bill of Rights), but he must actively participate and join in Anglican communion and worship.

In testimony of the requirement, Elizabeth II in 1953, and both her parents before her when they were crowned King George VI and Queen Elizabeth in 1937, received communion from the Archbishop of Canterbury as an integral part of their coronation services. However, whilst it has certainly been customary for monarchs to take communion in this way, the wording of the Act of Settlement does not actually stipulate that it is an act which must be performed as part of the coronation ceremony.

The oath to uphold the established English and Scottish Churches

Later in the same year as the Bill of Rights, Parliament enacted the Coronation Oath Act 1689. This required, and still does, a separate declaration to be made by a monarch during his coronation ceremony, which is to maintain the established Anglican Protestant Church.* In 1707, the Act of Union with Scotland modified the oath by adding a requirement with respect to Scotland, namely that the new monarch will swear to 'inviolably maintain and preserve' the established Presbyterian Church government in

---

* As originally drafted in the 1689 Act, the King had to swear to the utmost of his power to 'maintaine the Laws of God the true profession of the Gospell and the Protestant reformed religion established by law . . . and . . . preserve unto the bishops and clergy of this realm and to the churches committed to their charge all such rights and privileges as by law do and shall appertain unto them or any of them'. This wording has been subsequently changed: see above.

Scotland.* The content of the coronation oath, then, as will apply to Charles III under existing law is as follows:

The Archbishop standing before him shall administer the Coronation Oath, first asking the King,

Sir, is your Majesty willing to take the Oath?

And the King answering,

I am willing.

The Archbishop shall minister these questions; and the King, having a book in his hands, shall answer each question severally as follows:

Archbishop: Will you solemnly promise and swear to govern the Peoples of the United Kingdom of Great Britain and Northern Ireland, Canada, Australia, New Zealand . . . and of your Possessions and the other Territories to any of them belonging or pertaining, according to their respective laws and customs?

King: I solemnly promise so to do.

Archbishop: Will you to your power cause Law and Justice, in Mercy, to be executed in all your judgements?

King: I will.

Archbishop: Will you to the utmost of your power maintain the Laws of God and the true profession of the Gospel? Will you to the utmost of your power maintain in the United Kingdom the Protestant Reformed Religion established by law? Will you maintain and preserve inviolably the settlement of the Church of England, and the doctrine, worship, discipline, and government thereof, as by law established in England? And will you preserve unto the Bishops and Clergy of England, and to the Churches there committed to their charge, all such rights and privileges, as by law do or shall appertain to them or any of them?

King: All this I promise to do.

---

* The terms of this coronation oath, which also embraces the duty to govern according to law, have been slightly modified five times to reflect territorial developments including the Act of Union with Ireland, the disestablishment of the Irish Church, the Statute of Westminster and the Indian Independence Act 1947.

When the oath was changed in 1937 and 1953, specifically for the coronation ceremonies of George VI and Elizabeth II respectively, the change was effected not by Act of Parliament but simply by government action following consultation with other self-governing countries of the Commonwealth. For parliamentary discussion, see Hansard, HC Deb, 23 February 1953, cols 2091–3, when one MP, Mr E. Fletcher, said, 'In view of the fact that the Coronation Oath is a parliamentary creation, and is intended as a limitation on the prerogative, is it not desirable, though it may be inconvenient, that any changes that are proposed this year should have legislative sanction . . . It is a matter which affects the rights of Parliament, and not merely the rights of the Executive.'

Then the King arising out of his Chair, supported as before, the Sword of State being carried before him, shall go to the Altar, and make his solemn Oath in the sight of all the people to observe the premisses: laying his right hand upon the Holy Gospel in the great Bible (which was before carried in the procession and is now brought from the Altar by the Archbishop, and tendered to him as he kneels upon the steps), and saying these words:

The things which I have here before promised, I will perform and keep. So help me God.

Then the King shall kiss the Book and sign the Oath.[7]

Reform of the Act of Settlement

There is now widespread support for the proposition that the ancient prohibition on Roman Catholics, or persons marrying a Roman Catholic, becoming royal head of state should be abolished. This view has emerged as part of the wider historical context in which Roman Catholicism is no longer viewed as a threat to the political security of the state, as it was at the time three centuries ago when the Bill of Rights and Act of Settlement were passed. It is argued that leaving these antique statutes in force is offensive in terms of freedom of expression, religion and belief. They discriminate between different faiths within society, when the proper role of the monarchy should be to symbolise and represent the country as a whole.

Relations between Anglicanism and Catholicism

There have been great efforts, and numerous initiatives, in recent decades towards a closer mutual understanding and rapprochement between the Christian denominations of Anglicanism and Catholicism. There is a joint common purpose in helping re-evangelise Europe in our secular times.

The visit of a Pope, John Paul II, to England in 1982 had a huge impact in elevating the standing of the Catholic Church in the UK. It served as a powerful reminder to ordinary people that Roman Catholicism has a long-standing place in British national history and in a common European heritage of Christian civilisation. Perhaps above all, it visibly restored Catholicism to a place within the ruling establishment. The powerful scenes of inter-denominational fraternity started with the Pope being ceremo-niously being greeted at Gatwick Airport with open arms, and later he and Robert Runcie, then Archbishop of Canterbury, sat side by side at Canterbury Cathedral in a common service.

The 1990s witnessed setbacks in the ecumenical initiative, with some serious divisions becoming entrenched. This occurred particularly over the Church of England's decision to proceed with the ordination of women priests, which Catholic dogma completely rejected; and because of the two Churches' conservative–liberal parting of the ways over the issues of homosexuality, abortion and birth control. Yet the institutional momentum within Britain's corridors of power towards embracing Catholicism on an equal footing with Anglicanism has continued and gathered pace at a personal and diplomatic level. The doctrinal difficulties have, if anything, smoothed the passage of Catholic acceptance within the social and political establishment. According to the *Economist* in a social survey on the future of the church, 'Roman Catholicism is now seen as cool and classy among the country's social elite'.[8] There have been several high-profile conversions from Anglicanism to Catholicism in recent years, such as those of Ann Widdecombe, a leading Conservative MP, and Charles Moore, former editor of the *Daily Telegraph*.

It is well known that our Prime Minister, Tony Blair, is more than sympathetic to the Catholic Church. His wife and children are members of the Roman Catholic faith, and as a family they regularly attend Catholic services and mass. Indeed Mr Blair is reported to have regularly taken Catholic holy communion until 1996, when he was advised by the late Cardinal Basil Hume, Catholic Archbishop of Westminster, that it was inappropriate for him to do so. Later on, however, in February 2003, Mr Blair and his family attended mass with Pope John Paul II in his private chapel at the Vatican on the occasion of their visit to him in February 2003. According to press reports and Pope John Paul's biographer, Garry O'Connor, Mr Blair received holy communion personally from the Pope.[9] This appears to have been legitimate under a Catholic canon law proviso at the time, which allowed the administration of communion to non-Catholics 'on a unique occasion for joy or for sorrow in the life of a family'. This canon law proviso was subsequently repealed by the Roman curia only two weeks later, a forthcoming detail the Pope must have been aware of.

When John Paul II died in April 2005, his death and funeral prompted extraordinary outpourings of popular emotion towards this charismatic and missionary figure. As mentioned in Chapter 2, to his funeral service from Great Britain came not only the leaders of the Catholic Church, but the Prime Minister and his wife, Tony and Cherie Blair; Prince Charles, heir apparent, representing the Queen; and the Archbishop of Canterbury, Dr Rowan

Williams. Just over a fortnight later on 23 April, those in attendance at the inauguration of the new Pope, Benedict XVI, included the Queen's consort, Prince Philip; the Lord Chancellor, Lord Falconer; and, again, Dr Williams. It was first time since Henry VIII's break with Rome and the Reformation in the 1530s that the primate of the Protestant Church of England had graced the inauguration of a Roman Catholic Pope with his presence.

Prince Charles's backing for reform

It seems that the future Charles III is himself in favour of removing the religious provisions in the Act of Settlement. He may even support the case for disestablishment of the Church of England, or at least for transferring the headship and supreme governorship of the Church from the monarch to some other body. As he is famously known for saying, as King he would want to be seen by the country as the 'defender of faith', not Defender of *the* Faith. He expressed this view publicly in a BBC television interview with Jonathan Dimbleby in 1994. Of his future position as head of the Church of England, he said:

> I personally would much rather see it as 'defender of faith', not '*the* Faith', because it means just one particular interpretation of the faith, which, I think, is sometimes something that causes a great deal of a problem. People have fought each other to death over these things, which seems to me a peculiar waste of people's energy when we are all actually aiming for the same ultimate goal.[10]

Oddly, the actual title of Defender of the Faith, whose abbreviated form F. D. is still engraved today on our everyday coins against the monarch's name, was a title conferred upon the then Catholic Henry VIII before the Reformation by the Pope, for a scholarly tract written by Henry in defence of the Church against the Protestants.

A further expression of the future King's opinion on the matter has been indiscreetly given to us by Paddy Ashdown (now Lord Ashdown), the former leader of the Liberal Democrats, in his diaries published in 2000. In these, Mr Ashdown recounts travelling back on a flight from Israel five years earlier, where he and others had attended the funeral of the former Israeli Prime Minister Yitzhak Rabin. On board and engaging in the discussion with Lord Ashdown were Prince Charles, Tony Blair and Jonathan Sacks, the Chief Rabbi. The conversation turned to religious matters in the UK and the question of disestablishment of the Church of England, which Mr Ashdown

The Queen at eighty – Queen Elizabeth stands on the steps of St George's Chapel, Windsor, after a service of celebration in honour of her eightieth birthday on 23 April 2006. (*Reuters/Leon Neal*)

Constitutional monarch – The Queen addresses Parliament from the throne of the Chamber of the House of Lords, reading a speech every word of which is prepared by 10 Downing Street: 'Nothing could be more calculated to remind the monarch that he is only a figurehead,' observed ex-King Edward VIII. (*Matthew Fearn/PA/Empics*)

The British royal family – Queen Elizabeth waves at the crowd from the balcony at Buckingham Palace, the head of state's official residence, during the sixtieth anniversary of VE Day on 10 July 2005, while members of her family, the men dressed in military uniforms, look on. (*Reuters/Paul Hackett*)

The European royal family – Norway's King Harald V and Queen Sonja with Crown Prince Haakon and Crown Princess Mette Marit attend a state banquet at Buckingham Palace on 25 October 2005. The institution of hereditary monarchy still provides the ceremonial head of state in several other European nations, including Belgium, Denmark, the Netherlands, Spain and Sweden. (*Reuters/Matt Dunham*)

The royal line of succession – Princes William (*right*) and Harry, the sons of the heir apparent, Prince Charles, are now second and third in line of succession to the throne. During 2006, the year of Queen Elizabeth's eightieth birthday, Prince William turned twenty-four, just one year younger than the Queen when she acceded the throne as monarch in 1952. (*Reuters/Russell Boyce*)

The future King William V – An official portrait taken after Prince William's confirmation on 9 March 1997. He is seated centrally among his family, his mother, the late Diana, Princess of Wales, on his right. (*Reuters*)

The changing constitution – In 2005 Prince Charles received the united support of the British establishment following the announcement of his engagement to Mrs Parker Bowles. In striking contrast, the Queen's uncle, Edward VIII, and her sister, Princess Margaret, were told by 10 Downing Street, the Archbishop of Canterbury and government law officers that marriage to a divorcee was a fundamental breach of royal duty. In 1936 King Edward (*above*, with his wife, the former Mrs Wallis Simpson) was required to abdicate. In 1955 Princess Margaret (*below*, front row, at the theatre with her family and Capt. Peter Townsend, before their romance began) issued a public statement that, being 'mindful of the Church's teaching that Christian marriage is indissoluble', she had terminated her relationship with Capt. Townsend. (*PA News/PA/Empics*)

The royal wedding: public and private emotions – A few demonstrators with banners (*top left and bottom right*) situated themselves outside Windsor Guildhall, where the civil royal marriage took place on 9 April 2005, protesting against the prospect of 'King Charles and Queen Camilla', and calling for Prince William to succeed Queen Elizabeth as the next monarch. However, the great majority of people in the crowd throughout the day warmly cheered and congratulated the newly wed royal couple (*bottom left*). The marriage was the culmination of a long-standing romance that had encountered, in the Queen's words, 'all kinds of terrible obstacles'. (*Reuters/Darren Staples/John Schultz/Chris Young/PA*)

The royal wedding: civil register and Anglican blessing – The future King Charles III emerges from the Windsor Guildhall civil register marriage with his bride, newly entitled Her Royal Highness The Duchess of Cornwall, accompanied by the Duchess's son Tom Parker Bowles (*above*). Photographers were banned from the civil service, but permitted into the Anglican church blessing (*below*) that took place afterwards at St George's Chapel, Windsor, conducted by Dr Rowan Williams, Archbishop of Canterbury.
(*AP Photo/Stephen Hird/Chris Young/PA/Empics*)

The future King as public speaker – Charles addresses the World Health Assembly at the United Nations headquarters in Geneva in 2006, urging the adoption of complementary medicine, including acupuncture and homeopathy. The Prince said, 'I believe that the proper mix of proven complementary, traditional and modern remedies … can help create a powerful healing force in our world.' (*Reuters/Denis Balibouse*)

The future King as diplomat – The Prince and the Duchess of Cornwall on their first formal overseas tour together, with President George W. Bush and First Lady Laura Bush, at a White House state banquet in their honour in 2005. In his response to a toast from President Bush, Charles urged the US to take a lead on 'the most crucial issues that face our planet', implying environmental and climate change. (*Reuters/Jason Reed*)

The future King as defender of faith – As monarch Charles III will become head of the Church of England. The Prince has a deep interest in spiritual matters, famously commenting that as King he would like to be 'defender of faith', not '*the* Faith'. He is shown *top left* with the Archbishop of Canterbury, Dr Rowan Williams, at the latter's enthronement ceremony (*PA/Empics*); *top right* greeting the fourteenth Dalai Lama, the exiled Tibetan spiritual leader, during a visit to the UK (*Anwar Hussein/allactiondigital.com*); *bottom left* at a Network of Sikh Organisations event to commemorate the 400th anniversary of the Sikh holy book, the Guru Granth Sahib (*PA/Empics*); and *bottom right* with Archbishop James Harvey, head of papal protocol, at the Vatican prior to the funeral mass for Pope John Paul II on 8 April 2005, the day before the Prince's wedding (*Osservatore Romano/AP/Empics*).

expressed his support for. In response, Mr Ashdown records, 'Charles looked at me, smiled broadly and said, "I really can't think why we can't have Catholics on the throne." '[11]

Party political views and legislative blueprints
Meanwhile, across the political parties there is growing interest and support for removing the remaining historic relics of Catholic discrimination. Furthermore, this is not a policy of left or right, but one where support exists across the political spectrum.

Among Conservatives, in March 2005, shortly before the royal wedding, Michael Howard, when still leader of the Conservative Party, openly called for the abolition of the Catholic ban on royal succession. In an interview with the *Catholic Herald*, the Roman Catholic weekly newspaper, Mr Howard, himself of the Jewish faith, stated, 'It is an anachronism that Catholicism should be singled out.' In similar vein, Michael Forsyth, the Conservative Secretary of State for Scotland in the mid-1990s, made a high-profile speech on 26 January 1999, denouncing the 'grubby' and 'offensive' anti-Catholic provisions in the Act of Settlement. Saying that the Act treated 10 per cent of the British population as 'second-class citizens', he expressed the view that 'the Act is deeply discriminatory . . . It is the British constitution's grubby secret and nobody wants to tackle it.'[12]

Many Labour politicians support this reform in principle, but for practical political reasons, discussed below, have been and remain reluctant to tackle its implementation. The Liberal Democrats, as a matter of collective party policy, have said they are committed to reform of the royal succession. Their 2001 general election manifesto envisaged a programme of constitutional modernisation in which 'the Head of State will be able to be a member of any faith or none'. As individuals, both Charles Kennedy, former leader of the Liberal Democrats, and Baroness Williams, a prominent Liberal Democrat peer in the Lords, both Catholics themselves, have publicly advocated abolition of the Act of Settlement's religious restrictions.

In Scotland, feelings on the matter run higher than south of the border. A major debate on the Act of Settlement was held in the new Scottish Parliament in its first year of existence on 16 December 1999, on a motion put forward by Michael Russell calling for the repeal of the anti-Catholic provisions in the Act. Prior to the debate, Mr Russell had already secured the support of 70 per cent of MSPs eligible to sign the motion. Its passage was therefore a foregone conclusion, and the Parliament duly resolved:

that [it] believes that the discrimination contained in the Act of Settlement has no place in our modern society, expresses its wish that those discriminatory aspects of the Act be repealed, and affirms its view that Scottish society must not disbar participation in any aspect of our national life on the grounds of religion . . .

Strong rhetoric was used in the course of the wide-ranging debate, calling the anti-Catholic provisions in the Act of Settlement, and the other historic statutes involved, 'extremely offensive',[13] 'a denial of human rights'[14] and a 'tawdry little remnant of three centuries ago'.[15]

Similarly, the Equal Opportunities Committee of the Scottish Parliament published a statement in which it considers that the Act of Settlement has 'a negative impact on the equality of Scotland's people'.[16] Describing the Act as an anachronistic anomaly running contrary to the principles of inclusion and equality, the committee said that was 'an important matter', and urged the Westminster Parliament to consider the question of its repeal or reform.

There have been various attempts by parliamentarians in both Houses, by means of private members' Bills, to legislate in this area, all of which have failed, usually for lack of parliamentary time. The most ambitious of these was the Treason Felony, Act of Settlement and Parliamentary Oath Bill presented to the Commons by the MP Kevin McNamara in 2001.[17] This was under the ten-minute rule procedure, which allows the sponsoring member to make a short speech, which is then followed by a vote on a motion whether the Bill should be allowed and given a first reading or not. Describing the existing situation as 'extremely offensive' and enshrining a sectarianism that 'taints every aspect of life that it touches', Mr McNamara sought to amend the Act of Settlement to provide that persons in communion with the Roman Catholic church are able to succeed to the Crown. Other aims of his Bill were republican in sentiment: to remove the offence of treason for advocating abolition of the monarchy; and to amend the Oaths Act 1978 so that MPs were no longer required to swear an oath of loyalty to the monarch. Succeeding in the motion by 170 votes to 32, the Bill nonetheless failed to secure subsequent time for a second reading debate.

Rather than abolish the Catholic disqualification altogether, there was recently a joint Commons–Lords attempt at Westminster designed to repeal the disqualifying provisions relating to the spouse of a monarch. This was one of a package of three royal reforms in the Succession to the Crown Bills presented to both Houses of Parliament in 2004/05 by Lord Dubs in the Lords and Ann Taylor, the Labour MP and former government minister, in the Commons.[18] The other two royal reforms in the Bills were the removal of male preference in succession law and abolition of the Royal Marriages Act, both discussed elsewhere in Chapter 5. The case presented by Lord Dubs for his Bill – 'a breathtakingly modest and moderate' measure, as he described it – drew upon the report of a commission on the future of the monarchy set up by the Fabian Society, a think tank affiliated to the Labour Party.[19] On the disqualification from the throne for those marrying a Roman Catholic, Lord Dubs argued that this was an anachronism and 'unacceptable in this day and age'. He said the disqualification in our law was a complete anomaly since there was no bar on marriage to any other non-Anglican Christian denomination and no bar on marriage to a Hindu, Muslim or member of any other religion. In his view, the disqualifying provision in the Act of Settlement was 'an outdated piece of religious bigotry'.[20]

Also in the 2004/05 session, during the period of the royal engagement of Charles and Camilla, on 8 March 2005 the Conservative MP Edward Leigh utilised the ten-minute rule procedure to bring in a Royal Marriages (Freedom of Choice) Bill. This sought 'to allow any member of the Royal Family to marry a person of any religion or none'.[21] 'It is clearly not right', Mr Leigh said, 'for any country to have in its constitution a prohibition that apples to only one religion.'[22]

These private members' Bills made no progress in Parliament, but did throw up ideas and attitudes towards reform among our politicians. As with most private members' Bills, their real aim was to raise publicity for their cause and chivvy the government to take action. The debate on Lord Dubs's motion for a second reading of the Succession to the Crown Bill, subsequently withdrawn,* was particularly illuminating, especially for revealing – as discussed later in the chapter – the conflict of opinion among the Anglican bishops on the subject, and Labour government thinking on the matter and the obstacles to implementing reform.

The condemnation by Roman Catholics

Unsurprisingly, there are many within the ranks of the Catholic Church hierarchy who are strongly resentful of the Act of Settlement's provisions banning members of their faith from the position of head of state. The most vocal and high-profile Roman Catholic figure who has regularly condemned

---

* Out of deference to the view that a constitutional measure such as this should be effected by way of a government Bill.

the present situation is Cardinal Keith O'Brien, the leader of the Catholic Church in Scotland.

His message of personal support to Prince Charles and Camilla Parker Bowles in response to the announcement of the royal engagement on 10 February 2005 was coupled with a reference to the discriminatory provisions of the Act of Settlement and a call for their abolition.[23] A few days later at a summit on sectarianism hosted by the First Minister of Scotland, the cardinal took the opportunity to repeat his strong view that the Act of Settlement was a hindrance to religious tolerance and should be repealed or reformed.[24] He described 'its continued presence on the statute books as an offensive reminder to the whole Catholic community of a mentality which has no place in modern Britain'.

The cardinal went on to say:

> Although it may be argued that this is a piece of arcane legislation very unlikely to affect any of Scotland's Catholics directly, that would be to miss the point, which is that its effect is indirect. It causes offence and is hurtful. No other religious group in the UK is similarly excluded or stigmatised in law.

He reminded the summit of the effect the Act might have had on Prince Charles's marriage and family life, had Mrs Parker Bowles been a Roman Catholic. Again describing this legal situation as 'hurtful', he said, 'It is a matter of regret surely that had Mrs Parker Bowles been a Catholic, Prince Charles would have lost the right to succession to the throne and, similarly, if they had been going to have children they would have been excluded from the right of succession.'

Elsewhere in his speech to the summit, the Cardinal O'Brien called for a charter of religious freedoms, the effect of which would most certainly be to remove and liberate the restrictive effects of the Catholic disqualification provisions affecting succession to the Crown.

Conflict of opinion within the Anglican hierarchy
Meanwhile, mixed views are evident within the Anglican Church, though the majority holding office in the upper echelons are supportive of the status quo. This divergence of Anglican opinion became apparent during the debate on Lord Dubs's Succession to the Crown Bill last year, when the Lord Bishop of Winchester, representing the majority of his colleagues, spoke against the Bill, and the Lord Bishop of Worcester spoke in favour. It was

acknowledged by the Bishop of Worcester that his was the minority view within the church hierarchy, but he believed nonetheless it was important for him to take part in the debate to place on record his support for the comments and ideas of Lord Dubs on the matter.

Opposing reform, the Bishop of Winchester expressed his concern that the Bill, if adopted, would become the thin end of the wedge towards disestablishment of the Church of England.[25] The significance of this was not just a matter of the privileged position of the Anglican Church. For the bishop, the problem was that 'we should be embarking on a unique experiment for these islands of a state whose basis was explicitly secular'. The likely effect of disestablishment on the country as a whole, he believed, would be that it became 'markedly less tolerant and inclusive than our present arrangements', under which a priest of the established Anglican Church owes a pastoral duty to everyone in the parish he serves.

The bishop argued that key restrictions upon a Roman Catholic becoming head of the Church of England are in fact derived from Roman Catholic doctrine, rather than the Anglican Church. First, he pointed out, a Roman Catholic is prohibited from taking holy communion in the Church of England ('being joined in communion with the Church of England', as required by the Act of Settlement) by the Catholic Church, not the Church of England. Second, Roman Catholic doctrine would pressurise a Catholic consort of the monarch to bring the children of the marriage up in the Roman Catholic faith. And then consequentially, 'if the Bill became law and made in time for a Roman Catholic consort, in a generation we could therefore have a Roman Catholic heir to the throne who could not join in communion with the Church of England'. The bishop concluded his speech with his advice to the House of Lords that 'it is really not at all wise to give the noble Lord's Bill a second reading'.

Expressing dissent from his colleague, the Bishop of Worcester employed some powerful and vivid rhetoric.[26] He believed it was 'extremely important that this matter should be discussed – fearlessly so'. He was scornful of the suggestion that repeal of the Catholic disqualifications would lead to 'all sorts of other discussions' and believed 'there is no truth in the contention that a change of this kind will unravel the constitution'. 'There is absolutely no reason at all why a person married to a Roman Catholic could not be the Supreme Governor of the Church of England,' he argued. He pointed out that the Prime Minister, who advises the monarch on many Anglican Church matters, including the appointment of its bishops and archbishops, is not required to be of any particular faith and is subject to no religious disqualifications. By maintaining this discrimination, he went on to suggest, it was the British establishment that had to take responsibility for what had happened to relations between Catholics and non-Catholics. The offending legislation, in his view, was 'the last remaining grin of the Cheshire cat – but it is a pretty malicious grin if you consider our history'.

The Labour government's support in principle

The Labour government, as it happens, agrees. In principle, it would like to remove both the sex discrimination and the religious discrimination in the law relating to succession to the throne.

Certainly the Prime Minister, Tony Blair, would like to see the Catholic discrimination provisions repealed. He said as much in written correspondence during 1999 with James Douglas-Hamilton, a Scottish Conservative.[27] As mentioned above, although Mr Blair is an Anglican, at least for the time being, his wife Cherie Booth QC has been a devout Roman Catholic all her life and their four children have been brought up as practising Catholics, their eldest two sons attending the London Oratory School, which is part of the Roman Catholic church. Responding to a written parliamentary question from the Scottish Nationalist MP Roseanna Cunningham, when specifically asked on the subject, he said, 'The Government have always stood firmly against discrimination in all its forms, including against Roman Catholics, and it [sic] will continue to do so.'[28]

Several other senior Labour government ministers, particularly its Catholic members, have even more enthusiastically agreed in their public statements since taking office. Dr John Reid, formerly Scottish secretary and now Home Secretary, has told the Commons, 'As a Roman Catholic myself, I am only too well aware of the very deep feelings and passions which surround this issue. I recognise that the discrimination inherent in the Act of Settlement is offensive to many people in Scotland and perhaps more widely.'[29]

The strongest advocate of reform within Labour's senior ranks was Lord Williams of Mostyn QC, the former Attorney General, later Leader of the House of Lords, who died in 2003. In a published interview with the *Daily Telegraph* in 2001, he expressed personal views that the law should be amended to allow daughters of a monarch equal rights in succession to the throne, and that the bar on Roman Catholics should be abolished. 'I do not like any form of discrimination . . . My personal view is that there should not be any such bar.'[30]

On the Labour back benches of the House of Commons, as is discussed elsewhere,[31] the dominant view is that the monarchy as a whole is in need of reform and modernisation, with a significant number favouring republicanism. Within this group, almost all would favour reform of the Act of Settlement.

It is almost certain that, were government legislation to be introduced into Parliament to put into effect these royal reforms, a large majority of Labour members of Parliament would endorse and carry the Bill through. They would be joined by a substantial number of Conservatives, if allowed a free vote, as evidenced by the statements made when private members' Bills on the subject have been presented to Parliament.[32] Such a government Bill would also have the backing of the Liberal Democrats as a party, which has advocated in its policy documents and election manifestos both a single Equality Act outlawing all discrimination on grounds including sex and religion, and a commitment to separate Church and state.

Obstacles for the government in implementing reform

Legislative reform and the need for Commonwealth inter-governmental agreement

However, it seems the Labour leadership in government has been alternately defeated, stymied, exhausted or frightened by the prospect of taking the above reforms forward. It is all 'far too complicated' or 'too much trouble', seems to be the message from the top echelons of the New Labour government. This inactivity, despite assertions by certain ministers giving support in principle and speaking of the symbolic importance of the matter, is then given a curiously brittle support through expressions of this matter being 'not a priority'. The Lord Chancellor, Lord Falconer, said in 2005 he regards the reform as 'a complex and controversial undertaking', 'not a simple matter that can be tinkered with lightly' and 'not needed at the moment'.[33]

It is true that the law on the subject of royal succession does requires careful attention to statutory detail. There are a host of different Acts of Parliament which will need to be reformed along with the Act of Settlement. These include the Coronation Oath Act 1689, The Bill of Rights 1689, the Union with Scotland Act 1707, Princess Sophia's Precedence Act 1711, the Royal Marriages Act 1772, the Union with Ireland Act 1800, the Accession Declaration Act 1910 and the Regency Act 1937. But this complication would hardly bother the government's legislative draftsmen, known as 'parliamentary counsel'. As a constitutional measure, the Constitutional Reform Act 2005, transforming the office of Lord Chancellor and position of the Law Lords, was far more complex. The annual Finance Acts, dealing with the inter-woven minutiae of mind-boggling taxation details, are arguably much worse in terms of detail and comprehension.

It is also true that changes in the law of succession in the United Kingdom have to take into account their repercussion in those other Commonwealth countries where the British monarch is head of state. Under the Statute of Westminster 1931, the United Kingdom government is bound to obtain the assent of all the Parliaments of those countries before altering the law on succession:

> And whereas it is meet and proper to set out by way of preamble to this Act that, inasmuch as the Crown is the symbol of the free association of the members of the British Commonwealth of Nations, and as they are united by a common allegiance to the Crown, it would be in accord with the established constitutional position of all the members of the Commonwealth in relation to one another that any alteration in the law touching the Succession to the Throne or the Royal Style and Titles shall hereafter require the assent as well of the Parliaments of all the Dominions as of the Parliament of the United Kingdom.

In British law, the nature of this obligation is moral or one of honour only, because the need for these assents is stipulated in the preamble rather than the actual text of the 1931 statute. But nonetheless, this obligation is a powerful political convention. Indeed, in international terms across those Commonwealth countries affected, it is equivalent to a treaty. Absence of consultation by the UK government before it brought forward legislation to reform the succession laws would be regarded as high handed and arrogant, and it would cause serious offence in Australia, Canada and the other Commonwealth states where the Queen now reigns.

It would, in addition, upset all those who regard as important the existence and functioning of the Commonwealth itself as a unique international entity and organisation of more than fifty states. Though devoid of any genuine executive governmental functions, it is a unique forum for diplomatic and goodwill purposes. It is also highly significant to Queen Elizabeth herself as head of the Commonwealth. For, to a great extent, the Crown is the glue that holds these Commonwealth states together. As the Statute of Westminster itself puts it, 'they are united by a common allegiance to the Crown'.

What the attitude of the countries' Parliaments involved would be, especially those where there is a predominantly Anglican religious community, can currently only be speculated upon. It is worth keeping in mind the full list of countries involved. They are Antigua & Barbuda, Australia, the Bahamas, Barbados, Belize, Canada, Grenada, Jamaica, New Zealand, Papua New Guinea, St Christopher & Nevis, St Lucia, St Vincent & the Grenadines, the Solomon Islands and Tuvalu. It seems likely that several of these civil societies would harbour a more conservative and traditional attitude towards the monarchy, and towards matters of gender and religious faith, than those prevalent in the British Parliament today. If so, it would mean the British government proactively seeking to persuade and gather the necessary support for its reforming legislation.

Each country with its own independent legislature would have to enact the same alteration to its domestic constitutional laws to effect a unified change in the law of succession to the Crown. This process of consultation, agreement and national legislation across the Commonwealth on succession matters was vividly illustrated by events in 1936. This was the occasion when occupancy of and succession to the throne had to be changed in order to put into effect the abdication of Edward VIII and his replacement with his brother, who became George VI.

The British government, led by Stanley Baldwin, consulted the dominions at various stages between October and December 1936 on Edward's proposed marriage to the divorcee Wallis Simpson and its opinion that Edward must abdicate if he wished to go ahead with the marriage. The views from the dominions endorsed Mr Baldwin's stance on the matter. The Australian Prime Minister added, 'There would be outspoken hostility to His Majesty's proposed wife becoming Queen, while any proposal that she should become Consort and not Queen . . . would not be approved by my Government.'[34] Once the decision on abdication had been finalised, legislation entitled His Majesty's Declaration of Abdication Bill was introduced into the Westminster Parliament by the government on 10 December, to which all the self-governing dominions retaining the Crown expressly assented.[35] It was enacted the following day, and where necessary, implemented in the dominions by the appropriate legal forms under their national constitutions.

In the case of Canada, for example, an order in council was passed by the Canadian Privy Council, indicating its consent on 10 December 1936, followed the next month by the Succession to the Throne Act 1937 passed by the Canadian parliament.[36]

If such concurrence across the Commonwealth nations did not take place during this country's reform of the Act of Settlement, then in due course divergent lines of succession would occur under the different sets of national laws, and fragmentation of the Crown would ensue. This in fact has happened before, in 1837 concerning the kingdom of Hanover, from where George I had come to the British throne. Under its national Salic law, which excluded females from the dynastic succession, upon the death of William IV it was Queen Victoria's uncle, rather than Victoria herself, who succeeded to the Hanoverian throne.

In the parliamentary debate on Lord Dubs's Succession to the Crown Bill on 14 January 2005, the Conservative leader in the House of Lords, Lord Strathclyde, made it clear that the government had held no cross-party talks with him or his colleagues on royal reform. Lord Strathclyde asked Lord Falconer if any international consultations had taken place since the earlier debate on succession law in 1998, during which Lord Williams of Mostyn, then a Home Office minister, indicated that the government was 'considering how best to carry this forward'.[37] Lord Williams had then referred to the Statute of Westminster and need to consult the governments and legislatures of the fifteen other Commonwealth states affected. But Lord Falconer failed to answer the question. So it seems the Labour government have not initiated any inter-governmental consultations on the subject.

Concerns that removing the Catholic disqualification will lead to the disestablishment of the Church of England
There is no doubt that at the crux of the whole debate about reforming the Act of Settlement is whether the country, and the political elite of the country, wishes to maintain the established Church of England. These two issues – reform of the Act of Settlement and disestablishment of the Church of England – are, in truth, two sides of the same coin. Reform of the Act of Settlement and its related statutes would set in train an inevitable momentum towards disestablishment; and disestablishing the Church of England would automatically remove the rationale for the religious provisions binding succession to the Crown.

From a secular viewpoint, there is little difficulty in changing the laws on succession to remove any reference to religion (or gender) in eligibility to become King or Queen. But from a spiritual viewpoint, and for the Church of England, the changes that disestablishment would bring about in the Church's place, work and membership within British society following the repeal of the religious provisions in the royal succession law would be very considerable indeed.

How one evaluates the arguments over reform or repeal of the 1701 Act and its related ancient statutes, therefore, is largely coloured by the nature and degree of one's secular and/or spiritual outlook. An atheist is likely to have no problem with reform at all. A devout Catholic is likely to resent the lingering negative associations and disabilities of his or her faith in our constitutional law. A devout Anglican is likely to be cautious over reform of the 1701 Act and have a keener appreciation of the positive aspects of the established Church. The highest officials of the Church of England, of course, are sworn to uphold the established link that Anglicanism has with the state. Chief among these is Elizabeth II herself, who solemnly vowed at her coronation service in 1953 to protect the Protestant faith and uphold the established Church as its Supreme Governor.

The point is, of course, that if the religious provisions in the Act of Settlement and related statutes were repealed, then at some point in the future the person occupying the throne would be a non-Anglican, be they Catholic, Muslim, Jewish, of any other faith or belief, or of none at all. In terms of ecclesiastical governance, this of itself would not be a problem, for the Church is virtually self-governing, with the monarch performing a largely ceremonial role. The critical obstacle would be the theological absurdity of the situation, and the certain resentment that ordinary Anglican priests would feel in serving and swearing an oath of loyalty to a non-believer as Supreme Governor. In other words, even if the non-Anglican monarch was prepared to embrace his duties as Supreme Governor of the Church of England, the Church of England would not be prepared to embrace an individual who shared a very different religious ideology.

Arguments about disestablishing the Church of England

There is a high correlation between those who advocate repeal of the religious provisions in the Act of Settlement and those who favour disestablishment of the Church of England. The arguments for and against disestablishment are a subject for an entire book by itself, but the issues involved may be briefly set out as follows.

Disestablishment of the Church of England would automatically bring to an end the religious requirements and Catholic disqualification applicable to a British monarch. One cannot for certain gauge the nature and depth of the obligation felt by the present monarch, Queen Elizabeth, towards the established Church. She has, of course, sworn in her coronation service to uphold and maintain the Church. She has shown every indication of being a totally committed Anglican, dedicated to her position as Supreme Governor of the Church, highly conscious of its hugely important historical background. Formal breaches of the oath by previous monarchs have occurred before, such as when the Church of England was disestablished in Wales in 1920, and when the sister Church of Ireland was disestablished in 1871. But disestablishment of the Church of England *in England* – and in its entirety – strikes at the very heart of the monarch's solemn oath on taking office. It may well be that any move towards either or both reform of the Act of Settlement and disestablishment of the Anglican Church would be subject to considerable institutional resistance from the Queen and the Royal Household.

What establishment involves
The established Church of England was founded during the reign of Henry VIII in the sixteenth century. The Reformation, and its break with the institutional structure of the Roman Catholic church, was implemented through a series of parliamentary statutes, culminating in the Act of Supremacy 1534, which placed the King as 'the only supreme head in earth of the Church of England'. Today, this position is largely ceremonial, akin to the monarch's secular role in politics. It remains of considerable significance, nonetheless, that the monarchy holds the dual position of head of state and head of the Church.

The hierarchical authority of the Anglican Church is more similar in nature to that of the Catholic Church than most other Protestant faiths. Thus it is the Crown – the monarch acting on the advice of the Prime Minister – that directly appoints the senior officials of the Church of England, including the Archbishops of Canterbury and York and the senior bishops. The legal basis for this secular method of appointment is the Appointment of Bishops Act 1533, formerly known as the Second Statute of Annates.* The current

---

* The Statute Law Revision Act 1948 re-titled the statute.

procedure on appointment is that, first, a 'vacancy in see committee' is set up in the diocese concerned to gather together nominations. Since 1977, there has then been a process of selection and recommendation involving the Church authorities, rather than leaving the appointment to the discretion of 10 Downing Street altogether. Today the practice is that nominations are considered by the Standing Commission on Diocesan Vacancies, which comprises the Archbishops of Canterbury and York, three other clergymen of the Church of England, three laymen chosen by the Prime Minister and four representatives of the diocese concerned. This body then formulates recommendations by way of tendering two names, usually placed in order of preference, to the Prime Minister. The Prime Minister will then make the final choice. She or he has been known to prefer a second placed nominee of the Commission, and on occasion even to request that further names be submitted. When the Prime Minister's decision has been reached, she or he will 'advise' (in other words, direct) the monarch accordingly and the legal appointment is then made.

Establishment also involves secular control over the ecclesiastical laws of the Church. Under the Church of England Assembly (Powers) Act 1919, the General Synod of the Church legislates by way of 'measures'. These, following their passage, are submitted to Parliament for approval. The Ecclesiastical Committee, being a joint committee of both Houses of Parliament, whose membership is nominated by the Speaker and the Lord Chancellor, considers the draft measures and makes a report to both Houses. The Commons and Lords then vote on a motion to present each measure concerned up to the monarch for Royal Assent. Assent is given in the normal manner as for Bills. In this way, for example, the ordination of women and the introduction of *Common Worship* were enacted in Anglican canon law.

One of the most visible planks of establishment is the privilege and duty of the most senior Anglican bishops to sit and participate in the House of Lords. The 'Lords Spiritual' have sat in the upper chamber of Parliament since its evolution in medieval times, and since the sixteenth century have had their position provided for by Act of Parliament. The Archbishops of Canterbury and York, and the Bishops of London, Durham and Winchester, have an automatic right to sit in the House of Lords. Then under the Bishoprics Act 1878, a further twenty-one bishops are members of the Lords, selected in terms of their seniority within the Church. These memberships are ex officio, in other words the people concerned have the right to sit in Parliament whilst they continue to serve as bishop, and (since 1975) must retire before the age of 70 years. It is common for the former archbishops subsequently to be made barons for life under the Life Peerage Act 1958, such as (most recently) Lord Carey and Lord Hope.

The benefits of the established Church in society

The argument for retaining the established Church of England as now exists is that it promotes an inclusive, broad and tolerant brand of Christianity and religious attitude. It is obliged to adopt this general spiritual outlook, because in institutional terms it exists to cater for and serve the whole country.

It has been argued that disestablishment of the Church would almost certainly cause it to become far more insular. Its priests, especially at local level, might well start to claim that its membership was exclusive to those who attended and participated at church. Largely as a consequence, the doctrinal beliefs and requirements of the Church might tend to become more extreme in secular terms. The broad mass of British citizens who are not regularly church-goers, but who identify themselves as being members of the Church of England,* could become effectively disenfranchised from their most proximate faith. If this happened, major life events which a great many citizens call upon the Church to solemnise, such as births, deaths and marriages, would become even more secularised than at present.

This general view on disestablishment was put forward by the Bishop of Winchester, during a debate on removing disqualification from the throne for those marrying a Catholic:

> I want also to remind your Lordships – it seems fundamental – that a Church is established to serve, sustain and encourage the establishment of the Christian faith as the ultimate point of reference for government. Behind even this apparently quite unambitious Bill therefore lies this significant question: what kind of state have we, and what kind of state do we want? What kind of public life do we have, with what ultimate accountability for those who carry the honourable responsibilities of government? Were it to prove the case by some chance that the end product of the Bill – if it were somehow to become law – was the separation of the Crown from not only the Church of England but its anchorage in the Christian faith of this land, however expressed, we should be embarking on a unique experiment for these islands of a state whose basis was explicitly secular. The evidence of the nineteenth and twentieth centuries – indeed, of this century so far, and not far from here – is that such a state would be markedly less tolerant and inclusive than our present arrangements.[38]

---

* At the 2001 census, this numbered around 70 per cent of the British population.

The other general argument advanced in favour of keeping the established Church is that, because of the institutionalised links between church and state, the present situation provides a voice and an opportunity for spiritual and religious values to be expressed on national affairs. Because the Church is institutionally represented in Parliament, its moral values and more philosophical attitude on legislative matters and national policy can be brought to bear on subjects of parliamentary debate. In turn, the procedures enabling parliamentary consideration and approval to changes in Anglican ecclesiastical law and organisation provide a channel for ordinary secular values and concerns to be directed at the moral dogmas of the Church. In short, establishment allows God and Mammon to temper each other's more outlandish behaviour and find an accommodation.

Furthermore, it could be argued that the status quo actually liberates and keeps the Church more independent, precisely because it guarantees its position. Our leaders in political life are unable to hand-pick religious principles and supportive priests that best suit their vested interests, particular causes or needs of the moment. At times of national events, it *is* the Archbishop of Canterbury, Bishop of London or other representative of the national Church that will speak and pronounce on events that have occurred, or are being celebrated or mourned.

The arguments for disestablishment

The argument for disestablishing the Church of England is that secular involvement corrupts the integrity and purity of Christian moral values. The Church is constantly having to compromise with secular authorities and concerns. In the words of Tony Benn, 'Establishment necessarily involves a subtle corruption of the spirit of the church, because it is safely embedded in the wider establishment of society, which includes the privileged and the powerful.'[39]

According to this view, it is demeaning for Christian officials and bodies, including the General Synod and the Anglican members on the commission nominating candidates for bishoprics, to have to submit their deliberations and decisions for the approval of an external secular authority. 'The Church of England must be liberated from its subservience to the state,'[40] as Mr Benn puts it.

It is claimed that the office of Prime Minister is a totally inappropriate body for appointing the Church's senior officers. Political preferences and a desire to minimise Church criticism, or promote Church support, may influence their choice. The Prime Minister of the day may not even be an Anglican. Furthermore, it is argued, the individual who happens to succeed to the throne, and therefore become de facto head and Supreme Governor of the national Church, may not be a suitable or acceptable person in the eyes of its clergy to represent the Church and its values.

The debate over disestablishment is an old public issue, and one that was regularly debated in the nineteenth and twentieth centuries. Parts of the Church have been disestablished already, both in Ireland and in Wales, as mentioned earlier. A lively read on the subject from bygone days is Sidney Buxton MP's famous *Handbook to Political Questions of the Day*, first published in 1880. In his book, he argued both sides for and against political issues of the day, and included disestablishment of the Church as the second on his list. In favour of disestablishment, he said, 'The connection of Church and State causes, not the spiritualisation of the State, but simply the secularisation of the Church', adding, 'an Established Church is a Church in fetters.'[41]

More recently, there has been some overt political engagement with the issue. Mr Benn, a former Labour MP and Cabinet minister, has been a prominent advocate. In the 1980s he gave a series of speeches on the subject, culminating in a private member's Bill, the English Church Bill, that read:

> On the day after the expiration of six months, or such extended period as Her Majesty may fix by Order in Council, not being more than twelve months, after the passing of this Act, the Church of England shall cease to be established by law, and no person shall, after the passing of this Act, be appointed or nominated by Her Majesty or any person, by virtue of any existing right of patronage, to any ecclesiastical office in the Church of England.[42]

The Bill made no progress but had signatures of support from a number of backbench MPs, among them Chris Smith, Tony Banks, Dennis Skinner and Bernie Grant.

Leaders of the two major parties have consistently avoided the issue, but the Liberal Democrats have now adopted disestablishment as official party policy. Thus in its 2001 election manifesto, it promised to separate Church and state, saying, 'We will support the disestablishment of the Church of England to end political interference in the Church.'[43] The wording 'support' here is significant, by way of recognising that if and when such a reform proposal is to be seriously considered, it best comes from, or with the official backing of, the Church of England itself. Dismantling the established Church of England in the teeth of its own opposition would be a difficult and turbulent political undertaking.

Within the Church of England itself, in recent decades there has been a minority, but a vocal and persistent one, calling for disestablishment, or more subtly calling for abolition of one or more of the key components that constitute establishment. There are a number of well-known advocates, such as Canon Paul Oestreicher, who has written, 'The patchwork of customs and ancient statutes that tie the church to the apron strings of palace and parliament do nothing for the nation, limit the church's freedom to represent Christ to the people and, on a lighter note, have simply become faintly ridiculous.'[44]

Significantly, there have been a small number of Anglican bishops prepared to enter the fray on the side of loosening or removing secular control over the Church. Dr Colin Buchanan, the Bishop of Woolwich, is the best known of these.* In July 1994, he set down a private member's motion in the General Synod, carefully avoiding use of the term 'disestablishment', but addressing two principal components of establishment. His proposal was:

> That this Synod request the Standing Committee to bring forward proposals for the lifting of direct State control upon: (a) The Appointment of Diocesan Bishops; (b) Legislation coming from this Synod.

In November 2001, he proposed another motion on behalf of Southwark Diocesan Synod:

> That this Synod seek a reform in the method of appointing bishops in the Church of England so as to detach the process from any involvement with Downing Street and the Monarchy and to provide for a more participatory and open Church procedure than is currently possible.

---

* See also the set of recommendations published in a pamphlet by Iain McLean and Benjamin Linsley, *The Church of England and the State: Reforming Establishment for a Multi-faith Britain* (London: New Politics Network, 2004), with a foreword written by Dr Colin Buchanan. The proposals stop short of formal disestablishment, but would get rid of some of the central legal links between Church and state, removing both the restrictions on the monarch's religion and the bishops from the House of Lords, for example. Instead, they propose a United Kingdom Council of Faith to operate as an umbrella organisation to bring faith communities together. The future King Charles might well be keen to play a prominent role in the operation of such a multi-faith Council.

In both cases, the motions were overwhelmingly defeated. Nonetheless, the fact that they took place at all shows that the issue is a live one. During the course of wide-ranging debates, some strong opinions were expressed on both sides. Another bishop, Dr Peter Selby of Worcester, described the present system as 'wrong in principle, politically dangerous, ecumenically embarrassing and theologically indefensible'.

The personal and political effects of the Act of Settlement re-stated

Establishment aside, it is worth highlighting what the actual effects are, both of a personal and constitutional nature, of the Act of Settlement. On a personal level, the religious provisions do not dictate to those in succession to the throne or their spouses what their religion should be or whether they should get married or not. It simply provides, considered from a more positive perspective, that to be eligible to be a British monarch and the ex officio Head of the Church of England one must commit to the Anglican faith.

And not being eligible to be King in the twenty-first century is not such a terrible prospect as it might have been in long bygone days, when to all intents and purposes the King owned and ruled his national realm. There is no real comparison even with Edward VIII in the 1930s, who did regret having to abdicate. For in 1936 Edward stood to lose, and was made to suffer by having taken from him, his reputation and privileged position in British society – he was banished into exile abroad and treated like a social pariah. Nothing of this kind would happen in these 'classless' days of the twenty-first century. The ineligible would-be monarch would become a carefree and much sought-after celebrity, relieved from the weight of a demanding and in many ways frustrating job. Particularly now, given the transparency and thankless nature of public life combined with gross and limitless intrusions by the media into royal private lives, one can imagine that losing such eligibility would not be completely unwelcome.

From a political perspective, the significance of the Act of Settlement, as with the earlier Bill of Rights in 1689, was the acceptance of the primacy of Parliament over the Crown. It ended, once and for all, any lingering Stuart pretensions to absolutism and non-parliamentary rule. These historic statutes laid the foundations of our modern system of limited government and constitutional monarchy. Any real or purported prerogative powers of the King or Queen were accepted as subordinate to Parliament, which had the power to control, regulate or abolish them. Underpinning the entire settlement was the establishment of Parliament's authority to determine the royal succession and all rules and laws governing who might be monarch and head of state.

The New Labour government's inaction: the situation on reform as it stands

So will Parliament use its power to change the present law on succession, and if so, when? Parliament, we need to remind ourselves, virtually never acts as a cohesive entity itself. It is a reactive body that formalises decisions and legislation already prepared in the corridors of executive government, which is then debated and scrutinised by MPs and peers during the various procedural processes at the Palace of Westminster.

Law reform by way of the private member's Bill procedure, such as the Succession to the Crown Bill introduced by Lord Dubs in 2005, is only ever successful if at least tacitly supported by the government of the day, and stands no chance of success if actively opposed. Furthermore, there is a conventional view that legislation on matters of constitutional importance – such as who can and cannot become head of state – should be prepared, drafted and presented to Parliament by ministers by way of a government Bill. Indeed, this has been accepted by the sponsors of private members' Bills on succession law, who have simply sought to give publicity and parliamentary discussion to the issue in default of government initiative, not in any expectation of securing passage of their Bills.

But for the New Labour government, it is precisely the problems discussed above – the international dimension of succession and the underlying question of disestablishment of the Church of England – that make public discourse on the whole subject so sensitive. Furthermore, the New Labour leadership would need to rely on its party backbenchers in the House of Commons to carry the measure, if there was any opposition to it from the Conservatives. The problem for the government here is that it could with reasonable certainty anticipate a field day – indeed, a veritable jamboree – of republican sentiments to be enthusiastically expressed from along the wooden benches lined up behind where the Prime Minister and other government ministers sit.

So where lies government policy on the subject? The answer seems to be that, in principle, it is in favour of modernising the succession law – meaning abolition of gender preference in the common law of primogeniture, abolition of the religious requirements and Catholic disqualifications, and reform of the Royal Marriages Act. But in practice, it sees no advantage and a great deal of political grief to be had in attempting this modernisation of our royalty laws.

One can indeed appreciate why jobbing politicians in office, primarily driven by a mission and policy agenda in the field of social and economic affairs, continue to give the Act of Settlement a wide berth, even if as individuals they personally support reform. For it would not only fuel an unwanted bonanza of royal sensationalism in the mass media, but it would almost certainly

- outrage many priests in the Church of England as well as Protestant traditionalists;
- upset the Queen, who has sworn to uphold the established Church and has taken her Anglican duties deeply seriously;
- require delicate diplomacy in securing international agreement from the other fifteen Commonwealth countries affected;
- consume a huge amount of parliamentary time, to the exclusion of other government business, and provide a platform for republicans and others seeking wider royal reform.

In conclusion, this measure is more easily stated than implemented. As with many royal laws, it is embedded in a deep network of constitutional complications and conflicting claims upon what is expected of, and for, the Crown.

5

Modernisation of the monarchy: the way forward under King Charles

Will the institution of monarchy survive?

Monarchy is essentially a creature of the past and at some point in the future is very likely to collapse. It is unrealistic to think it can last forever and it is remarkable that the institution endured through the course of the twentieth century. The cause or timing of the institution's future demise cannot be predicted with any degree of confidence. If and when it occurs, it is most likely to involve one or more of the following factors:

- a collapse in popular support for the monarch of the day;
- those in line of succession to the throne being unwilling to accept the burdens of office as head of state;*
- the abuse or misuse of the constitutional powers of the Crown by the monarch of the day, causing parliamentary resentment;
- the developing international governmental structure within which the country operates rendering the position of a hereditary monarchy in the UK inappropriate or redundant.

---

* It is a fundamental mistake to think that those in succession to the throne would necessarily be opposed to political pressures or a government policy on abolition of the institution of monarchy. As the Duke of Edinburgh said in a rare media interview in 1994, 'There's a perfectly reasonable alternative which is a republic . . . What it is not is a desperate attempt by a family to hold onto some sort of situation. Because that isn't the point. I don't think anyone would actively volunteer for this sort of job.' (*Daily Telegraph*, 17 October 1994.) A major force driving modernisation of the monarchy is to make the 'job' less unattractive and offputting at a personal level and easier for a human being to perform.

It must be emphasised, however, that in the present circumstances replacement of the monarchy is not a practical proposition, even if republicanism were advocated as a principle. On the right, the Conservative Party has been the most loyally royalist at Westminster. The Liberal Democrats too continue to support the monarchy, and under their ambitious long-term reform agenda they have said they would circumscribe it within their proposed written constitution. On the left, Tony Blair as Labour leader and Prime Minister has often professed his admiration for the Queen and given his backing to the institution of the monarchy.[1]

None of the political parties is close to espousing a republican agenda. This is so for several powerful practical political reasons, whatever ideological views may be harboured by individual left-of-centre parliamentarians. There are two principal reasons why republicanism is impractical today:

- the large scale of government and parliamentary work involved in any move towards a republic, which would seriously disrupt implementation of and time available for public reforms and acts of greater social and economic importance;
- the continuing high level of popular support for the institution of monarchy in the country throughout the reign of Elizabeth II.*

If we accept that monarchy cannot endure forever, we should be mindful that in shaping the institution of monarchy for tomorrow, into its space one day, after the monarchic institution has collapsed, will most likely step an elected or appointed president. It is in everyone's interests that this transition, whenever it occurs, can be effected as smoothly and with as little disruption to the normal working of the political, legal and constitutional process as possible. The role, functions and powers of a one-day future president would, almost certainly, become precisely the same as those of the monarch as head of state today. Only the associated institution of the royal family would be lost, apart from the small social role performed by the president's spouse at ceremonial occasions. The document – a 'written constitution' – that would be necessary to replace the Crown as the basis of the constitution would otherwise codify our existing body of public law;

---

* A MORI poll taken during 7–9 April 2005 on the question 'Would you favour Britain becoming a republic or remaining a monarchy?' showed that 65 per cent favoured the existing monarchy, 22 per cent supported a republic and 13 per cent did not know. Omitting the 'don't knows' the equation between supporters to abolitionists was therefore 75 per cent to 25 per cent.

though this could, if desired, be an opportunity for further constitutional reforms to be made.

Turning to the more immediate prospects for the reign of Charles III, an agenda for modernisation will arise. This chapter deals firstly with the process of reform and change. It considers opinion within the present governing party, and how the way forward will need to accommodate – and may be galvanised by – changing attitudes, including those within the Anglican community and across the Commonwealth. A selection of inter-related modernisation issues and proposals are then discussed, together with the relevance of the Human Rights Act in certain areas. These reform subjects are concerned with matters relating to succession to the throne and royal marriages, and the exercise and codification of the monarch's prerogative powers and constitutional duties.

The Labour Party and the monarchy

Tucked away inside the Labour Party's 1997 general election manifesto, positioned at the end of its section on House of Lords reform, was a one-sentence paragraph: 'We have no plans to replace the monarchy.' This was a carefully worded statement. As a public policy and expression of principle, it fell considerably short of a ringing endorsement of the institution of monarchy in New Labour's programme of constitutional modernisation. As Prime Minister, Tony Blair has taken care to give his full endorsement to the Queen, personally and professionally. In his speech at the government banquet to celebrate her golden wedding anniversary, for example, he referred to Elizabeth II, perhaps a little condescendingly, as 'simply the best of British'.[2]

Elsewhere within the Labour Party, however, there is a large contingent that favours a republic, at least in principle. A newspaper poll of Labour MPs in 1994 showed that 44 per cent wanted to replace the monarchy with a republic, with the vast majority of the others favouring sweeping changes to the institution and to its powers and style of public conduct.[3] In the year immediately prior to the 1997 election that brought New Labour into office, its MPs were far less constrained in expressing their personal views on such matters, whereas since then, the leadership has frowned on negative comments being made about the monarchy and royal affairs. And indeed, there are prominent members of the present Labour government, including in the Cabinet, who are well known for having earlier made controversial suggestions or stinging remarks about the monarchy or royal family before taking office.

The Cabinet minister Jack Straw, for example, called in 1994 for a slimmed-down Scandinavian-style monarchy in a BBC *Panorama* programme.[4] Elsewhere, writing in a book on the monarchy debate, he said:

> There is now a widespread understanding that things cannot remain as they are. The monarchy might be good for tourism, but it is bad for citizenship . . . I am not in favour of the complete upheaval which a republic would bring. But we do need a new Act of Settlement, to establish the Crown and the monarchy in a more modern form.[5]

The same year, Kim Howells, now a minister of state at the Foreign Office, said during a debate in BBC's *Question Time* that the royal family had become 'a scandal-ridden anachronism'.[6] Similarly, Peter Hain, now Secretary of State for Northern Ireland and Wales, wrote in his book *Ayes to the Left*, published in 1995, 'It is extraordinary, not simply that we have a monarch who de facto believes in her divine right to reign over us, but that we accept such nonsense . . . As part of a strategy for reforming and modernising the British constitution, the left should adopt a policy of pragmatic republicanism.'[7]

Within the ranks of the Labour Party there lies more overt republicanism. One open advocate is Paul Flynn, who in 1996 presented an Elected Head of State (Referendums) Bill to the House of Commons.[8] This sought to have a referendum held, in which electors would be asked if they wished the monarchy to continue after the Queen's death and, if not, whether they would prefer a president chosen by members of Parliament or through a popular vote. Another famous republican, who retired from the House of Commons in 2001, is Tony Benn, the former Labour Cabinet minister. He presented several Commonwealth of Britain Bills into the Commons, as blueprints for a republican written constitution, arguing that 'the Crown is a totally insupportable basis for a constitution'.[9] Yet another high-profile radical royal reformer, and a republican in principle, is the former deputy leader of the Labour Party Roy Hattersley, who has written regularly on the subject in the pages of the *Guardian*.[10] As he once memorably wrote on the need to reduce and circumscribe the role of royalty in public affairs, 'flummery is the farce that dances attendance on privilege. The monarchy breeds both and, if it is to survive, it must consciously abandon the more blatant manifestations of an ancient class division.'[11]

The relevance of these radical underlying attitudes towards the monarchy as a whole is that virtually any royal reform measure that is brought before Parliament by the government, however narrow in scope or subject matter, is bound to get side-tracked into a general debate on modernisation or abolition. A great many Labour MPs lose no opportunity to voice objections to the monarchy (which then in turn prompt exaggerated retaliatory interventions of support for the institution from high Tories) or call for wide-ranging reform, whenever some point of royalty arises, however non-contentious. For example, when the then Prime Minister, John Major, announced the official separation of the Prince and Princess of Wales, the response of the veteran Labour member for Bolsover, Dennis Skinner, was not to offer any personal commiseration to the family, but to berate the institution to which they belonged:

> Does the Prime Minister realise that probably the most controversial part of what he said was that there would be no constitutional changes? Would not it be fair to say that, as a result of the occurrences in recent months and the pushing of the self-destruct button by the monarchy, we could now be witnessing the end of the monarchy and that the reigning Queen could be the last? That could not be blamed on those of us who believe that there is no need for a monarchy in this land now.[12]

Understandably therefore, in recent decades Buckingham Palace has never been keen on the prospect of legislation or public debate on royal affairs, because of the sensationalised nature and destabilising influence of today's mass media coverage that would go along with it. And the New Labour government, despite its wide-ranging reforms of the constitution in other respects, has had no appetite for tackling the reform of royal affairs. For not only is it nervous of upsetting the Palace, but it is uncertain of how successful it would be in containing the republican rhetoric, volatile attitude and potentially maverick voting of its own back benches.

Events that may galvanise modernisation and implementation of royal reform

A different context for reform in the reign of Charles III
The accession of King Charles III will radically change the context for modernisation and reform of the monarchy.

At the outset of his reign, the new King – who, as already discussed, wishes to be seen as 'defender of faith', not Defender of *the* Faith[13] – will encounter and be immediately involved with ceremony for his coronation. This will raise the spiritual aspects of monarchy, together with the obligations and restrictions upon the monarch, which he himself has queried, as mentioned earlier.[14] Charles's coronation arrangements will have already been contemplated by him and the royal officials who organise the event, and it is likely the future King already has some clear ideas about what he wants. At the very least, it is predictable that the future King Charles will want a prominent role in the ceremony to be found for the leaders of non-Christian faiths, especially Islam and Judaism, and for the leaders of the Roman Catholic and other leading Christian denominations.

Attitudes among the Anglican clergy towards the monarchy and establishment may well shift considerably upon the Queen's demise. If members of the Church of England are less than enthusiastic about Charles III as their head and Supreme Governor, this could develop into a slow parting of the ways for church and state. This would be magnified if King Charles proves noticeably less active in his devotion to Anglicanism than his mother. There is no doubt that the circumstances of the future King's matrimonial breakdown and divorce in 1996, and then his re-marriage to Camilla Parker Bowles in 2005, considerably strained the loyalties of many Anglican priests. How keen and genuinely willing will they be on his accession to swear their clerical oaths of loyalty and obedience to him personally as their Supreme Governor? The oath they must swear to the monarch is, 'I accept your Majesty as the sole source of ecclesiastical, spiritual and temporal power.'

In secular society, it is clear that a sea change in the public mood and underlying sentiments towards the monarchy will occur when Charles III ascends the throne. As has already been commented upon, how people view or evaluate the institution of monarchy is closely bound up with how they view or evaluate the individual person who happens to be the monarch. Indeed for many, it amounts to the same thing. Such thinking will powerfully determine popular views on the desirability and shape of future developments, change or reform.

In this new context with Charles III on the throne, it is foreseeable that there will be considerably less support, to the minds of government, public opinion and new monarch alike, for continuing with some of the more antiquated ceremonial trappings of monarchic office. There will be less deference in the national mind towards the new King than that which has been a hallmark in popular affection towards Queen Elizabeth; and the new King, as the product of a later generation, will be better equipped to represent the here and now.

The enthusiasm and high regard in terms of support, endearment and celebrity that Prince William has acquired in the popular imagination will be a significant factor too. This could prove an instrument for reform itself. For example, if by fortune or chance it happened that William's personal faith or romantic liaisons with a Catholic stood to disqualify him from succession to the throne, it is extremely likely there would be a public outcry. It is certain that in such circumstances there would be public, press and broadcasting demands to abolish the 1701 Act and other such discriminatory provisions. Furthermore, if the political establishment had an overriding preference for William to follow his father as King, rather than Prince Harry (being the next in line to the throne after William), then this could well provide the catalyst for action in government that has hitherto been singularly lacking.

Winds of change across the Commonwealth

A major change of context for the monarchy at the accession of King Charles will be determined by events in the other Commonwealth countries where the British sovereign is retained as head of state. For many years now, in several of these self-governing countries there have been vociferous republican movements and a growing political desire for a fully fledged national identity separate from the British crown.

Political and popular opinion in those countries on severing their constitutional ties with Britain and establishing their own head of state has fluctuated but overall has steadily grown over the past ten years or so. In Canada in 1998, those who said they were in favour of an indigenous head of state outnumbered those who preferred things as they are by 48 per cent to 39. A recent report of the Canadian House of Commons Standing Committee on Government Operations and Estimates recommended a review of the office of Governor General. If acted upon, this will inevitably open up a wider debate on the monarchy itself within the heart of the Canadian political establishment.*[15]

---

* The report's recommendations included:
  1. That the Parliament of Canada take the necessary measures to conduct a review and initiate a debate on the mandate, constitutional role, responsibilities, and future evolution of the Office of Governor General of Canada (the Head of State) in which all Canadians be included.

[cont.

Within the Caribbean, in Barbados in 2003, the Prime Minister, Owen Arthur, announced plans to turn his country into a republic at the earliest opportunity, following a referendum. The reasoning, which he set out in a speech in 2005, echoed the sentiments of many others in Commonwealth states where the future King Charles will reign. Mr Arthur said:

> We must move to a new level of maturity as a nation. It is in this context that in our fortieth year [2006] Barbadians will be afforded the opportunity by way of a referendum to decide whether we will fundamentally change our system of government by having a Barbadian rather than the Queen of England to be our head of state . . .
>
> We are building a nation. That exercise is not alone about how much goods and service we can produce, how many jobs we can create. It is also more fundamentally about creating a sense of national identity, based on our sense of confidence in who we are as a people under God, and what we stand for.
>
> We need also to be able to hold up symbols of our Barbadianness as inspirations for our people. And must stop seeking foreign validation of the symbols of our national identity and of our way of life. We must also become a land of genuine opportunity in which any child, no matter how humble his or her origin, can aspire to hold the highest office in the land.
>
> Why should we, in this land of opportunity, perpetuate a situation where the highest office in the land, our head of state, is beyond the reach of each and every born Bajan? . . . I view the proposal to move to a republic status as a statement of confidence in our future.[16]

The republican debates abroad have been watched most keenly within the United Kingdom with regard to Australia. In 1995 the Prime Minister of Australia, the Labor Party leader Paul Keating, announced to the House of Representatives that 'it is the government's view that Australia's head of state should be an Australian – that Australia should become a republic by the year 2001'.[17] A referendum was then held in 1999 on the question of whether 'to alter the Constitution to establish the Commonwealth of

---

2. That the Parliament of Canada conduct a review of the process for selecting and appointing the Governor General (Head of State) of Canada.

3. That the Parliament of Canada ensure that the necessary measures are taken to improve the financial transparency and accountability of the Office of the Governor General (Head of State).

4. That the Parliament of Canada consider whether it should terminate the constitutional exemption of the Governor General (Head of State) from reporting to Parliament.

Australia as a republic with the Queen and Governor General being replaced by a president appointed by a two-thirds majority of the members of the Commonwealth Parliament'. The government's republican recommendation was defeated, with 54.87 per cent opposing the change and 45.13 per cent supporting the end of the monarchy. This result was a personal victory for John Howard, the Conservative opposition leader at that time, who had campaigned vigorously for a 'no' vote during the referendum.

However, a highly significant expression of political opinion took place during the Queen's tour of Australia in 2006. Mr Howard, now Prime Minister, gave a surprisingly candid television interview with the BBC, in which he was willing to speak publicly about the future of the monarchy in Australia. In this interview, broadcast on 14 March, the pro-monarchist Mr Howard drew a line between Elizabeth II and Charles III in terms of the future of the monarchy. Describing the constitutional monarchy as a 'very good institution for delivering a non-political head of state', he went on to say, 'I do not believe Australia will become a republic while the Queen is on the throne.' He then added, 'Beyond that, I do not know.'

This could be interpreted as suggesting that such loyalty and support for the monarchy as exists in Australia, itself fairly fragile and largely to be found on the conservative side of the political divide, is firmly attached to the person of Queen Elizabeth. Clearly, it is questionable whether the monarchy will survive in Australia, or be wanted by the political establishment there, when Charles III becomes the King of Australia at the same time as monarch of the UK. This need not necessarily suggest lack of enthusiasm at the prospect of King Charles personally. For the end of one reign and beginning of another is clearly a convenient time for transition from monarchy to republic if the country as a whole, or a consensus of opinion, is ready to move towards its own fully nationalised constitution and is simply awaiting a suitable moment to implement the change.

There are wider implications too. Elsewhere across the Commonwealth, almost certainly in the Caribbean and probably in Canada and New Zealand, republican initiatives are likely to move to the forefront of public debate, especially if majority opinion or the governing party at the time of King Charles's accession happens to favour a home-grown head of state. Furthermore, if a 'domino process' of dismantling the monarchy in these countries does take place on the Queen's demise, its knock-on effects will undoubtedly be felt in the United Kingdom as well. Both at home and abroad, therefore, the end of the reign of Elizabeth II and the accession of

Charles III will prove a catalyst for change. It will provide the opportunity and timing for modernisation plans to be realised.

The initiative, formulation and implementation of royal reform

If there is to be serious consideration given to measures seeking to modernise the monarchy, from whom or what quarter should proposals be prepared and put forward? There is no shortage of ideas or proposals on royal reform. The shelves of any good library are filled with books containing journalistic or academic recommendations on individual matters affecting the monarchy such as Crown finance,[18] or on how to create a slimmed-down Scandinavian-style monarchy, or advocating outright abolition and the creation of a new British republic.[19] Policy institute 'think tanks' have had their say too, including Demos,[20] the Fabian Society[21] and Charter 88.[22] High-profile politicians, past and present, have presented their individual views in speeches, articles and pamphlets.[23] But it is not ideas that are at a premium if royal reform is to be taken further than mere talk.

Real change will only occur when 10 Downing Street and Buckingham Palace in combination agree a way forward. Relations between these two pivotal agencies of the constitution are wary of each other at the best of times. Indeed, in our contemporary history, it is precisely the awkwardness of Crown–government relations that has created the existing reluctance and inactivity over measures to modernise the monarchy.

There are different fears and motivations on each side, too. From the Palace's perspective, it fears that any initiative it brings forward on reform may unleash a process – especially in Parliament – that it will then be unable to control and which will eventually go far further than the original intentions envisaged. For the government, there are major practical complexities to overcome involving reform of the monarchy and their inter-woven nature with other parts of the constitution, which it does not wish to deal with. It too fears opening a Pandora's box of legislative and diplomatic difficulties, and sacrificing a huge amount of its time, in both government and Parliament, over issues that may prove an electoral liability.

The arrival of King Charles III into this equation could prove the catalyst for momentum. Whereas his parents' natural conservatism and caution is unlikely to provide the trigger for a modernising initiative in her reign, the future Caroline regime at Buckingham Palace could change everything in this respect. The personality and outlook of the new King would be able to approach the subject in a way that has clearly been more difficult for the

Queen, because of the depth of her personal commitment to the value structures, ideology and loyalties she inherited from her father in the 1950s.

The initiative, formulation and implementation of a programme of royal modernisation could then take shape. The Palace might communicate its interest in some modernisation initiative and measures taking place. The Royal Household could initiate talks with the Prime Minister's office, making clear the new King's willingness to entertain significant changes. Once broad areas for resolution are agreed upon, the government, probably through a Cabinet committee established for the purpose with one or more royal officials co-opted to its membership, could set out the agreed elements for a way forward.

If Buckingham Palace were left to formulate and shape royal reform itself, this could prove disastrous. Any broad-ranging review of Crown affairs would necessarily have implications for areas of government activity that were highly political and contentious across the parties. These might include, for example, the prerogative powers exercised by ministers (treaty making, defence etc.), election law (the timing of general elections, now conducted under the royal power of dissolution) and European human rights law (religious equality and non-discrimination). These are areas where the King and his advisers would be constitutionally unsuited and politically unqualified to make value judgements on behalf of the country.

The detailed preparation of any reforming legislation, therefore, would have to come from the government. So too would the general management of its passage, including at an early stage the various consultation processes. These consultations might be formal (such as with foreign governments if the law on succession was affected),[24] national (such as with interested groups, for example the Church of England) or parliamentary (especially where a draft Bill was prepared for scrutiny by the Constitution Committee and the Constitutional Affairs Committee). The creation of some sort of commission (royal commission, ministerial committee of inquiry etc.) to offer independent views and recommendations would not be helpful, since the foundations of any modernisation programme must be an agreed platform of principles agreed between Buckingham Palace and 10 Downing Street.

Strong personal leadership by the Prime Minister would be necessary, to pilot the management of the reforming legislation through Parliament and limit the scope for the process becoming derailed by the proposal of wider royal reforms. A referendum on modernisation of the monarchy would be inappropriate, and would at once become a test of public opinion on the existence and continuation of the monarchy versus republicanism.

The male preference in succession to the throne

The questions of who becomes monarch, and how succession to the throne and therefore head of state is effected, are determined through a mixture of feudal common-law principles and ancient parliamentary statutes. In legal theory 'the monarch never dies'. To use the more popular expression, 'The King is dead, long live the King!' At the very moment George VI died in his sleep at Sandringham during the early hours of 6 February 1952, his eldest daughter Princess Elizabeth, then visiting Kenya with her husband, the Duke of Edinburgh, instantly and automatically became Queen Elizabeth II. The same simultaneous process will occur at the death of Queen Elizabeth and assumption of the throne by King Charles III.

Accession law and politics

Contrary to popular imagination, envisaging grandiose, long-drawn-out ceremonial occasions through which the heir to the throne is acclaimed and crowned King, a coronation is not actually required before a person becomes King or Queen. Edward VIII reigned for ten months as head of state, without ever being crowned at a coronation ceremony. Royal books and articles discussing succession to the throne tend to dwell on the elaborate details of the assorted ceremonies that have accompanied the accession of a new monarch in the past. These are often written about as though there is some mandatory force to the traditions and customs of earlier accessions. In truth, however, most of the events accompanying or following accessions in the modern era, including in 1952, have simply followed what had happened the last time as a matter of habit or precedent for 'how these things are done' – not a set of procedures prescribed by law.

Clearly some political process needs to supervise the change-over, so as to intervene in cases of difficulty. Most immediately, the Privy Council constitutes itself as an Accession Council, under the direction of the government, represented by the President of the Council and the Lord Privy Seal, both of whom are Cabinet members and usually Leaders of the House of Lords and House of Commons respectively. Arrangements are made for the presence of high commissioners from the Commonwealth countries where the monarch is retained as head of state, senior clergymen of the Church of England, and ceremonial officers from the City of London, the Palace of Westminster and elsewhere. The traditional method of publishing the council's proclamation recognising the new monarch is by way of it being physically read out in various places, notably at St James's Palace in London by the Garter King of Arms, and being published in the *London Gazette*.

In 1952, the meeting of the Accession Council took place at St James's Palace within two days of George VI's death. On that occasion, as previously, the aristocratic peers of the realm were invited and played a high-profile role. Today, by contrast, the hereditary peerage has no role to play in the political processes of the country and since 1999 has lost its automatic right to membership of Parliament. It is impossible to imagine an identical procedure to 1952 being followed when the Queen dies, for both practical reasons and ones of constitutional modernity. It will be 10 Downing Street, not any aristocratic cabal, that is the political force for determining any dispute about royal lineage or suitability to succeed in the future.

The ultimate legal authority on matters relating to succession to the throne is Parliament. It has been a fundamental constitutional principle since 1689 that the common law of inheritance to the Crown is subject to parliamentary modification. As we have seen, two historic statutes, the Act of Settlement 1701 and Act of Union 1707, exclude Roman Catholics and persons marrying Roman Catholics from the succession. The monarch must be in communion with the Church of England, of which he or she is Supreme Governor, and must swear to uphold the established Church.[25] Under the terms of the Statute of Westminster 1931, the succession can only be altered by the common consent of all member states of the Commonwealth which retain the monarch as their head of state. Such an alteration happened in practice in 1936, when King Edward refused to accept the advice of the Cabinet not to marry Wallis Simpson.

Common-law male primogeniture
The hereditary principles of monarchy are ones of primogeniture: eldest preferred, sons before daughters. If the heir apparent (Prince Charles) predeceases his parent on the throne (Queen Elizabeth), then the heir of the heir apparent (Prince William) takes in preference to the next remaining child (Prince Andrew) of the reigning King or Queen. The order of succession among the Queen's issue at the time of writing is therefore Prince Charles, then in turn his sons Prince William and Prince Harry; Prince Andrew, then his daughters Princess Beatrice and Princess Eugenie; Prince Edward, then his daughter Lady Louise Windsor; then the Princess Royal, and in turn her children Peter Phillips and Zara Phillips.[26]

One theoretical legal conundrum arose in 1952 upon the death of George VI. Strictly speaking, according to the feudal property law of primogeniture, if there are no sons and more than one daughter of the departing monarch, then the daughters are considered equal in law, regardless of age, and succeed to their father's estate jointly. This combination arose for the first time ever in 1952, when King George left two daughters, the Princesses Elizabeth and Margaret. However, no claim was made by Princess Margaret, or others on her behalf, for joint sovereignty. The Accession Council simply proclaimed Elizabeth the sole Queen and head of state, and Parliament then confirmed the succession to Queen Elizabeth alone.

Gender equality: removing the sex discrimination

Today, the practice is condemned of treating some people less favourably than others on grounds of their gender or sexuality in virtually all matters of a public nature, especially in holding public office. The principle is enshrined in post-war statutes such as the Sex Discrimination Acts and in western international human rights treaties such as the European Convention on Human Rights. Clearly, in this context, the present male preference in the law of succession to royal and aristocratic titles looks an anomaly.

Unsurprisingly therefore, there have been numerous calls to remove this item of sex discrimination, including from parliamentarians in both Houses of Parliament, so that it would become simply the eldest child of the monarch who succeeds to the throne. On 3 July 1991, for example, the MPs Simon Hughes and Peter Archer obtained leave from the House of Commons to bring in a Bill under the ten-minute rule procedure, 'so that females have the same opportunity as males to ascend the British throne'.[27] Mr Hughes was successful in persuading colleagues in the House that 'no honourable Member would, on reflection, oppose the application of the principle of equal opportunities to the top job in the land'. However, as with all other private members' Bills on the matter since, he was unsuccessful in persuading the government to back the Bill, which therefore lapsed for want of parliamentary time.

On 27 February 1998, Lord Archer secured a debate in the House of Lords on this reform proposal. His Succession to the Crown Bill provided that 'in determining the line of succession to the Crown and to all the rights, privileges and dignities belonging thereto no account shall be taken of gender, notwithstanding any custom or rule of law to the contrary'.[28]

As with most advocates of the reform, his speech started by emphasising his great support for the monarchy and that his Bill sought to strengthen the institution, not detract from it:

> I am a supporter of the Royal Family and a believer in this country having a monarch. There are no conditions in which I would favour a president for Britain. However, that does not mean that as we approach the 21st century we should not consider any changes to a system that has served us so well for centuries.

The speeches that followed made reference to the excellence of female monarchs of the past, notably Elizabeth I, Anne, Victoria and the present monarch, Elizabeth II.

What made this particular event of real significance and special interest was that the reform proposal appeared to carry the express support of the Queen herself. This was indicated by the minister responding to the Bill on behalf of the government, Lord Williams. He told the House:

> I should make it clear straight away that before reaching a view the government of course consulted the Queen. Her Majesty had no objection to the government's view that in determining the line of succession to the throne daughters and sons should be treated in the same way. There can be no real reason for not giving equal treatment to men and women in this respect.[29]

When challenged by a peer that it was constitutionally improper for the views of the monarch to be made public on legislation before the House, Lord Williams replied that the text of his speech 'has been specifically cleared with those to whom reference has been made'.

The government opposed Lord Archer's Bill on the basis that such a measure should be handled by way of government legislation. On the assumption that the government would take things forward on this issue, Lord Archer withdrew the Bill, though it is highly unlikely it would have proceeded further in the Lords anyway. On the government's intentions, Lord Williams said:

> We do not think that, whatever its merits, a private peer's Bill is an appropriate vehicle for so important a change as the one we have been debating. A major constitutional measure of this sort ought properly to be the subject of a government Bill. We shall be considering how best to carry this forward within government and in consultation with the Royal Family.

The most recent reform attempts on this subject have been by way of two similar Succession to the Crown Bills, prepared and introduced into Parliament by Lord Dubs in the Lords and by Ann Taylor in the Commons between December 2004 and January 2005.[30] Clause 1(1) of the two Bills was phrased identically to the provision in Lord Archer's earlier Bill. No Commons debate on the Bill took place, but in the Lords more parliamentary discussion was held. As in earlier debates, Lord Dubs argued that after fifty years of Elizabeth II on the throne it was absurd to think that the job of head of state cannot be done by a woman. 'Indeed, by all account, the Queen has done the job extremely well,' he commented.[31] But his main case rested upon the simple proposition that the monarchy should symbolise the national values of the United Kingdom, and male preference in the selection of a head of state was out of kilter with contemporary society's notions of equality between the sexes. One rather weak argument employed by Lord Falconer, the Constitutional Affairs Secretary and Lord Chancellor, speaking in opposition to the Bill was to say that Lord Dubs proposed legislation would throw up calls for a re-examination of succession to aristocratic titles generally.[32] For most royal modernisers, this would be a positive, not negative, consequence of the reform.

So in this area of royal affairs, therefore, the government has deliberately chosen, or preferred, not to act. Government ministers have blocked succession reform Bills brought forward by backbench members of the Lords and Commons on the basis that such a reform should be effected by way of a government Bill, yet they have done nothing themselves to provide a solution. The reality seems to be that all attempts to change the law within the corridors of power have so far foundered on inertia in the face of the inter-woven legal, constitutional and practical difficulties involved in legislating on royal affairs.*

Reform of the monarchy and the Human Rights Act

The Guardian's *republican campaign, its utilisation of the Human Rights Act and the Treason Felony Act 1848*
Some have maintained that the Human Rights Act could effectively amend the Act of Settlement and its religious provisions governing succession to the

* See above, pp. 125–8.

throne. In 2000, the *Guardian* newspaper launched a campaign to have the Act of Settlement and related statutes banning Roman Catholics and other non-Protestants from the throne removed from the statute book on the grounds that they were in breach of fundamental human rights as protected by the Human Rights Act.

This in fact has been part of a wider campaign by the *Guardian* for a national debate on the future of the monarchy. Its leading article on 6 December 2000 expressed the hope that 'in time we will move – by democratic consensus – to become a republic'. To enable the paper to air robust republican views, its editor, Alan Rusbridger, was concerned about his and his staff's possible liability under the ancient treason laws, notably the Treason Felony Act 1848. Under the original terms of this statute those convicted faced the prospect of being deported for life, but amending legislation changed this to imprisonment for life or shorter period.[33] The wording of the 1848 statute provides:

If any person whatsoever shall, within the United Kingdom or without, compass, imagine, invent, devise, or intend to deprive or depose our Most Gracious Lady the Queen . . . from the style, honour, or royal name of the imperial crown of the United Kingdom, or of any other of her Majesty's dominions and countries, or to levy war against her Majesty . . . within any part of the United Kingdom, in order by force or constraint to compel her . . . to change her . . . measures or counsels, or in order to put any force or constraint upon or in order to intimidate or overawe both Houses or either House of Parliament, or to move or stir any foreigner or stranger with force to invade the United Kingdom or any other of her Majesty's dominions or countries under the obeisance of her Majesty . . . and such compassings, imaginations, inventions, devices, or intentions, or any of them, shall express, utter, or declare, by publishing any printing or writing . . . or by any overt act or deed, every person so offending shall be guilty of felony, and being convicted thereof shall be liable . . . to be transported beyond the seas for the term of his or her natural life.

Consequently Mr Rusbridger sought an undertaking from the Attorney General that he and his journalists would not be prosecuted under the Act for any republican sentiments they or others expressed in the newspaper. This was refused by the Attorney General of the day, Lord Williams, on the basis that 'it is not for any attorney general to disapply an Act of Parliament; that is a matter for Parliament itself'. Mr Rusbridger thereupon commenced a legal action in the courts for a judicial declaration that the 1848 Act was in breach of his human right to freedom of expression. He relied upon Article 10 of the European Convention on Human Rights, incorporated into British domestic law by the Human Rights Act 1998, which reads,

> Everyone has the right to freedom of expression. This right shall include freedom to hold opinions and to receive and impart information and ideas without interference by public authority . . . The exercise of these freedoms, since it carries duties and responsibilities, may be subject to such formalities, conditions, restrictions or penalties as are prescribed by law and are necessary in a democratic society.

This odd legal case went all the way through appeals up to the House of Lords, which handed down its judgment on 26 June 2003. Rejecting the *Guardian*'s claims, the court declined to intervene over a hypothetical situation, namely that a prosecution for treason under the Act might actually at some point be brought against a *Guardian* writer. Furthermore the Attorney General had astutely declined to lay before the *Guardian* or the court any prosecution policy on the application of the 1848 Act which might have then been the subject of judicial review. As Lord Hutton said, 'it is not the function of the courts to decide hypothetical questions which do not impact on the parties before them'. And Lord Steyn commented that the courts should not be used as an instrument for chivvying Parliament into 'spring cleaning the statute book'.

Although the *Guardian* therefore lost its case, the Law Lords made it clear that if a prosecution was brought, it was most unlikely to be regarded as compatible with the right to freedom of expression under the European Human Rights Convention. Lord Scott spelt this out most clearly, saying:

> The respondents [the *Guardian* staff] have said that they fear that if they advocate the abolition of the monarchy and its replacement by a republic, all by peaceful and constitutional means, they may be prosecuted for treason pursuant to Section 3 of the Treason Felony Act 1848. They refer to the 'chilling effect' that section has upon the freedom of expression guaranteed by Article 10 of the European Convention on Human Rights.
>
> My Lords, I do not believe a word of it. It is plain as a pike staff to the respondents and everyone else that no one who advocates the peaceful abolition of the monarchy and its replacement by a republican form of government is at any risk of prosecution. Whatever may be the correct construction of Section 3, taken by itself, it is clear

beyond any peradventure first, that the section would now be 'read down' as required by Section 3 of the Human Rights Act 1998 so that the advocacy contemplated by the respondents could not constitute a criminal offence, and second, that no Attorney General or Director of Public Prosecutions would or could authorize a prosecution for such advocacy without becoming a laughing stock. To do so would plainly be an unlawful act under Section 6(1) of the 1998 Act. . .

I have already expressed my non-belief in the reality of the respondents' alleged fear of prosecution. I repeat it. I do not suppose there is any school debating society that has not regularly debated the issue of monarchy versus republic. Everyone who reads newspapers or magazines will have read numerous articles and letters extolling the advantages of a republic over a monarchy and advocating a change – and vice versa, of course. These articles and letters have not led to prosecution or any threat of it. Nor have those responsible for school debating societies received visits from the Special Branch. This has been the state of affairs throughout my adult life but it is, I do not doubt, of longer standing than that. There has been no prosecution under the Act since 1883. The enactment and coming into force of the Human Rights Act 1998 made the tolerance de facto of advocacy of peaceful political change a tolerance de jure.[34]

The legality of the royal succession laws under the Human Rights Act

The *Guardian's* aspirations to have the Act of Settlement and law on primogeniture in succession declared incompatible with fundamental human rights under the Human Rights Act have been widely debated but are most unlikely to succeed. Ostensibly, it seemed to have powerful legal support, with two eminent QCs, Geoffrey Robertson and Keir Starmer, from Doughty Street Chambers, championing their cause. In an article in 1999, Mr Robertson argued,

Both Britain and Australia endorse human rights principles which disavow discrimination in public office on grounds of race or sex or religion or birth. How anachronistic, then, that the highest public office in both countries should be defined by a law – the Act of Settlement 1701 – which provides that the Crown shall 'be, remain and continue to the most excellent Princess Sophie, Electress of Hanover, and the heirs of her body, being Protestant'.

This law breaches three fundamental tenets of the new Human Rights Act. Firstly, it enshrines religious intolerance: any monarch who becomes or even marries a Roman Catholic (heaven forbid a Muslim or Jew or a Hindu) is automatically unthroned. Secondly, it breaches the rule against sex discrimination, because the Crown descends as did property in feudal times by male primogeniture, i.e. to men before women.

Thirdly, it embodies racial discrimination, since the office of head of state is open only to white Anglo-German Protestants, members of the Saxe-Coburg-Gotha family (the name was changed to Windsor in 1917 to disguise its German origins).

However, in their published comments over the next three years, it transpired that Messrs Robertson and Starmer appeared hopeful only with respect to challenging the gender and non-Christian discrimination in the rules on royal succession.[35] Mr Robertson was quoted in the press as saying no more than that it was 'possible' that they were affected by the Human Rights Act. Both QCs have also been quoted as saying that the 'express virulence' against Roman Catholics in succession to the throne could be removed only by parliamentary legislation.

There are a number of reasons why the Human Rights Act is unlikely to be used successfully to challenge the Act of Settlement. The first major issue is that the principle of non-discrimination as set out in Article 14 of the European Convention on Human Rights, whose articles are incorporated by the Human Rights Act, applies only in the enjoyment of the *other* rights and freedoms in the convention. Article 14 reads:

> The enjoyment of the rights and freedoms set forth in this Convention shall be secured without discrimination on any ground such as sex, race, colour, language, religion, political or other opinion, national or social origin, association with a national minority, property, birth or other status.

The problematic question then arises: precisely which human rights could a future monarch, such as King William V, or his prospective wife, who might be Catholic, assert before a court of law in defiance of the Act of Settlement's provisions? What convention rights could Prince Charles and the Duchess of Cornwall assert now, if the former Mrs Parker Bowles had been, or was, in fact a Roman Catholic, as had – inaccurately – been believed in some quarters? What rights might the future William V's eldest daughter assert to give her primacy in the law of succession in preference to a younger brother?

None fits easily in to this personal equation for members of the British royal family. There is no human right in the European Convention on

Human Rights expressed specifically on the ability to hold public office free from discrimination on grounds of religious belief or gender. However, there are some other human rights which could conceivably have the meaning of their wording stretched far enough to embrace the royal succession laws. One is the human right to 'freedom of thought, conscience and religion' in Article 9 of the convention, discussed elsewhere in the context of the future King Charles's conscience over legislative affairs. This right to freedom of religious belief may be legitimately restricted, according to the convention, only by legal measures that are 'necessary in a democratic society' or 'for the protection of the rights and freedoms of others'.

There is also the human right to 'protection of property' and 'the peaceful enjoyment of possessions' as set out in Protocol 1, Article 1 of the convention. Clearly, this is mainly concerned with situations such as the compulsory deprivation of land, belongings or money. However, loss of a work position or job title could arguably fall within the category of 'possessions'. The European Court of Human Rights has certainly adopted a flexible and broad approach on precisely what constitutes a 'possession'. There is also the factor that a British monarch is entitled to the vast royal estates, wealth and properties that go to the person who succeeds to the throne.

On the particular point of male preference, a human rights complaint about male primogeniture was in fact brought before the European Court of Human Rights by some Spanish aristocratic ladies a few years ago.[36] The four applicants, all of them the first-born child of noble Spanish families, challenged the transmission of their father's aristocratic title to their younger brothers. In the Spanish domestic courts, the appeal decided by the Constitutional Court went against daughters, holding that the relevant legal provisions on succession of titles did not offend against the constitutional principle of non-discrimination. In the view of the Spanish court, amending the rules of law governing the noble titles' transmission in order to comply with the principle of the equality of the sexes would be to interfere with what was essentially an anachronism and a practice moulded by history.

The Spanish noble ladies then took their human rights claims to the European Court of Human Rights at Strasbourg. Here, their case was deemed inadmissible *ratione materiae*. It was held that Protocol 1, Article 1 only applied to existing possessions and did not guarantee the right to acquire possessions by way of succession. Such noble titles, furthermore, did not constitute a 'possession' for the purposes of the convention. The court similarly rejected the Spanish noble ladies' claims that male primogeniture breached their 'right to respect for private and family life' under Article 8 of the convention, which they had pleaded alongside their 'deprivation of property' argument. The court held that, unlike surnames and forenames, noble titles did not fall within the scope of Article 8 of the convention. It pointed to the fact that in the Spanish civil register, such titles were only recorded as 'additional information', not as the aristocrats' principal name(s). Consequently, as no human right contained in the convention was held to apply, it automatically followed that the prohibition on discrimination in the enjoyment of convention rights, as drafted in Article 14, did not apply.

The situation regarding a claim for gender or religious discrimination might be different if a newly drafted protocol to the convention – Protocol 12 – was accepted and ratified by the United Kingdom government. This is a general free-standing equality article, not dependent upon establishing some other convention right that had been treated in a discriminatory fashion. Article 1 of this protocol reads:

> 1. The enjoyment of any right set forth by law shall be secured without discrimination on any ground such as sex, race, colour, language, religion, political or other opinion, national or social origin, association with a national minority, property, birth or other status.
> 2. No one shall be discriminated by any public authority on any ground such as those mentioned in paragraph 1.

This protocol has now come into operation, on being ratified by ten member states of the Council of Europe. But it only applies in those states which have ratified it. The British government has defended its failure to do so, on the basis that 'in the absence of any case law from the European Court of Human Rights, [it] considers that there remain unacceptable uncertainties regarding the impact of Protocol 12 if it were incorporated into UK law'.

Some might think that government fears for the impact of such an equality provision might include stirring up the political difficulties over constitutional reform to the monarchy and its succession laws, where it presently prefers to leave well alone. However, in fact it is still unlikely that even an equality provision such as that contained in the new Protocol 12 would lead to a judicial declaration that the Act of Settlement was incompatible with human rights law. For one thing, under the Human Rights Act a case before the courts may only be brought by a 'victim' of a human rights violation. In other words, the royal personage who found him or herself disqualified from succeeding to the throne would have to launch the legal challenge. There would be no 'public interest' grounds of standing under the Act to enable others to bring proceedings because they themselves had principled objections to the law.

Another factor, particularly relevant before the European Court of Human Rights, is its 'margin of appreciation' doctrine. This is a position adopted by the court which accepts that national governments may legitimately take into account special indigenous factors in limiting human rights within its jurisdiction, when in normal circumstances such limitations would be regarded as a violation.[37] It is extremely difficult to imagine that the Strasbourg court would ever declare a fundamental constitutional law of this country upholding the established Church of England to be invalid as contrary to international human rights law.

An indication of the likely deep-rooted aversion of the judiciary to become embroiled in disputes over royal succession laws may be gleaned from a test case brought three years ago in Canada. The applicant in this case was Tony O'Donohue, a Canadian citizen and Roman Catholic. He brought legal proceedings before the Ontario superior court of justice, seeking to have those parts of the Act of Settlement, in so far as they refer to Roman Catholics, declared to be in breach of the Canadian Charter of Rights and Freedoms. Section 15 of the Charter has a strong non-discrimination provision which reads:

> Every individual is equal before and under the law and has the right to the equal protection and equal benefit of the law without discrimination and, in particular, without discrimination based on race, national or ethnic origin, colour, religion, sex, age or mental or physical disability.*

The case was struck out on a preliminary consideration of whether such a claim was justiciable at all; in other words, whether the statutory provisions concerned contained the type of subject matter a court would review. The reasoning of Judge Rouleau emphasised that the monarchy was at the root of the country's constitutional structure. Canada shared the Crown with the

---

* Subsection 2 of Section 15 contains an affirmative action provision: 'Subsection 1 does not preclude any law, program or activity that has as its object the amelioration of conditions of disadvantaged individuals or groups including those that are disadvantaged because of race, national or ethnic origin, colour, religion, sex, age or mental or physical disability.' This might assist public-interest actions though such a claim failed in the O'Donohue case.

United Kingdom and certain other Commonwealth states under a commitment to symmetry and union. The court, even if it wished to do so, could not invalidate the Act of Settlement, which would require a constitutional amendment in Canada, and concurrent changes in the law of the United Kingdom:

> These rules of succession, and the requirement that they be the same as those of Great Britain, are necessary to the proper functioning of our constitutional monarchy and, therefore, the rules are not subject to charter scrutiny.
>
> In the present case the court is being asked to apply the charter not to rule on the validity of acts of decisions of the Crown, one of the branches of our government, but rather to disrupt the core of how the monarchy functions, namely the rules by which succession is determined. To do this would make the constitutional principle of union under the British Crown together with other Commonwealth countries unworkable, [and] would defeat a manifest intention expressed in the preamble of our Constitution.

The judge, in conclusion, firmly emphasised that judicial review of the nature sought by Mr O'Donohue 'would have the courts overstep their role in our democratic structure'.

At home in the UK, some have urged the government to follow its earlier dubious constitutional practice of simply making a ministerial declaration 'clarifying' the law on the matter.[38] Such a course of action would involve the publication of a statement in Parliament, setting out what the Lord Chancellor believed the law to be, or had become, in the light of the Human Rights Act. What is envisaged is that the Lord Chancellor declares that the Act of Settlement's discriminatory provisions, and the common law of male primogeniture to the throne, had simply been re-written by the Human Rights Act. In consequence and reliance on this statement, the political and royal establishment could proceed upon the basis of it. Armed with the Attorney General's office, a battery of top QCs and unlimited financial funding, it would be prepared to meet all those who challenged its interpretation of the law in the High Court.

Such a course of action would be unwise. It would not face up to the practical difficulties in securing Commonwealth consent, and it would be effectively changing the legal position of the monarchy without a proper debate on the implications of reform, especially those affecting the established Church. This novel procedure of a ministerial statement, in any event, should properly be regarded as an undemocratic 'quick fix' form of law reform, and not conclusive as to its validity without being tested in the courts.

A regency for the future King's conscience?

Curiously, until 1937 our constitutional law had no permanent provision for the possibility of a regent to cover the situation of a monarch being incapable of performing his or her duties, being a minor or becoming incapacitated in some way.[39]

Historically in common law the incapacity of 'minority' – being under the age of eighteen years (previously twenty-one)[40] – as applicable to everyone else was not recognised in the person of the sovereign.* So no question of legal guardianship of the monarch could arise. Occasions of minority and illness have not been uncommon in our history, and each had to be dealt with by some temporary expedient. So long as the monarch was a minor as opposed to an infant, or not so physically infirm that he could not speak or put a signature to a document, then routine functions could easily be delegated by the monarch to a council of advisers, as in the minorities of Edward III and Henry VI, or to a commission, as under George V when he was seriously ill in 1928. Insanity proved a more difficult problem, especially since statutory authorisation for a regent required the monarch's own Royal Assent. On two occasions, in 1454 in the reign of Henry VI, and in 1810 during the reign of George III, legal fictions were resorted to for the formal appearance of assent to measures in substance passed upon the authority of the Commons and Lords alone.

The Regency Act
It was the debilitating illness of George V from February 1935 until his death on 20 January 1936 (he suffered from chronic bronchitis) which provided the immediate momentum for a rationalisation of the procedures for a regency, which were enacted in the Regency Act 1937. The preamble to the

---

*As Sir Edward Coke reasoned: 'In judgment of law the King, as King, cannot be said to be a minor: for when the royall bodie politique of the King doth meete with the naturall capacity in one person, the whole bodie shall have the qualitie of the royall politique, which is the greater and more worthy, and wherein is no minoritie.' The Institutes of the Laws of England, 9th edn (1684), Part I: 'Commentary on Littleton', p. 43.

Act, which recites the background to the legislation, reads in the conventional form of extreme deference, and emphasises that the initiative for this particular reform – a modernising measure, well overdue – came from Buckingham Palace itself:

> Whereas Your Majesty, by Your Majesty's Royal Message to both Houses of Parliament, has been pleased to recommend that provision should be made for a Regency in certain events:
>
> And whereas Your Majesty in the same Message put both Houses of Parliament in mind of the difficulties which arose in relation to the exercise of the Royal Authority at the time of the illness of His late Majesty King George the Fifth in the year nineteen hundred and twenty-eight and of His last illness in the month of January nineteen hundred and thirty-six, and recommended that Parliament should consider whether it be not expedient to make permanent provision for the purpose of securing the exercise of the Royal Authority as well in the event of the incapacity of the Sovereign as in the event of the minority of the Sovereign on His accession and in certain other circumstances:
>
> Now therefore we, Your Majesty's most dutiful and loyal subjects, the Lords Spiritual and Temporal, and the Commons, in Parliament assembled, do most humbly beseech Your Majesty that it be enacted by the King's most Excellent Majesty, by and with the advice and consent of the Lords Spiritual and Temporal, and the Commons, in this present Parliament assembled, and by the authority of the same, as follows.

Since that Act was passed in 1937, no statutory regency has actually been created. But for the future, one will arise, firstly, if the person inheriting the throne is under the age of eighteen, until he or she attains that age (Section 1). Secondly, there is to be a regency if the monarch 'by reason of infirmity of mind or body' is incapable of performing the royal functions, and until he or she recovers (Section 2).

There is thirdly a very interesting additional ground within the drafting of Section 2 of the Act. This is that a regency arises if 'the Sovereign is for some definite cause not available for the performance of those functions'. What exactly does this mean, and what types of situation does it cover?

Non-availability on physical grounds
Clearly, it was intended to cover extreme situations where the monarch

might find it physically impossible to perform his or her royal duties. Thus when the clause in the Regency Bill was presented to the House of Commons for approval in 1937, the then Home Secretary, Sir John Simon, offered two examples of what might constitute non-availability. These were where a monarch was taken prisoner of war, or where a monarch was shipwrecked when abroad.[41] Obviously, both these examples are extremely unlikely.

Simply being physically outside the country is insufficient, because modern communications technology means the monarch can keep in personal contact with London wherever she or he happens to be in the world. Most routine royal functions can be delegated by the monarch before her or his departure to counsellors of state by letters patent under the Great Seal.[42] Those royal powers that cannot be delegated in this way, namely the award of peerages and instructions for the dissolution of Parliament, can be exercised by fax or same-day courier mail services. An example of this occurred in spring 1966, when the then Prime Minister, Harold Wilson, wanted a general election. In his memoirs Mr Wilson wrote:

> In my latest audience with the Queen on 27th January, before she left for her Caribbean tour, I had informally mentioned the probability that I should be recommending a dissolution for the early days of March, by which time she would be back in London. She agreed that the formal recommendation to enable the forthcoming dissolution to be announced could be sent by secure telegram. A fortnight before this was sent I wrote a letter setting out my recommendations, to which the Queen replied in her own hand.[43]

Non-availability on human rights grounds

A very new scenario which almost certainly falls within the scope of 'non-availability' today, giving rise to a regency, is where the monarch is prohibited on human rights grounds of conscience from performing a particular public act expected of him or her.

Into this category would fall the possible future situation of Charles III, or any other future monarch, being presented with a parliamentary Bill to sign which he found morally abhorrent, and to which his conscience forbade him to give Royal Assent. The prospect of such circumstances arising after Elizabeth II's demise was considered in Chapter 3. Such a situation would bear some resemblance to the justification with which King Baudouin of Belgium declined to sign an abortion law reform in 1990, causing him to abdicate for a day and a half, his legislative duties being performed instead by a council of state in his absence (see p. 93).

This extraordinary procedure, whatever its desirability or otherwise,* has only arisen as a possibility in the past five years since the Human Rights Act came into force. This is because Section 3 of the Human Rights Act now dictates that 'so far as it is possible to do so' all statutory provisions 'must be read and given effect in a way which is compatible with' the human rights articles of the European Convention on Human Rights. It is therefore now perfectly feasible to construe the wording of the Regency Act broadly enough to encompass non-availability due to fundamental human rights grounds of conscience. The monarch would be deemed incapacitated and 'not available' for carrying out the functions in the task of giving his or her Royal Assent, thereby enabling a temporary regent to be appointed in his or her place. The regent would serve in office for the short duration in which the Bill in question could be assented to by him or her, whereupon the regency would be terminated and the monarch restored as royal head of state.

Such an interpretation would be decided upon not by a court of law but through a special procedure set out in the Regency Act for determining whether the statutory grounds for a regency, including non-availability, exist. This is that a written certificate of 'non-availability' is to be issued by three or more persons drawn from any or all of the following: the spouse of the monarch, the Lord Chancellor, the Speaker of the House of Commons, the Lord Chief Justice and the Master of the Rolls. The reasoning behind this certificate's conclusion of non-availability, regardless of the process being essentially a political rather than judicial one, would still nonetheless draw support from the legal and constitutional principles of the Human Rights Act. Indeed, assuming these designated people were sympathetic to the King, they would be even more likely than an ordinary court of law to adopt this human rights interpretation, not less.

Furthermore, this approach to a crisis of this nature would be consistent with the government's novel reliance on the Human Rights Act in Crown affairs during the much-publicised controversy over whether Prince Charles and Camilla Parker Bowles could contract a lawful marriage under the terms of the Marriage Act 1949. This dispute over the state of the law, detailed

---

*The view of the author is that the principles and procedures on Royal Assent as set out on p. 94 should be followed. However, in the event of a King declining to give Assent for reasons of conscience, the Regency Acts now provide a way forward that may be preferable to abdication.

earlier in the book,[44] was resolved in the future King Charles's favour through a process of ministerial statement to Parliament by the Lord Chancellor, which rested heavily on the residual legal authority of the Human Rights Act. As recited earlier, in his statement the Lord Chancellor said:

> The Human Rights Act has since 2000 required legislation to be interpreted wherever possible in a way that is compatible with the right to marry (Article 12) and with the right to enjoy that right without discrimination (Article 14). This, in our view, puts the modern meaning of the 1949 Act beyond doubt . . . [in support of] . . . the view that has been taken by the Government on the lawfulness of the proposed marriage between the Prince of Wales and Mrs Parker Bowles.[45]

Who becomes regent in a crisis? The Regency Act stipulates that the regent will generally be the person next in line of succession to the throne. A person is disqualified from serving as regent if they are under eighteen years of age, or not a British subject, or not domiciled in the United Kingdom, or a Roman Catholic. The anticipated regent would therefore be Prince William in the case of King Charles III ever becoming 'not available'. If Prince William were himself 'not available' because he shared his father's fundamental objection to the Bill requiring Royal Assent, then in present circumstances the choice of regent would fall upon Prince Harry.

Repeal or modernisation of the Royal Marriages Act?

Under the ancient common law, the monarch has a duty and right of care over the upbringing of his or her close relatives, particularly his or her children, grandchildren, nephews and nieces. This general authority over the royal family in times past tended to be exercised with regard to matters of education and tutors, choice of servants and the approval of marriages. The clarity and degree of seriousness with which the monarch could, if he or she wished, control the marital unions of his or her close relatives was buttressed by passage of the Royal Marriages Act in 1772. This statute, declaratory in effect of the existing law, was prompted directly as the result of George III's outrage at the unsuitable matches, in his eyes, of his two brothers: the Duke of Cumberland to Mrs Horton, and the Duke of Gloucester to Lady Waldegrave.

The provisions of the 1772 statute commence with a preamble declaring the principle that 'marriages in the royal family are of the highest importance to the state, and that therefore the Kings of this realm have ever been entrusted with the care and approbation thereof'. The way in which the statute was drafted was that after 1772, any member of the royal family, defined as any descendent of the then King's father, George II, had to obtain the formal written consent of the monarch in council before entering into matrimony. Without such consent, a ceremony of marriage entered into by a royal descendant of George II would be invalid:

> No descendant of the body of his late majesty King George the Second, male or female, (other than the issue of princesses who have married, or may hereafter marry, into foreign families) shall be capable of contracting matrimony without the previous consent of his Majesty, his heirs, or successors, signified under the great seal, and declared in council, (which consent, to preserve the memory thereof is hereby directed to be set out in the licence and register of marriage, and to be entered in the books of the privy council); and that every marriage, or matrimonial contract, of any such descendant, without such consent first had and obtained, shall be null and void, to all intents and purposes whatsoever.

However, there is a proviso to this control by the reigning monarch over the marriages of his or her relatives. In the case of members of the royal family who are aged twenty-five or more, in the event of a refusal by the monarch they can effectively appeal over the head of the sovereign to the Houses of Parliament. Such a procedure under the Act operates by way of the royal member giving notice to the Privy Council of his or her intention to marry, and then waiting twelve months before going ahead and doing so, during which time it is open to Parliament to express its disapproval. If both Houses of Parliament do express their disagreement with the marriage, then again, any such ceremony entered into would be invalid. As worded, if a royal descendant,

> above the age of twenty-five years, shall persist in his or her resolution to contract a marriage disapproved of or dissented from, by the King, his heirs, or successors; that then such descendant, upon giving notice to the King's privy council . . . may, at any time from the expiration of twelve calendar months after such notice given to the privy council as aforesaid, contract such marriage; and his or her marriage with the person before proposed, and rejected, may be duly solemnized, without the previous

consent of his Majesty, his heirs, or successors; and such marriage shall be good, as if this act had never been made, unless both houses of parliament shall, before the expiration of the said twelve months, expressly declare their disapprobation of such intended marriage.

So how precisely did the Royal Marriages Act apply to the proposed and eventual wedding of Prince Charles and Camilla Parker Bowles in 2005? This was a question regularly posed during previous years. Legally under the Act, Prince Charles was required to ask and obtain the Queen's consent to marry.* Constitutionally by convention, the Queen solicited and followed the political advice of the Prime Minister on how this power of consent or refusal should be exercised.† If consent to the marriage was refused by the Queen, acting on the advice of the Prime Minister, on the grounds of it being inappropriate or contrary to the national interest, then Prince Charles could then have appealed to Parliament.

To do so, he would have needed to give notice to the Privy Council of his intention to marry regardless of the objection of the monarch and the Prime Minister, and within the following twelve months parliamentarians in the Commons and Lords could have legitimately debated the issue. If they had supported the marriage or took no steps to oppose it, then no further action would have been necessary and the Prince and Mrs Parker Bowles could have proceeded with their wedding plans. But if Parliament had collectively resolved to endorse the objection of the monarch and Prime Minister, and disagreed with the wedding taking place, then this would have had the effect of vetoing Prince Charles lawfully marrying Mrs Parker Bowles whilst he remained Prince of Wales.

Had the situation of his re-marriage arisen after Charles had become King, of course, the Royal Marriages Act would no longer have been applicable. Instead, Charles would have been subject to the same constitutional subordination to the opinion of the Prime Minister that had obliged Edward VIII to abdicate in 1936. In other words, like King Edward, Charles could have legally proceeded to contract the marriage, but in the face of prime

---

* This was granted and proclaimed on 2 March 2005; see above, p. 42.
† For formal purposes the following phraseological formula was drafted by Harold Wilson as Prime Minister in 1967: 'The Cabinet have advised The Queen to give her consent and Her Majesty has signified her intention to do so.' Contemporary history, including in 2005, suggests that in fact it is the Prime Minister alone rather than Cabinet collectively that interprets and conveys the elected government's view on any royal marriage.

ministerial opposition to the union he would have been constitutionally obliged to vacate the office of royal head of state.

Over time, the literal state of the Royal Marriages Act, as regards its extent and the number of royal relatives affected, has become ridiculous. The proliferation of issue in descent from George II has become a veritable multitude, the great mass of whom the monarch can have no concern with. The Act's reach of control over royal relatives has gone far further than the common law, of which the Act in 1772 was intended to be confirmatory, ever contemplated.

Some people maintain that, as a piece of legal machinery applicable to today's monarchy, the Act as a whole has become an anachronism. The two private members' Bills presented by Lord Dubs and Ann Taylor (now Baroness Taylor of Bolton) in 2004–5* sought to repeal the Royal Marriages Act in its entirety. During the debate on his Bill in the Lords, Lord Dubs referred to the 1772 Act as 'archaic', 'badly drafted', 'complicated' and 'bizarre'.[46] However, apart from offering rhetorical abuse towards the Act, Lord Dubs gave no actual reasoning or coherent argument in favour of complete abolition. Indeed, he seemed to misunderstand the scope of the Act when he proceeded to give as an example of its operation the abdication crisis of 1936. This involved the wish of Edward VIII to marry Mrs Wallis Simpson in circumstances where Edward as King needed no one's legal permission under the terms of the Act.[†]

There is no question but that the Royal Marriages Act is in need of some modernisation. Obviously there is no need for the hundreds of descendants of George II now covered by the Act's requirement to have the suitability of each and every one of their marriages to go through a formal legal process involving the head of state and the Privy Council. The issue is whether the Act should be repealed altogether, as Lord Dubs and Lady Taylor believe, or whether it should be reformed and replaced by some modern formal procedure appropriate to those closest to the throne. If replaced, its scope

---

* See above, pp. 120–1 and 154.

† In Lord Dubs's view what is required is 'none of the complicated rigmarole of legislation, just a simple dialogue between the monarch and government': Hansard, HL Deb, 14 January 2005, vol. 668, col. 497. Certainly it was such a dialogue, between Stanley Baldwin as Prime Minister and Edward VIII as monarch, that led to the abdication. As regards the application of the Royal Marriages Act to Edward VIII *after* his abdication, when he became the Duke of Windsor, the statute putting into effect his abdication, His Majesty's Declaration of Abdication Act 1936, included a provision that the Royal Marriages Act would not apply to Edward when he was no longer monarch (s.1(3)).

could be limited simply to the children of the reigning monarch and those of the heir apparent. Alternatively, the limitation could be by reference to a specific number of persons, perhaps three, who are at the head of the line of succession to the throne at the time in question.

The idea that there should be some form of constitutional control over who becomes the spouse of the reigning or prospective head of state is self-evidently a prevalent one. It drove Edward VIII into abdication and exile in 1936, and prohibited Princess Margaret from marrying a divorcee in the mid-1950s. More recently, the same notion was the underlying assumption driving the extensive public debate and controversy on whether Prince Charles should marry Camilla Parker Bowles. The logic behind this idea is that the personality and personal life of the individual who is or may become head of state is a matter of profound public interest to the well-being of the government and the country. The head of state's consort is inter-woven into this public interest in good governance, for he or she not only has considerable de facto official, ceremonial and diplomatic functions to perform, but normally will be the father or mother of the subsequent heir apparent. A comparative glance at monarchies elsewhere in the world indicates that similar notions often operate there too. Both Spain and Sweden, for example, have constitutional provisions debarring from the throne those who proceed with a royal marriage which is not approved by the government.

As with other issues of royal reform, however, a legislative solution to the outdatedness of the Royal Marriages Act encounters practical problems which are unattractive to government ministers. There is no burning desire for reform, and no votes to be had in it. It will be a distraction, attracting a wholly disproportionate amount of public and parliamentary attention and taking valuable legislative time away from the government's more pressing mainstream social reform programme. And, perhaps above all, unravelling one knot of the legal thread that binds the current law relating to the Crown together serves to tease at other knots that the government would much prefer to leave well alone. In responding to Lord Dubs's Bill to repeal the 1772 Act, the present Lord Chancellor and Constitutional Affairs Secretary, Lord Falconer, said, 'The government have not said that the laws we have considered today should never be changed. They do not rule out change in the future, but have no immediate plans to legislate in this area.'[47]

Codification and reform of the monarch's constitutional duties

There exists today the worrying prospect of theories of royal activism, perpetuated by academic and establishment exponents of a monarch's 'personal prerogatives', being combined with the reality of the future King Charles's propensity for asserting strong personal views and involving himself in matters of government policy and public affairs. This has the makings of a political crisis, if nothing is done to clarify, circumscribe and, where necessary, codify the role and duties of a British monarch operating in 21st-century conditions.

So long as the proper existing conventions, as set out in Chapter 3, are adopted and followed by the Palace, there is no powerful case for reforming the royal acts of prime ministerial appointment and the legislative assent by way of legal reform. In other words, the official publication of a non-legal codification of the conventions will solve most problems. This could be implemented by way of a Conference on Royal Affairs initiated by the Palace, representing 10 Downing Street and both Houses of Parliament as well as the Crown. A public document of this sort could indicate that the act of Royal Assent is a procedure limited to certifying that a Bill has duly passed through all its parliamentary stages. On prime ministerial appointment under a hung Parliament, the codification document could indicate that under current procedure the incumbent Prime Minister remains in office so long as he is not defeated in a no-confidence motion following the Address, in which case the leader of the opposition is sent for.

However, a question may arise in the future as to the substance of the constitutional rule applicable to which party leader wins a general election. There is a case for arguing that, in principle, the leader of the party with the largest number of elected MPs should have first opportunity to form a government, rather than the incumbent Prime Minister, which is the rule at present.[48] If this change of rule was adopted as a new item of constitutional policy to be implemented, then an Act of Parliament would be necessary to effect such a reform.

There are foreseeable circumstances in which a proposal of this nature – one standing a realistic chance of success – might emerge. This is in the context of a referendum being held and won on reform of the voting system. The Labour government promised a referendum on reform of the voting system in its 1997 party election manifesto. Later the same year, the Prime Minister established a Commission on the Voting System under the chairmanship of Lord Jenkins of Hillhead. In the commission's subsequent report, published in 1998, it recommended a more representative alternative to the existing 'first past the post' system, which it called 'AV top-up'.[49] Most recently, in its 2005 election manifesto, the Labour government reiterated that a referendum remained the right way to agree a change on the voting system.

If the promised referendum does endorse electoral reform, and the existing 'first past the post' voting system is to be replaced by a new system incorporating an element of proportional representation (which 'AV top-up' does), then hung Parliaments, where there is no overall majority for a single party, will become significantly more likely. The awareness of this consequential effect might well lead ministers and parliamentarians to think that the Bill implementing the new electoral system should at the same time set down a clear statutory procedure for resolving disputed claims as to the premiership in the outcome process of a general election. In determining this procedure, it is quite likely that a majority of people will support the proposition that the leader of the largest party elected has the greatest democratic claim to have the first attempt at forming a government.

As regards the royal power of dissolution of Parliament, there are two strong arguments in support of the case for abolishing it altogether and replacing it with a system of fixed intervals between elections, as is common elsewhere in the world. One is the unsatisfactory position regarding the constitutional conventions and precise role of the monarch in dissolution affairs, where a great deal of uncertainty and 'grey areas' are widely believed to exist, even though these are set out and explained clearly in Chapter 3 (see p. 100). As earlier discussed in that chapter, the lack of public clarity on a monarch's constitutional duties is largely the fault of lingering theories about a King's 'personal prerogatives' still being propagated at senior levels in academe and establishment circles.

The second argument, of a different nature, is simply the grossly unfair electoral advantage the present position hands to the party leader in office as Prime Minister over the other political parties. As the present chairman of the House of Lords Constitution Committee, Lord Holme once put it, a general election is 'a race in which the Prime Minister is allowed to approach it with his running shoes in one hand and his starting pistol in the other'.[50] Under the existing arrangements, a Prime Minister can advise the monarch to dissolve Parliament at whatever moment he or she likes. Occasionally this has been done for some specific constitutional purpose, such as where the

Prime Minister wishes to put an item of major public policy to the country. Elections of this quasi-referendum nature were held in 1910 (called by Herbert Asquith over the House of Lords), in 1923 (called by Stanley Baldwin over tariff reform) and in February 1974 (called by Edward Heath over the miners' strike and 'who governs Britain' – the government or the trade unions).

But most commonly, a general election is called at a particular time simply because it is when the Prime Minister thinks he or she is most likely to win it (or conversely, least likely to lose it). The Prime Minister and his or her closest strategy advisers can plan and pace events, in conjunction with a keen eye on the public opinion polls, to calculate and manipulate the best chances of success. Electioneering arrangements such as ensuring sufficient funds are in place, preparing broadcasts and booking advertising billboards can all be planned carefully. By contrast, opposition parties are left guessing when the election date will be: they receive no advance notice of the announcement, which takes place a mere five weeks before polling day itself.

One of the great constitutional lawyers of the twentieth century, Professor Owen Hood Phillips, described this feature of our democratic life in the following terms:

> The practice is for the Prime Minister . . . before the end of the statutory period of five years, after consulting his party henchmen and nowadays the public opinion polls, to choose a date for the dissolution – published as short a time as possible beforehand – that he thinks will be most advantageous to the government party and most disadvantageous to the opposition party. Since the Prime Minister and his fellow conspirators alone know when that date will be, they can juggle with direct and indirect taxes and manipulate the economy in such a way as to favour their chances at the general election. Any unpopular measures will have been taken in the earlier part of their term of office. This squalid practice of the leaders of both main parties as it has developed is the least creditable aspect of the British constitution.[51]

It can indeed be argued that the state of the law on electoral timing adversely affects the fairness and integrity of our democratic process as a whole. More generally, it feeds the existing sense of public cynicism about the motivation of its political leaders.

Unsurprisingly a governing party tends to be more successful in British general elections than opposition parties. In the eight most recent general elections, the government has lost only twice. More widely, this feature of our political process feeds the executive domination of the constitution. Our system of electoral timing is one whereby 'an elective dictatorship has proved more and more powerful, and more and more liable to perpetuate itself', as Lord Hailsham, a former Conservative Lord Chancellor, once said.[52] Since political control over dissolution belongs specifically to the Prime Minister, in recent times it has facilitated over-long tenures in that office which in other constitutional systems would be regarded as democratically unhealthy. Margaret Thatcher ruled for eleven years from 1979 to 1990. Tony Blair, elected in 1997, has already surpassed the maximum tenure of eight years permitted for the presidency under the United States Constitution, and looks set to match Baroness Thatcher's record before stepping down prior to the next general election.

What signs are there of this reform coming about? There have been several serious proposals for fixed Parliaments made during the past two decades.[53] The Labour leadership has toyed with the idea in the past. In 1991, the then Labour Party leader, Neil Kinnock, promised in his speech to the party conference that an incoming Labour government would establish fixed intervals between general elections, so as to do away with the unfair advantage possessed by a Prime Minister to control the election date. The 1992 Labour election manifesto subsequently read:

> The general election was called only after months of on-again, off-again dithering which damaged our economy and weakened our democracy. No government with a majority should be allowed to put the interests of party above country as the Conservatives have done. Although an early election will sometimes be necessary, we will introduce as a general rule a fixed parliamentary term.[54]

Labour's policy documents have been quiet on the matter since. However, it has become established as a Liberal Democrat commitment; there have been a number of private members' Bills presented to the Commons advocating a fixed-term Parliament; and such opinion polls as have been taken on the issue indicate it would have strong public support.[55] The most significant recent development is that the Conservative leader, David Cameron, has indicated his personal interest in this as a constitutional reform policy, during a speech he gave at the Carlton Club. He said:

> If we're looking for ways to redress the balance between a weak legislature and an overmighty executive, I believe it's time we looked seriously at fixed-term parliaments.

Is it really right that one person should be able to set the date of the general election? To decide the whole timetable of political discourse?[56]

Since the 1997 election any rationale for the existing system has become ever more tenuous. Thus, for example, the purported justification that the prerogative of dissolution permits the government some mechanism whereby it may test electoral opinion on some major item of public policy has now evaporated with the government's espousal of the institution of referendums in contemporary politics. In the newly created Scottish Parliament, a fixed four year term applies[57] and there was never any question of utilising the prerogative or an Order in Council as the basis for election timing there.

The adoption of fixed as opposed to floating election dates for the Westminster Parliament would involve the abolition of the prerogative of dissolution and the enactment of an Act of Parliament prescribing the new arrangements. One important detail will be to set down the circumstances and procedures through which an earlier election might be permitted within the fixed term period. There has to be some such safety valve, as is common in such arrangements elsewhere, such as in Germany. It would address those exceptional or crisis situations where, for example, the government lost the confidence of the Commons but the opposition were unable or unwilling to take office either as a minority party or in coalition with other parties.

The other essential matter is to agree the appropriate length of the fixed interval between elections. Elsewhere in the world, members of legislatures or office holders in government tend to stay in post for between two and six years. In the USA, members of the House of Representatives (the lower House in Congress) are elected every two years, the President holds office for four years, and members of the Senate (the second chamber of Congress) serve for six-year terms. The House of Representatives in both Australia and New Zealand operate three-year terms between elections. French law has the French President being elected every fifth year, members of the French second chamber (the Senate) being elected for six-year terms, and National Assembly elections being every fifth year. In Sweden, members of the Rikstag serve for three-year terms. But the majority of European countries, including Denmark, the Netherlands, Germany, Norway, Portugal and Austria, all regulate the intervals between their parliamentary elections at the period of four years.

For the United Kingdom, there can be little doubt that the period between general elections should be four years. The proposal for fixed-term

Parliament as a whole should fit as closely as possible into existing constitutional expectations. The idea that four years is about the right length of time between elections is very prevalent, and this simply reflects the reality that the average duration between general elections in recent decades has indeed been about four years. Furthermore, it was the period expressly approved of as being normal in practice, when the Parliament Act set the period of five years as a maximum.[58]

A reform of this nature, then, would take the political role of the monarchy out of the electoral process altogether, to everyone's benefit. From the Palace's perspective, such a development should be welcomed. For it will better safeguard the monarch from becoming embroiled in politics in the event of difficult or controversial political circumstances, from which it stands to gain only the hostility of the party against whose interests the prerogative was used. The office of head of state filled by a hereditary monarch – whatever personality succeeds to the throne – would continue in its largely ceremonial capacity, its constitutional role being to ensure that established lawful processes are followed by the government.

Afterwords

Queen Camilla or Princess Consort?

Few public issues in recent years have suggested that Britain is still obsessed with social rank and status quite so much as the over-hyped controversy on whether the Duchess of Cornwall may one day bear the title 'Queen Camilla'. Ever since 1997, the mass media have latched onto this subject, coming back to it time and again. It has been commented on at length across the television screens and in yards of columns in the press, as though it was a constitutional question of profound importance to the life of the nation.

In terms of popular opinion, polls taken during the years prior to 2005 seemed to indicate, curiously, that this was the key objection that most opponents had to the royal wedding as a whole. During the period of the engagement, most people did not object to the wedding per se, and indeed favoured the Prince and Mrs Parker Bowles getting married.[1] It was the idea of Camilla becoming Queen that the majority objected to. In an earlier NOP poll for the BBC in October 2002, 52 per cent were opposed to her becoming Queen, with 30 per cent in favour (18 per cent did not know); so 63 per cent of those expressing an opinion were against the royal title of 'Queen Camilla'.[2] In July 2004, six months prior to the engagement, a Populus poll for the *Sun* indicated a three-to-one level of opposition, 74 per cent disliking the idea, with 21 per cent being in favour (5 per cent undecided).

The public question had therefore become not so much 'will the country stand for Mrs Parker Bowles marrying the heir to the throne', as 'will the country stand for Mrs Parker Bowles being called Queen'. According to a leading article in the *Daily Express*,[3]

> Prince Charles and his court have been hoping that, on the terrible day this country's present sovereign is no more, we will have become indifferent to the idea of Camilla as Queen. He is taking a dreadful risk. If he allows Camilla to be crowned, he is going to create the most unpopular monarchy since the early 19th century when the Prince Regent's coach was stoned by the mob as it travelled through London.

Even the BBC's flagship current affairs programme, *Panorama*, devoted an entire edition to the question, entitled 'Queen Camilla?', broadcast on 27 October 2002, treating the question as though a constitutional crisis of great proportions was on the horizon. The same question featured again in two subsequent *Panorama* programmes on the royal marriage broadcast in 2005, on 13 February ('Lawful Impediment?') and 2 October ('A Right Royal Shambles?'), shortly before and after the wedding.

In recognition of popular feeling in the country, at least in part, a decision on a royal title for Camilla when King Charles III ascends the throne was announced at the same time as the engagement announcement on 10 Feburary 2005. This declared the intention that when Charles becomes King, his wife, shortly to become Her Royal Highness the Duchess of Cornwall, should use the title 'HRH The Princess Consort'. This has met with broad popular approval. A Populus poll taken for the *Times* in April 2006, just before the Prince and Duchess's first wedding anniversary, showed that 56 per cent of respondents preferred the royal title of 'Princess Consort', with only 21 per cent content for her to be called 'Queen'.

The fact is that whatever title a husband or wife of the head of state is given is purely titular and ceremonial. It is devoid of any occupational significance over and above that which would attach in any event to the spouse of the head of state, whatever he or she was called. The wife of a King remains a private citizen. She has no right to participate in the coronation of her husband or be crowned herself, which is a matter to be decided by the new King acting on the advice of his government.*[4] Such prerogatives and

---

* One source of opposition to Camilla becoming 'Queen' lies in the consequential question mark over whether she might then wish to be crowned at the coronation service, similarly to the wife of George VI, Queen Elizabeth. The coronation service is a sacred ceremony for the Church of England that anoints and consecrates the new sovereign as its Supreme Governor. Any suggestion

[cont]

privileges as have customarily been said to attach to the Queen consort are virtually all of a redundant or archaic nature today,[5] and most of these arguably attach to the wife of the King whatever her title may be. Even the Treason Act 1351, by which the offence of treason is committed where a person 'doth compass or imagine the death of our lord the King, or our lady his Queen', is subject to an alternative statutory text in existence where the term 'wife' is used instead of 'Queen'.[6] In the event of a regency, it is the 'wife' of a male monarch who is involved in determining questions of availability, not specifically the 'Queen'.[7] In other words, whether or not the Duchess of Cornwall becomes known as Queen Camilla in due course is a legal, constitutional and political non-issue.

Confusion and misunderstandings have arisen over the related question of whether the spouse of a King has any option on what she will be called. Clearly, the view from Clarence House is that there is an option, or it would not have stipulated that the Duchess will become Princess Consort. However, many have argued that there is no discretion over the matter and the wife of a King must be entitled 'Queen' whether she and/or the King like it or not. A leading academic advocate of this view is Dr Stephen Cretney, the Oxford legal historian and family lawyer who also, unsuccessfully, argued during the royal engagement in February 2005 that it was legally impossible for Charles and Camilla to be married by way of a civil register office service.[8] This view relies heavily on the opinions of law officers expressed in 1936, now available in the National Archives at Kew, to the effect that Wallis Simpson would automatically have become 'Queen Wallis' if Edward VIII had married her whilst head of state. It is true that Stanley Baldwin publicly stated this to be a legal fact at the time. But it was the moral and constitutional reservations of the government and the Church of England that set their face against King Edward's marriage. This undoubtedly coloured their interpretation of the common law on titles for the wife of a King and indeed the legal obstacles as a whole to King Edward's proposed marriage to a twice-divorced American citizen.

Convention and law in this question must not be muddled. Certainly it has been the conventional practice in the past for the wife of a King regnant to be called Queen, but it has also been customary over the past two

---

of Camilla being crowned as part of the coronation, therefore, would be highly problematic for the Church, given that the new King and Queen had not been married in an Anglican religious ceremony. For the views of the former Archbishop of York, Lord Hope, on the matter, see the *Times*, 8 November 2005.

centuries for the husband of a Queen regnant to be called Prince. The best precedent on the matter is the most recent, namely the manner and style of the title afforded to Elizabeth II's spouse, Prince Philip, the Duke of Edinburgh. Prior to the Queen's accession, Philip had already been given the titles 'His Royal Highness' and 'Duke of Edinburgh' by George VI. On his wife's accession in 1952, he was simply granted by the Queen the right of ceremonial precedence after Elizabeth herself. The Duke of Edinburgh did not participate in the coronation, and he was not crowned King. He was not even made Prince Consort, in the manner of Queen Victoria's husband Albert, as is intended in its female form for the Duchess of Cornwall. Only subsequently by royal act of letters patent on 22 February 1957, did Queen Elizabeth confer the title of 'Prince of the United Kingdom' upon her husband. Today one can neither assume nor expect differential treatment according to the gender of the head of state.

In conclusion, first, nothing in our constitutional history has removed the legal prerogative right of the Crown as the common-law fountain of honours and titles to confer and dictate whatever title it thinks fit upon the spouse of the head of state. Second, it is consistent with customary practice as viewed in today's context for the spouse of a reigning head of state to be known as Prince or Princess, if such title is thought more appropriate than King or Queen by the monarch and government to the circumstances of the particular case.

The situation as explained to the press and public by the government has been rather unclear, attempting to tread a middle way and leaving the door open to the Duchess of Cornwall becoming 'Queen Camilla'. On being pressed on the matter in the House of Commons by the Labour backbencher Andrew Mackinlay, the constitutional affairs minister Christopher Leslie correctly stated that the marriage was not 'morganatic', in other words one where special rules displaced the normal application of the law on royal titles.[9] Ministers have avoided responding directly to the situation when King Charles III ascends the throne, but in a statement regarding the similar principle and analogous entitlement of the Duchess at present to being called 'Princess of Wales', Mr Leslie told Mr Mackinlay, 'She will be Princess of Wales but will not use the title.'[10]

Further indication of the government's mentality on the matter may be gleaned from quotations to the press by government 'spokesmen'.[11] Thus, responding to the suggestion that the Duchess will become 'Queen Camilla', the press were told by an unnamed Department for Constitutional Affairs spokesman:

> I think traditionally that is probably the case because in all similar circumstances in past royal marriages that is what has happened. But I think she is not going to be referred to as Queen. She will be referred to as Princess Consort. I think you are right in thinking it would require legislation for her not to be Queen.

Similarly, on 21 March 2005 the Prime Minister's official spokesman told reporters, 'The position at the moment is limited to what the title would be on her marriage. In terms of any future events, let us wait until future events arise.' When a reporter suggested to him that Camilla Parker Bowles would automatically become Queen unless there was legislation enacted to the contrary, the spokesman replied, 'I am not disputing what you have said.'

The government's position on the matter, therefore, has been hesitant and not very authoritative. It has chosen to prevaricate on the issue, or use informal channels to hint at what its view is, despite intense media interest and publicity. The indications are that the government accepts the legal case that the Duchess will in theory be 'Queen Camilla', perhaps out of deference to the legal opinions expressed by its own law officers in 1936, especially as their significance proved devastating to the fortune of the reigning King at the time. But simultaneously ministers wish to avoid conflict with the current popular view that the title of 'Queen Camilla' is inappropriate and that of 'Princess Consort' preferable. The question is therefore being left open until King Charles III actually ascends the throne.

Leapfrogging a generation: King William V as the next monarch?

The views of Diana, Princess of Wales, on the prospect of King Charles III formed a much-publicised component of her famous BBC *Panorama* interview with Martin Bashir on 5 November 1995.

> *Bashir*: Do you think the Prince of Wales will ever be King?
> *Diana*: I don't think any of us know the answer to that. And obviously it's a question that's in everybody's head. But who knows, who knows what fate will produce, who knows what circumstances will provoke?

Bashir: But you would know him better than most people. Do you think he would wish to be King?

Diana: There was always conflict on that subject with him when we discussed it, and I understood that conflict, because it's a very demanding role, being Prince of Wales, but it's an equally demanding role being King. And being Prince of Wales produces more freedom now, and being King would be a little bit more suffocating. And because I know the character I would think that the top job, as I call it, would bring enormous limitations to him, and I don't know whether he could adapt to that.

Bashir: Do you think it would make more sense in the light of the marital difficulties that you and the Prince of Wales have had if the position of monarch passed directly to your son Prince William?

Diana: Well, then, you have to see that William's very young at the moment [he was aged thirteen at the time of the interview], so do you want a burden like that to be put on his shoulders at such an age? So I can't answer that question.

Bashir: Would it be your wish that when Prince William comes of age that he were to succeed the Queen rather than the current Prince of Wales?

Diana: My wish is that my husband finds peace of mind, and from that follows other things, yes.

The suggestion seemed to be, therefore, that Prince Charles might prefer not to be King, because it would stifle his individuality and freedom to express himself and his opinions even more restrictively than at present – intolerably so, perhaps. The conclusion Diana pointed to was that Prince William should step forward as the next prospective monarch, at least once he had reached a suitable age of maturity, presumably on graduating from full-time university education shortly after reaching the age of twenty-one.*

Speculation on the royal succession skipping a generation has been rife

---

* According to the memoirs of Sir Max Hastings, former editor of the *Daily Telegraph*, Princess Diana's personal opinion was that the throne should indeed pass from the Queen to Prince William. At a meeting in 1994, she reportedly told him, 'I am absolutely determined to see William succeed the Queen. I just don't think Charles should do it.' (Max Hastings, *Editor: An Inside Story of Newspapers* (London: Macmillan, 2002), p. 338). In the memoirs of another former newspaper editor, Piers Morgan of the *Daily Mirror*, Morgan recounts a lunch-time conversation on 16 May 1996 with Princess Diana and Prince William, when in response to the question 'Do you think Charles will become King one day?', she replied, 'I think he thinks he will, but I think he would be happier living in Tuscany or Provence, to be honest.' (Piers Morgan, *The Insider* (London: Ebury Press, 2005), p. 122.)

over the years since that interview took place, fuelled by the controversies and implications of the Prince's affair with Camilla Parker Bowles. Prince William, born on 21 June 1982, graduated with an honours degree from St Andrew's University in 2004. Since his twenty-first birthday, he has undertaken limited public engagements, raising his profile as a public figure, and popular opinion has clearly warmed to him as a prospective head of state. In 2006, the year of Queen Elizabeth's eightieth birthday, Prince William turns twenty-four years of age, just one year younger than the Queen herself when she became monarch in 1952. He exudes charm, robust health and good looks, and he has a noticeably more easy-going and fluent manner with the press and television media than his father.

Opinion polling has reflected this momentum towards a preference for Prince William succeeding to the throne. In 2002, 48 per cent of respondents thought Charles should succeed the Queen, and 28 per cent said William. In 2003, when William turned twenty-one, the relative views were 38 per cent for Charles and 37 per cent for William. On 11 February 2005, the day of the royal engagement, popular opinion was slightly in favour of William succeeding the Queen, with 41 per cent of the respondents favouring this option, 37 per cent believing it should still be Charles, and 3 per cent undecided.[12] The remaining 19 per cent were republicans and said there should be no monarch after Elizabeth II.

The personal difficulties faced by a King Charles III

Prince William has grown into his public role more successfully than anyone could have hoped for. Meanwhile, his father has entered late middle age, more outspoken on public issues than ever before and seemingly less tolerant of the media and the irritants that go with being heir to the throne. A vivid example of the two different directions in which father and son are travelling in their professional lives occurred on 31 March 2005 at the customary annual photo-shoot of Prince Charles with William and Harry on the snow slopes at Klosters, the Swiss ski resort. On this occasion, the event came less than a fortnight before the Prince's pending marriage, causing him no doubt to be more emotional than otherwise. As reported on the front page of the *Daily Telegraph*, the most supportive of royal newspapers, 'the full extent of the Prince of Wales' contempt for the media was revealed yesterday, transforming what should have been an innocuous pre-wedding photo-call into a public relations disaster.'

Clearly audible by the microphones brandished by the assembled mêlée of reporters and cameramen, Prince Charles made a number of negative comments about the photo-shoot and the fifty or so journalists present. While Prince Charles was heard uttering 'I hate doing this' and 'I hate these people', Prince William told him to 'keep smiling, keep smiling' and lightened things up by joking about his father's sunglasses and saying he was 'very happy, very pleased' about his father's forthcoming wedding.

The heir apparent's most caustic comments were reserved for the BBC's royal correspondent, Nicholas Witchell, to whom he first made a sarcastic reply to the question whether he was looking forward to the wedding: 'I am very glad you have heard of it, anyway.' Then he added, 'These bloody people. I can't bear that man. I mean, he's so awful, he really is.' Meanwhile, William took over, light-heartedly telling reporters he was looking forward to his father's big day, and 'so long as I do not lose the ring, it will be all right'. The front page headlines the next day were epitomised by the *Daily Telegraph*'s ' "Bloody people": Charles rages at reporters'.

This of course served even more to fuel the press and media sensationalism of royal affairs. Even though Charles's flash of annoyance was perfectly understandable in terms of a human being feeling hounded by the media, he was widely condemned for losing his dignity. The distinguished journalist and former *Daily Telegraph* editor Sir Max Hastings spoke of 'the damage his self-pitying petulance has done to the monarchy',[13] saying that 'he should step aside' if he could not make more of a success of his appearances surrounding the forthcoming wedding and other public duties. More abrasively, the film director Michael Winner, writing in the *News of the World*, complained:

> I object that he is so unprofessional. Doesn't he know he has a job to do? To be a figurehead. To charm people. At a time of crisis for the royal family isn't it unbelievable that at his age and with his experience Charles sits po-faced knowing he has a microphone attached to him and insults the very press and media representatives he needs on his side . . .? I implore him to do the decent thing. Renounce the crown and disappear quietly into a world of talking to plants. And keep out of sight.[14]

It may well be that Prince Charles has a declining appetite to be King. Or more likely, as Princess Diana intimated, he may well increasingly feel the inherent conflict stemming from his desire as a human being in a position of influence wanting to make a difference by speaking out and lobbying for special interests. As King, on the other hand, he will be required to subordinate his private views to his public duties. Furthermore, he must suppress his personal views and only ever express them with utter discretion, so the public is kept unaware of his own personal and true feelings. If this is too much to bear, then he may desire to step aside. He could do so in the knowledge that his talented elder son, Prince William, is popular in the country and within the political establishment and appears to have all the necessary personal qualities to make an excellent head of state in succession to Elizabeth II.

The adaptable nature of contemporary constitutional practice

The weight of tradition and custom rests heavily against the idea of changing the person who is next in line to the throne, unless there are circumstances of disqualification, legal or constitutional. Automatic succession from one generation to the next is regarded as fixed practice. The official line from Buckingham Palace or any other official royal source, therefore, will not depart from this doctrine or enter into any discussion of whether Prince William might ever 'leapfrog' his father to become King.

However, as has been discussed elsewhere, the weight of constitutional tradition today is of a far lighter nature than when Queen Elizabeth ascended the throne. In the immediate aftermath of the Second World War, as before it going back into the Victorian era, the British constitution operated as a hugely inert set of processes, almost entirely upon the basis of historical precedents that were universally praised and regarded as of near-biblical authority. Such veneration for the political ways of our past began to be seriously questioned in the 1960s, and over the period since has gone into a state of gradual decline. This weakening of constitutional tradition has been accelerated since 1997 by the Blair administration's constitutional reform programme. What started with devolution and the Human Rights Act has developed into a permanent, rolling process of 'modernisation' of government. New Labour's agenda for changing the constitutional furniture of state has included, for example, transforming the House of Lords and the office of Lord Chancellor. Constitutional modernisation is now part of the mission statement of a new department of state created in 2003 by the Prime Minister specially for the purpose, the Department for Constitutional Affairs.

In short, many actions affecting the composition and working of our political system which would have been unthinkable fifty years ago are now to be evaluated upon the basis of existing circumstances, exigencies or advantage. There would certainly be nothing 'unconstitutional' in putting into effect a proposal that Prince William succeed Queen Elizabeth, rather than his father Prince Charles.

The terms of such an arrangement would require collaboration and agreement by all parties concerned. It would be for Prince Charles to suggest that the throne be passed on direct to his son, no doubt on the basis that he was near or past the age of normal retirement, whereas his son was in his prime. It would be for Prince William to determine his willingness to assume the mantle of King, on which he would be strongly influenced no doubt by his father. And it would be for 10 Downing Street to express its constitutional advice and political preferences on the matter, in which it would sound out opinion across the Commonwealth, whilst paying close attention to public opinion at home within the UK.

The detailed content and manner of the formalities would be determined to some extent by the timing of this arrangement, whether taking place prior to or immediately following the demise of Queen Elizabeth. In either case, however, the procedures would be relatively simple and straightforward. First, there would be a public declaration by Prince Charles, stipulating his intent and desire to step aside, combined with his reasoning for doing so expressed in terms of public duty. Then, an Instrument of Renunciation – a better term than 'abdication' with its negative historical overtones – would be signed by Charles, witnessed by signatures of the closest members of the royal family, certainly including Princes William and Harry. A Succession to the Throne Bill would then be prepared by the government for approval and enactment by Parliament, putting into legal effect that Prince Charles had vacated the throne which therefore passed to the next in line of succession, Prince William.

Notes

Chapter 1

1. *HRH The Prince of Wales v Associated Newspapers* (2006) EWHC 522 (Ch), 17 March 2006. See p. 19.
2. *Daily Telegraph* YouGov poll, published 25 February 2006.
3. 'Ministers from Blair down have protected Charles from himself', *Times*, 23 February 2006.
4. These provisions and their possible reform are discussed in Chapter 4.
5. On the legality of the civil royal marriage, see below, p. 54.
6. The constitutional exercise of these royal acts is the subject of Chapter 3 below.
7. *A King's Story* (1965), documentary film.
8. See Robert Blackburn, 'The Queen and Ministerial Responsibility', *Public Law* (1985), vol. 30, p. 361.
9. See House of Commons Public Administration Select Committee, *Taming the Prerogative: Strengthening Ministerial Accountability to Parliament*, Fourth Report, 2003–04, HC 422.
10. See p. 101, where Prime Ministers have expressed appreciation for the Queen's views.
11. Anthony Sampson, *Who Runs this Place?: The Anatomy of Britain in the 21st Century* (London: John Murray, 2004), p. 36.
12. To take three recent instances, on government policy towards complementary healthcare: 'We have become allergic to our western way of life', *Guardian*, 28 February 2004; on government and European fishing policy, 'We must act now – before the world runs out of fish', *Daily Telegraph*, 6 December 2004; and on government overseas aid policy, 'We must never forget the tsunami victims', *Sunday Telegraph*, 6 March 2005.
13. For examples see Jonathan Dimbleby, *The Prince of Wales* (London: Little, Brown, 1994), pp. 405, 433–8, 543; *Mail on Sunday*, 29 September 2002.
14. Interview with the *Observer*, 29 September 2002.
15. From the letters as reproduced in the *Mail on Sunday*, 29 September 2002.
16. *Times*, 30 September 2002.
17. Quoted in Dimbleby, *Prince of Wales*, pp. 455–6.
18. Dimbleby, *Prince of Wales*, pp. 320–3.
19. *Sunday Times*, 29 September 2002.
20. *Daily Telegraph*, 22 October 1999; *Sunday Times*, 24 October 1999.

21. Witness statement, 18 January 2006, in the Prince's legal proceedings against Associated Newspapers: see below.
22. 23 October 1999.
23. 24 October 1999.
24. Extracts from this journal were published in the *Mail on Sunday*, 13 November 2005.
25. *The English Constitution* (London: Fontana, [1867] 1963), p. 111: more precisely, Bagehot wrote that a 'sovereign has, under a constitutional monarchy such as ours, three rights – the right to be consulted, the right to encourage, the right to warn. And a king of great sense and sagacity would want no others.'
26. Dimbleby, *Prince of Wales*, p. 544. See Rodney Brazier, 'The Constitutional Position of the Prince of Wales', *Public Law* (1995), vol. 30, p. 401.
27. Dimbleby, *Prince of Wales*, p. 554.
28. Confidential letter of Prince Charles, quoted in Dimbleby, *Prince of Wales*, p. 405.
29. Populus, fieldwork 7 and 11 January 2005.
30. For an account of relations between the Queen and Mrs Thatcher with regard to Commonwealth meetings, see the shrewd analysis in Ben Pimlott, *The Queen: A Biography of Queen Elizabeth II* (London: HarperCollins, 1996), especially pp. 462–9. The 1986 episode involved a report in the *Sunday Times*, 27 July 1986: see Rodney Brazier, *Constitutional Practice*, 2nd edn (Oxford: Clarendon Press, 1994), pp. 184-5.
31. *Times*, 24 December 2005.
32. This was included in Mr Bolland's witness statement published during the trial of the Prince of Wales's action against Associated Newspapers in February 2006 (see above).
33. This section closely follows earlier writing by Robert Blackburn and Raymond Plant in 'Monarchy and the Royal Prerogative', in Robert Blackburn and Raymond Plant (eds), *Constitutional Reform: The Labour Government's Constitutional Reform Agenda* (London: Longman, 1999), pp. 141–2.
34. Dimbleby, *Prince of Wales*, p. 234.

Chapter 2
1. *Charles: The Private Man, the Public Role*, Carlton, 29 June 1994, made by Jonathan Dimbleby. In Mr Dimbleby's subsequent book, *The Prince of Wales: A Biography* (London: Little, Brown, 1994), he identified Mrs Parker Bowles as the person to whom Prince Charles had been referring.
2. Also the co-author with Ken Wharfe, Princess Diana's former personal protection officer, of *Diana: Closely Guarded Secret* (London: Michael O'Mara, 2002).
3. See below.
4. *Guardian*, 11 February 2005.
5. All quotes in this paragraph from the *Evening Standard*, 10 February 2005.
6. These legal and constitutional problems are discussed below.
7. *Guardian*, 1 July 2004.
8. See Public Accounts Committee, *The Accounts of the Duchies of Cornwall and Lancaster*, Nineteenth Report, Session 2004–05, Oral Evidence, HC 313-I, Q. 224.
9. *Independent*, 11 February 2005.
10. *Sun*, 11 February 2005.
11. Address by the Archbishop of Canterbury, Robert Runcie, at the marriage of the Prince of Wales and the Lady Diana Spencer, 29 July 1981, from Jonathan Dimbleby, *The Prince of Wales* (London: Little, Brown, 1994), p. 290.

12. Dimbleby, *Prince of Wales*, p. 395.
13. Hansard, HC Deb, 9 December 1992, vol. 215, col. 845.
14. *Report of the Committee on Privacy and Related Matters (No. 2)*, Cm 2135, 1993.
15. ' Let them divorce', *Daily Mail*, 16 November 1995.
16. Quoted in Robert Rhodes James, *A Spirit Undaunted: The Political Role of George VI* (London: Little, Brown, 1998), p. 115.
17. Ibid., p. 107.
18. *Guardian*, 5 June 2000.
19. 18 June 2000.
20. For an account of the Church of England's regulations on this, see *The Canons of the Church of England*, 6th edn (2000, first supplement 2005), Canon B30, p. 51, Holy Matrimony; and Supplementary Material, Advice to clergy concerning marriage and the divorced (November 2002).
21. Quoted in *Christian Today*, 15 March 2005.
22. Quoted in the *Daily Express* wedding supplement, 9 April 2005.
23. *Times*, 11 February 2005.
24. For those who did attend and a narrative of the occasion, see below.
25. *Daily Telegraph*, 3 April 2005.
26. Extracted in the *Times*, 4 June 2004.
27. *Times*, 4 June 2004.
28. *Daily Telegraph*, 28 March 2005; and see note 20 above.
29. Source: Archbishops House/Scottish Catholic Media Office.
30. The Act of Settlement's provisions are discussed in Chapter 4.
31. *Christian Today*, 11 February 2005.
32. Quoted in the *Daily Telegraph*, 15 February 2005.
33. See below, pp. 62–5.
34. *Evening Standard*, 10 February 2005; *Guardian*, 11 February 2005.
35. Hansard, HC Deb, 10 February 2005, vol. 430, cols 1658–61.
36. *Evening Standard*, 10 February 2005.
37. As reported in the *Daily Mail*, 19 July 1997. At the start of the week, from among the Cabinet ministers then holding office, he met with the Chancellor, Gordon Brown, the Scottish secretary, Donald Dewar, and the education secretary, David Blunkett, at public events. On the Wednesday, he had a private meeting with John Prescott, the newly appointed deputy Prime Minister. Later the same day he met with the health secretary, Frank Dobson, the culture secretary, Chris Smith, and the defence secretary, George Robertson. On the Friday he met the Foreign Secretary, Robin Cook.
38. *The Daily Mail*, 19 July 1997; the report suggested that Dr Wright as a PPS to the Lord Chancellor was representing the views of the Prime Minister, the Lord Chancellor and the government on the matter, but to the contrary he emphasised that he was expressing a personal opinion.
39. Edward, Duke of Windsor, *A King's Story: The Memoirs of HRH the Duke of Windsor, KG* (London: Cassell, 1951), p. 373.
40. Delivered in an address on the BBC; see Philip Ziegler, *King Edward VIII: The Official Biography* (London: Collins, 1990), p. 338.
41. Rev. J. A. Jardine, a 'turbulent priest from Darlington', offered his services after Edward found it impossible to recruit any of the royal chaplains: Ziegler, *King Edward VIII*, p. 363.
42. *Daily Mirror*, 17 July 1953.
43. 'Getting public backing will be toughest hurdle', *Times*, 11 February 2005.

44. *This Morning*, ITV, 10 February 2005.
45. The question whether the Duchess of Cornwall will become Queen in due course is considered below in the Afterwords; and on polls taken on 'Queen Camilla' see p. 178.
46. Source: Populus, fieldwork 24–5 April 2005, published in the *Times*, 29 April 2005.
47. Source: Populus, fieldwork 10–11 February 2005, published in the *Times*, 12 February 2005.
48. See pp. 36–7.
49. *The English Constitution* (London: Fontana, [1867] 1963), p. 86.
50. Quoted by Joshua Rozenberg, *Daily Telegraph*, 22 February 2005; and *PM*, BBC Radio 4, 21 February 2005.
51. *Independent*, 11 February 2005.
52. Hansard, HL Deb, 24 February 2005, cols WS87–8.
53. *Daily Mail*, 9 April 2005; *Daily Telegraph*, 24 February 2005.
54. *Observer*, 6 March 2005.
55. *Daily Telegraph*, 9 March 2005.
56. *Mail on Sunday*, 10 April 2005.
57. SI 1995/510, Schedule 1, para. 2.
58. Quoted in the *Daily Telegraph*, 18 February 2005.
59. Quoted in BBC News, 15 March 2005: 'Media barred from Royal Wedding'. It was reported in many media outlets that the Queen was deeply unhappy about the wedding arrangements (e.g. 'The Queen was said to be furious at Prince Charles's decision to switch his wedding venue to a "common" town hall', *Edinburgh Evening News*, 15 March 2005), which were widely portrayed in the media as having been 'confusion from the moment they named the day' (*Daily Telegraph*, 23 February 2005) and whose 'sloppy preparation has left the happy event close to shambles' (*Guardian*, 25 February 2005). See pp. 43–4 for the views of the Queen and Buckingham Palace and her non-attendance at the civil marriage.
60. SI 1995/510, Schedule 2, para. 12.
61. Under Schedule 2, para. 6(1)(b) of the regulations, the general registrar may attach 'such further conditions as it considers reasonable in order to ensure that the facilities provided at the premises are suitable and that the solemnization of marriages on the premises does not give rise to a nuisance of any kind'.
62. Public Order Act 1986, Criminal Justice and Public Order Act 1994, Criminal Justice and Police Act 2001 and Serious Organised Crime and Police Act 2005. The last of these, for example, enables the government simply to designate sites which are then banned from entry by the public 'on grounds of national security' (Section 128).
63. See p. 75.
64. Reported in the *Times*, 11 April 2005, whose reporter Alan Hamilton also commented, 'It seemed a heavy-handed response to a peaceful and legitimate protest.'
65. *People*, 10 April 2005.
66. See p. 43–4.
67. *Sunday Times*, 27 February 2005.
68. *Mail on Sunday*, 10 April 2005.
69. Quoted in the *Times*, 11 April 2005.
70. Quoted in the *Daily Mail*, 11 April 2005.
71. *Daily Mirror*, 11 April 2005: Exclusive, 'The royal wedding', by Jane Kerr, royal reporter.
72. According to the *Daily Mail*, 11 April 2005.
73. *Daily Mail*, 11 April 2005.
74. For example, the *Daily Telegraph* on 8 April 2005 reproduced the form and lists from the Clarence House press pack virtually unchanged.

75.   Lord Bragg, quoted in the *Mail on Sunday*, 10 April 2005.

76.   'A Right Royal Shambles', *Panorama*, BBC1, 2 October 2005.

77.   Quoted in the *Sunday Times*, 10 April 2005.

78.   John Cannon and Ralph Griffiths, *Oxford Illustrated History of the British Monarchy* (Oxford: Oxford University Press, 1988), p. 624.

79.   *Daily Mirror*, 11 April 2005.

Chapter 3

1.   A. W. Bradley and K. D. Ewing, *Constitutional and Administrative Law*, 13th edn (Harlow: Longman, 2003), ch. 12; Christopher Vincenzi, *Crown Powers, Subjects and Citizens* (London: Pinter, 1998), ch. 1; Maurice Sunkin and Sebastian Payne (eds), *The Nature of the Crown: A Legal and Political Analysis* (Oxford: Oxford University Press, 1999), ch. 4.

2.   See also Chapter 1, pp. 12–13.

3.   Thus those who argue for a wholesale codification of the Crown prerogatives are virtually in the same camp as those making the case for a written constitution. See Institute for Public Policy Research, *A Written Constitution for the United Kingdom* (London: Mansell, 1993); and for a recent parliamentary inquiry, Public Administration Select Committee, *Taming the Prerogative: Strengthening Ministerial Accountability to Parliament*, Fourth Report, Session 2003–04, HC 422.

4.   Sir William Blackstone, *Commentaries on the Laws of England*, 14th edn, p. 239.

5.   The High Court's treatment of prerogative powers is therefore at variance to its approach towards statutory powers, the exercise of which is most certainly reviewable on grounds such as improper purpose or irrationality of discretion. Since the 'GCHQ case', *Council of Civil Service Unions v. Minister for the Civil Service* [1985] AC 374, the courts have inquired into the exercise of some low level prerogative acts such as the issue of passports, whilst making it clear they would certainly not encroach into the sphere of the monarch's prerogatives or high matters of state such as treaty-making.

6.   Triennial Act 1664; the earlier statute was the Triennial Act 1641.

7.   See Chapter 5, where the author suggests a novel use of this statute in the light of the Human Rights Act.

8.   Ivor Jennings, *Cabinet Government*, 2nd edn (Cambridge: Cambridge University Press, 1951), p. 368. The phrase Sir Ivor quotes in his first sentence belongs to Walter Bagehot, *The English Constitution* (1867). The first 1936 edition of *Cabinet Government* was followed by a second in 1951 and a third in 1959, all published by Cambridge University Press. His other two classic works are *The Law and the Constitution* (London: University of London Press, 1933) and *Parliament* (Cambridge: Cambridge University Press, 1939).

9.   27 February 1984.

10.   3 July 1984.

11.   Vernon Bogdanor, *The Monarchy and the Constitution* (Oxford: Clarendon Press, 1995), p. 75.

12.   Reginald Bassett, *1931: Political Crisis* (London: Macmillan, 1958).

13.   The Labour member and LSE political scientist Professor Harold Laski famously described the National Government as having been 'born of a Palace revolution': *The Crisis and the Constitution: 1931 and After* (London: Fabian Society, 1932), p. 34.

14.   Jennings, *Cabinet Government*, 2nd edn, p. 21; 3rd edn, p. 21.

15.   Ibid., 2nd edn, p. 355; 3rd edn, p. 382.

16. Ibid., 2nd edn, p. 368; 3rd edn, p. 394.
17. Rodney Brazier, *Constitutional Practice*, (Oxford: Clarendon Press, 1988), p. 24.
18. Ibid., p. 43.
19. Brazier, *Constitutional Practice*, 2nd edn (Oxford: Clarendon Press, 1994), p. 37.
20. See David Butler, *Governing without a Majority: Dilemmas for Hung Parliaments in Britain* (London: Collins, 1983; 2nd edn, Basingstoke: Macmillan, 1986).
21. Questions of reform are considered in Chapter 5.
22. On the legislative powers of the Lords and the Parliament Acts 1911–49, see Robert Blackburn and Andrew Kennon, *Griffith and Ryle on Parliament: Functions, Practice and Procedures*, 2nd edn (London: Sweet and Maxwell, 2003), Chapter 12.
23. Formerly authorised by the Royal Assent by Commission Act 1541, now repealed and superseded by the Royal Assent Act 1967.
24. 2nd edn, p. 380; 3rd edn, p. 412.
25. Brazier, *Constitutional Practice*, 2nd edn; his list of situations is at pp. 190–2.
26. Such as the Anti-Terrorism, Crime and Security Act 2001 and the Prevention of Terrorism Act 2005.
27. House of Lords Act 1999.
28. See Chapter 5 for how our present constitutional law might address this situation, utilising the Human Rights Act; and also Robert Blackburn, 'The Royal Assent to Legislation and a Monarch's Fundamental Human Rights', *Public Law* (2003), vol. 48, p. 205.
29. See Chapter 2.
30. Section 7, amending the earlier Septennial Act 1715, which had provided for seven-year parliaments.
31. Jean-Louis de Lolme, *The Constitution of England*, 4th edn (London, 1790), pp. 414–15.
32. On the law and procedure, see Robert Blackburn, *The Meeting of Parliament: A Study of the Law and Practice relating to the Frequency and Duration of the United Kingdom Parliament* (Aldershot: Dartmouth, 1990).
33. See Blackburn, *Meeting of Parliament*, Chapter 5, and Geoffrey Marshall, *Constitutional Conventions: The Rules and Forms of Political Accountability* (Oxford: Clarendon Press, 1984), Chapter 3, on the historical evolution of this convention.
34. Harold Wilson, *The Governance of Britain* (London: Weidenfeld and Nicolson / Michael Joseph, 1976), p. 38.
35. Jennings, *Cabinet Government*, 2nd edn, p. 368; 3rd edn, p. 394.
36. Peter Hennessy, *The Hidden Wiring: Unearthing the British Constitution* (London: Victor Gollancz, 1995), p. 62.
37. Vernon Bogdanor, *No Overall Majority: Forming a Government in a Multi-party Parliament* (London: Constitutional Reform Centre, 1986), see especially pp. 16–22.
38. On censure motions, see Robert Blackburn and Andrew Kennon, *Griffith and Ryle on Parliament: Functions, Practice and Procedures*, 2nd edn (London: Sweet and Maxwell, 2003), pp. 58–62, 484–7.
39. See Chapter 1 on the hereditary principle.
40. Lord Hailsham, *The Dilemma of Democracy: Diagnosis and Prescription* (London: Collins, 1978), p. 193.
41. 'How the Queen picks her man', *Times*, 8 April 1992.
42. *The Back of the Envelope: Hung Parliaments, the Queen and the Constitution*, Strathclyde Analysis Paper No. 5 (1991).
43. Hennessy, *Hidden Wiring*, pp. 61 & 221.
44. Letter to the *Times*, 11 May 1974.

45. *Times*, 12 September 1985.
46. *Guardian*, 12 September 1985.
47. Quoted by Trevor Kavanagh, *Sun*, 17 October 2003.
48. Ibid.

Chapter 4

1. Added by way of an appendix to the Act.
2. The tortuous wording of this important statutory provision, which is still today the foundation of the royal succession, is: 'For a further provision of the succession of the Crown in the Protestant line, we Your Majesty's most dutiful and loyal subjects, the Lords Spiritual and Temporal, and Commons, in this present Parliament assembled, do beseech Your Majesty that it may be enacted and declared, and be it enacted and declared by the King's most excellent majesty, by and with the advice and consent of the Lords Spiritual and Temporal, and Commons, in this present Parliament assembled, and by the authority of the same, That the most excellent Princess Sophia, Electress and Duchess Dowager of Hanover, daughter of the most excellent Princess Elizabeth, late Queen of Bohemia, daughter of our late sovereign lord King James the First, of happy memory, be and is hereby declared to be the next in succession, in the Protestant line, to the imperial Crown and dignity of the said Realms of England, France, and Ireland, with the dominions and territories thereunto belonging, after His Majesty, and the Princess Anne of Denmark, and in default of issue of the said Princess Anne, and of His Majesty respectively: and that from and after the deceases of His said Majesty, our now sovereign lord, and of Her Royal Highness the Princess Anne of Denmark, and for default of issue of the said Princess Anne, and of His Majesty respectively, the Crown and regal government of the said Kingdoms of England, France, and Ireland, and of the dominions thereunto belonging, with the royal state and dignity of the said Realms, and all honours, styles, titles, regalities, prerogatives, powers, jurisdictions and authorities, to the same belonging and appertaining, shall be, remain, and continue to the said most excellent Princess Sophia, and the heirs of her body, being Protestants: and thereunto the said Lords Spiritual and Temporal, and Commons, shall and will in the name of all the people of this Realm, most humbly and faithfully submit themselves, their heirs and posterities: and do faithfully promise, that after the deceases of His Majesty, and Her Royal Highness, and the failure of the heirs of their respective bodies, to stand to, maintain, and defend the said Princess Sophia, and the heirs of her body, being Protestants, according to the limitation and succession of the Crown in this act specified and contained, to the utmost of their powers, with their lives and estates, against all persons whatsoever that shall attempt anything to the contrary.'
3. Laura Peek, 'Uberto, the man who could have been King', *Times*, 14 February 2005.
4. 'Let them marry', *Spectator*, 18–25 December 2004, p. 7.
5. Private correspondence.
6. Section 3.
7. From the official edition of *The Coronation of Her Most Excellent Majesty Queen Elizabeth II* (By Order of Her Majesty's Stationary Office, 1953), pp. 14–15, adapted to substitute masculine terminology.
8. *Economist*, 9 April 2005.
9. 'Revealed: Tony Blair's Catholic secret', *Daily Telegraph*, 9 April 2005, and Garry O'Connor, quoted in the *Mail on Sunday*, 10 April 2005. His biography is *Universal Father: A Life of Pope John Paul II* (London: Bloomsbury, 2005).

10. *Charles: The Private Man, the Public Role*, BBC documentary by Jonathan Dimbleby, 29 June 1994.
11. Paddy Ashdown, *The Ashdown Diaries, vol. 1: 1988–1997* (London: Allen Lane, 2000), as extracted in the *Guardian*, 24 October 2000.
12. Speech to the Institute of Economic Affairs, 26 January 1999, as reported in the *Daily Telegraph*, 27 January 1999.
13. Scottish Parliament Official Report, 16 December 1999, vol. 03, no. 16, col. 1633; and on the resolution passed, col. 1754.
14. Ibid, col. 1666.
15. Ibid, col. 1662. An early day motion expressed in similar terms to the one passed by the Scottish Parliament was set down in the Westminster Parliament on 4 November 1999 by the Scottish Nationalist MP Roseanna Cunningham, but was never debated (Session 1998–99, EDM 985).
16. Scottish Parliament, Equal Opportunities Committee, 9th meeting 1999 (Session 1), 14 December 1999, statement: The Act of Settlement.
17. Hansard, HC Deb, 19 December 2001, vol. 377, col. 319. See also the earlier brief discussion in the House of Lords when Lord Forsyth set down a motion 'to remove the bar on a person who is not, or who is married to a person who is not, a Protestant to succeed to the Crown', responded to by Lord St John of Fawsley: Succession to the Crown (Amendment), *Lords Hansard*, 2 December 1999, vol. 607, col. 917.
18. Session 2004–05, HL 11; Succession to the Crown (No. 2) Bill, session 2004–05, HC 36.
19. *The Future of the Monarchy* (London: Fabian Society, 2003). No debate was held on Ms Taylor's Bill in the Commons.
20. His view as expressed in an article shortly before the debate, *Guardian*, 9 December 2004.
21. Session 2004–05, HC 79.
22. Hansard, HC Deb, 8 March 2005, vol. 431, col. 1392.
23. See Chapter 2, p. 46.
24. Address to Summit on Sectarianism, Scottish Catholic Media Office, 14 February 2004.
25. Hansard, HL Deb, 14 January 2005, vol. 668, cols 500–2.
26. Ibid., cols 502–3.
27. Reported in the *Sunday Times*, 31 October 1999.
28. Hansard, HC Deb, 13 December 1999, vol. 341, cols 57–58W.
29. Hansard, HC Deb, 9 November 1999, vol. 337, cols 865–6.
30. *Daily Telegraph* interview with Rachel Sylvester, 10 March 2001.
31. See Chapter 5.
32. p. 121.
33. Hansard, HL Deb, 14 January 2005, vol. 668, cols 510–12.
34. Quoted in Philip Ziegler, *King Edward VIII: The Official Biography* (London: Collins, 1990), pp. 305–6. For Stanley Baldwin's account of the political stages through which the decision on abdication was reached, see his speech to the House of Commons: Hansard, HC Deb, 10 December 1936.
35. On the complex law governing the situation across the Commonwealth states at that time, and the application of 'imperial statutes' under the Statute of Westminster 1931, see R. T. E. Latham, *The Law and the Commonwealth* (London: Oxford University Press, 1937), Appendix: 'The Abdication of King Edward VIII in Commonwealth Law and Convention'.
36. On the constitutional steps taken at home and in the Commonwealth leading to the abdication, see A. Berriedale Keith, *The Constitution of England from Queen Victoria to George VI* (2 vols; London: Macmillan, 1940), vol. 1, pp. 29–34.

37. Hansard, HL Deb, 27 February 1998, vol. 586, col. 917.
38. Succession to the Crown Bill, Session 2004–05, HL 11; Hansard, HL Deb, 14 January 2005, vol. 668, col. 500.
39. Speech at St James's Church, Piccadilly, London, 2 March 1983.
40. 'A Case for the Disestablishment of the Church of England', in Donald Reeves (ed.), *The Church and the State* (London: Hodder and Stoughton, 1984).
41. Sidney Buxton: *Handbook to Political Questions of the Day, Being the Arguments on Either Side*, 9th edn, (London: John Murray, 1892), pp. 42–3.
42. English Church Bill, Session 1987–88, HC 156.
43. p. 14.
44. 'Free the Church', *Guardian*, 12 December 2000.

Chapter 5

1. For his comments on the Queen, for example see p. 101. On the institution of monarchy, for example in an interview for *Queen and Country*, BBC, 23 May 2002, he said, 'A lot of people of my generation have decided in part because of how important a unifier for the country the Queen has been that actually this [the monarchy] is a better system – rationally, not simply emotionally or as part of tradition – but rationally this is a better system.'
2. 20 November 1997. See Robert Blackburn and Raymond Plant, 'Monarchy and the Royal Prerogative', in Robert Blackburn and Raymond Plant (eds), *Constitutional Reform: The Labour Government's Constitutional Reform Agenda* (London: Longman, 1999), from which an extract is included in this section.
3. *Independent on Sunday*, 23 October 1994. A later poll conducted for the *Independent* on 18 February 1996 showed that only eleven Labour MPs supported the monarchy 'without serious reservation'.
4. 5 December 1994; see also his comments in *Tribune*, 5 February 1993.
5. 'Abolish the Royal Prerogative', in Anthony Barnett (ed.), *Power and the Throne* (London: Vintage, 1994), p.128.
6. 17 March 1994.
7. Peter Hain, *Ayes to the Left: A Future for Socialism* (London: Lawrence and Wishart, 1995). Extract published in the *Guardian*, 5 March 1996.
8. Session 1995–96, HC 115.
9. Session 1990–91, HC 161; Hansard, HC Deb, 17 May 1991, vol. 191, col. 554.
10. See for example, 'About time we grew up', 5 January 1996.
11. 'Bogus mystique of monarchy', *Observer*, 13 December 1992.
12. Hansard, HC Deb, 9 December 1992, vol. 215, col. 847.
13. See Chapter 4, p. 118.
14. p. 20.
15. *The Governor General of Canada: Role, Duties and Funding for Activities*, Second Report, Session 2003–04.
16. Message on the thirty-ninth anniversary of Barbados's independence, 2005.
17. House of Representatives, 7 June 1995.
18. For example Phillip Hall, *Royal Fortune: Tax, Money and the Monarchy* (London: Bloomsbury, 1992).
19. The best known of these is Jonathan Freedland, *Bring Home the Revolution: The Case for a British Republic* (London: 4th Estate, 1998).
20. Tim Hames and Mark Leonard, *Modernising the Monarchy* (London: Demos, 1998).

21. *The Future of the Monarchy* (London: Fabian Society, 2003).

22. Anthony Barnett (ed.), *Power and the Throne: The Monarchy Debate* (London: Vintage, 1994).

23. Roy Hattersley, 'Bogus mystique of monarchy', *Observer*, 13 December 1992; Tony Benn and Andrew Hood, *Common Sense: A New Constitution for Britain* (London: Hutchinson, 1993).

24. See pp. 125–8.

25. The issue of Catholic disqualification is discussed further below.

26. A longer list is usefully shown in the annual *Whitaker's Almanack* (London: A. and C. Black).

27. Constitutional Reform Bill, session 1990–91, HC 204; Hansard, HC Deb, 3 July 1991, vol. 194, cols 340–2.

28. Session 1997–98, HL 86.

29. Hansard, HL Deb, 27 February 1998, vol. 586, cols 916–17.

30. Succession to the Crown Bill, session 2004–05, HL 11; Succession to the Crown (No. 2) Bill, session 2004–05, HC 36.

31. Hansard, HL Deb, 14 January 2005, vol. 668, col. 496.

32. Ibid., col. 511.

33. Penal Servitude Act 1857 and Criminal Justice Act 1948.

34. *R. v. Her Majesty's Attorney General ex parte Rusbridger and another*, 26 June 2003, paras 39, 40, 45.

35. Keir Starmer, 'The last blatantly anti-Catholic piece of legislation', *Guardian*, 31 May 2002; Geoffrey Robertson quoted in Clare Dyer, 'Law on succession to throne may be incompatible with Human Rights Act', *Guardian*, 6 December 2000.

36. *Cierva Osorio de Moscovo v. Spain* (No. 41127/98), *Fernandez de Cordoba v. Spain* (No. 41503/98), *Roca y Fernandez Miranda v. Spain* (No. 41717/98), *O'Neill Castrillo v. Spain* (No. 45726/99), decision 28 October 1999, Section IV of the Court.

37. See Robert Blackburn, 'The Institutions and Processes of the Convention', in Robert Blackburn and Jorg Polakiewicz (eds), *Fundamental Rights in Europe: The ECHR and its Member States 1950-2000* (Oxford: Oxford University Press, 2001), pp. 24–25.

38. See pp. 60–61 for the ministerial statement in 2005 which declared the state of the law regarding civil royal marriages.

39. The following paragraphs draw on the author's earlier work *The Meeting of Parliament: A Study of the Law and Practice Relating to the Frequency and Duration of the United Kingdom Parliament* (Aldershot: Dartmouth, 1990), pp. 54–6.

40. Regency Act 1953, Family Law Reform Act 1969.

41. Hansard, HC Deb, 1 March 1937, cols 107–11.

42. Provided for in Section 6 of the Regency Act 1937.

43. Harold Wilson, *The Labour Government 1964-70: A Personal Record* (London: Weidenfeld and Nicolson, 1971), p. 215.

44. See p. 54.

45. Hansard, HL Deb, 24 February 2005, vol. 669, col. WS87.

46. Hansard, HL Deb, 14 January 2005, vol. 668, col. 497.

47. Ibid., col. 512.

48. See Chapter 3 for an explanation of the status quo.

49. *Report of the Independent Commission on the Voting System* (Jenkins report), Cm 4090, 1998. On proportional representation and its constitutional consequences, see Robert Blackburn, *The Electoral System in Britain* (London: Macmillan, 1995).

50. Hansard, HL Deb, 22 May 1991, col. 245.

51.   Owen Hood Phillips, *Reform of the Constitution* (London: Chatto and Windus, 1970), p. 52.

52.   'Elective Dictatorship', BBC Richard Dimbleby Lecture 1976.

53.   These are in addition to those of the author: see Blackburn, *Meeting of Parliament* and *Electoral System in Britain*, which latter contains a suggested draft Bill.

54.   Labour election manifesto 1992, p. 25.

55.   'A programme for Conservative constitutional reform', 26 July 2005.

56.   See for example Liberal Democrats, *Here We Stand: Liberal Democrat Proposals for Modernising Britain's Democracy* (Dorchester: Liberal Democrats, 1993), p. 15; Fixed Parliaments Bill, session 1986–87, HC 64.

57.   Scotland Act 1998, Sections 2 and 3.

58.   On the parliamentary context of the 1911 amendment of the Septennial Act, see Blackburn, *Meeting of Parliament*, p. 22.

Afterwords

1.   See pp. 51–2.

2.   Interestingly, another result of the poll was that 57 per cent thought it was 'acceptable for him [Charles] to live with Camilla rather than marry her', with 32 per cent saying it was unacceptable, and 11 per cent not knowing. The poll was of 996 people conducted on 27 October 2002.

3.   22 March 2005.

4.   *Queen Caroline's Claim to be Crowned* (1821) 1 State Tr NS 949.

5.   See *Halsbury's Laws of England*, 4th edn (London: Butterworths, 1973–87), vol. 12(1), paras 28–31.

6.   *Halsbury's Statutes*, 4th edn (London: Butterworths, 1985–92), Treason Act 1351.

7.   Regency Acts 1937 and 1953.

8.   See the *Times*, 22 February 2005.

9.   Hansard, HC Deb, 17 March 2005, vol. 432, col. 462W. The position and entitlement of Camilla's children by her first marriage, Tom and Laura, appear to remain unaffected by the royal marriage and whatever title she adopts.

10.   Hansard, HC Deb, 4 April 2005, vol. 432, col. 1228W.

11.   *Daily Telegraph*, 22 March 2005; *Guardian*, 22 March 2005; *Times*, 22 March 2005 (whose front page headline read 'Camilla will be Queen unless MPs change law').

12.   YouGov poll published in the *Daily Telegraph*, 11 February 2005.

13.   *Daily Mail*, 2 April 2005.

14.   10 April 2005.

Index